The World Trade Organisation

A Guide to the Framework for International Trade

About the Author

BHAGIRATH LAL DAS served in the Indian Administrative Service, from where he retired as a Secretary to the Government of India. He has had a long association with international trade issues, participating directly in a large number of bilateral and multilateral trade negotiations. He was India's Ambassador and Permanent Representative to GATT and Deputy Permanent Representative to UNCTAD in Geneva. During that period he also functioned as Chairman of the GATT Council and of the GATT Contracting Parties. Later he spent five years with UNCTAD as its Director of International Trade Programmes. In that capacity, along with his other responsibilities, he organised and coordinated UNCTAD's technical assistance programme for developing countries to facilitate their participation in the Uruguay Round of Multilateral Trade Negotiations which culminated in the setting up of the World Trade Organisation. His earlier books are *An Introduction to the WTO Agreements* and *The WTO Agreements: Deficiencies, Imbalances and Required Changes*. He now provides consultancy services to various institutions

The World Trade Organisation
A Guide to the Framework for International Trade

Bhagirath Lal Das

ZED BOOKS
London, New York

TWN
THIRD WORLD NETWORK
Penang, Malaysia

BOOKWELL
New Delhi, India

This book is reprinted from *The World Trade Organisation: A Guide to the Framework for International Trade* originally published by Third World Network and Zed Books Ltd

ISBN: 81-89640-23-2

This edition is published in india in 2007 by:

BOOKWELL

Sales Office

24/4800, Ansari Road,
Darya Ganj,
New Delhi-110002, India
Ph: 91-11-23268786

Head Office:

2/72, Nirankari Colony,
Delhi-110009, India
Ph: 91-11-27251283
Fax: 91-11-23281315

E-mail: bkwell@nde.vsnl.net.in
bookwell@vsnl.net

To my father

Pandit Shree Madhava Lal Das

Explanatory Notes:

AT several places in this text, the terms "country", "countries", "Member country" and "Member countries" occur. These terms have been used for simplicity and convenience, though it is well recognised that the territories of some Members of the WTO may not fit exactly into this category.

In the endnotes, BISD II/12, for example, denotes Basic Instruments and Selected Documents, volume II, page 12, of GATT, WTO, Geneva. Similarly, BISD 35S/245, 289-290 denotes 35th supplement of BISD, pages 245, 289-290, of GATT, WTO, Geneva. References have been made in the endnotes to similar other volumes of BISD.

In the text, frequent reference is made to "WTO agreements." This expression is meant to include all agreements covered by the WTO, i.e., GATT 1994, other agreements on goods, the agreements on trade in services and trade-related intellectual property rights, the Trade Policy Review Mechanism and the Dispute Settlement Understanding. It should be distinguished from the "WTO Agreement", which has been more formally called the Marrakesh Agreement Establishing the World Trade Organisation.

CONTENTS

PREFACE xv

PART I: BACKGROUND AND INTRODUCTION

Chapter I.1 Background and Introduction 3
Origin 3
Further Developments 4
Development Dimension 5
Tokyo Round 5
Uruguay Round 6
General Trends 7
How to Read WTO Agreements 9
General Scheme of Agreements 11

PART II : GENERAL PRINCIPLES

Chapter II.1 Most-Favoured-Nation (MFN) Treatment 15
Introduction and Broad Definition 15
Forms of Benefit 16
Coverage of Benefit 17
Some Important Concepts 18
Some Important Considerations 21
Exceptions 23
Importance of MFN Principle for Multilateralism and Erosion of the Principle 27

Chapter II.2 National Treatment 29
Introduction 29
Main Elements 30
Some Important Concepts 33
Some Important Considerations 40
Exceptions 43
Emerging Problems 45

Chapter II.3 Other General Principles 47
Obligations Relating to Regional Governments 47
Status of Laws and Regulations 48
Transparency 50

PART III : MARKET ACCESS

Chapter III.1 Tariffs 55
Introduction 55
Main Disciplines 56
Types of Tariff 56
Classification 57
Binding of Tariffs 59
Increase in Tariff Beyond Binding 63
Schedule 66
Tariff Quota 67
Preferential Tariff 67
Other Matters 68

Chapter III.2 Safeguards 71
Introduction 71
Nature of Safeguard Measures 72
Preconditions for Taking Safeguard Measures 73
Procedure for Taking Safeguard Measures 76
Special Disciplines Regarding Quantitative Restrictions 80
Limitations and General Disciplines 83
Termination of Pre-Existing Measures 90
Grey-Area Measures 90
Non-Discrimination or Selectivity 92
Notification 94
Provisions for Developing Countries 95
Dispute Settlement 96
Special Safeguard Provisions 96

Chapter III.3 Balance-of-Payments Provisions (Article XVIIIB of GATT 1994) 99
Introduction 99
General Conditions for Use of Article XVIII of GATT 1994 100
Permissible Action Under Article XVIIIB 103
Limitations on Action Under Article XVIIIB 104
Notification 105
Consultations 106
Emerging Issues 113

Chapter III.4 Technical Barriers to Trade 115
Introduction 115
Definitions and Procedure 116
Exclusion of Coverage 117
Disciplines on Technical Regulations 118
Formulation of Standards 123
Assessment of Conformity 126
Developing Countries 127
Other Provisions 128
Emerging Issues 129

Chapter III.5 Sanitary and Phytosanitary Measures 131
Introduction 131
Definitions 131
Nature of SPS Measures 132
Limitations on SPS Measures 132
Conformity with International Standards 133
Assessment of Risk 134
Provisional Measures 134
Transparency, Publication, Notification, Enquiry Point 134
Other Provisions 136

Chapter III.6 Trade-Related Investment Measures (TRIMs) 139
Introduction 139
Prohibited Measures 140
Flexibility for Developing Country Members 142
Elimination of Existing Measures 143

Introduction of New Measures 144
Notification and Transparency 144
Committee, Consultation and Dispute Settlement 145
Review 145

Chapter III.7 General Exceptions 147
Introduction 147
Main Elements 147
Recent Issues 149

PART IV : MEASURES AGAINST UNFAIR TRADE

Chapter IV.1 Subsidies and Countervailing Measures 153
Introduction 153
Disciplines 154
What is a Subsidy? 155
Permissible (Non-Actionable) Subsidies 157
Prohibited Subsidies 162
Actionable Subsidies 165
Remedies 170
Determination of Injury 181
Imposition of Countervailing Duty 188
Intermediate Steps 192
Some Other Provisions 195
Special Provisions for Developing Countries 196
Countries in Transition 202

Chapter IV.2 Anti-Dumping 205
Introduction 205
Effects of Dumping, Varying Interests and Pressures 205
Dumping 207
Export Price 207
Normal Value 208
Comparison of Export Price and Normal Value 214
Investigation for Dumping and Injury 216
Newcomers 221

Dispute Settlement Process 221
Other Provisions 223

PART V : SOME SPECIFIC SECTORS

Chapter V.1 Agriculture 227
Introduction 227
Areas of Commitments 229
Market Access 230
Domestic Support 241
Export Subsidy 249
Export Restriction 252
Limitations on Action Against Subsidy 253
Other Provisions 254

Chapter V.2 Textiles and Clothing 257
Introduction 257
Progressive Liberalisation 260
Continuing Restrictions 263
Safeguards 264
Circumvention 272
Sectoral Balance of Rights and Obligations 275
Textiles Monitoring Body 275
Termination of the Agreement 276

PART VI : PROCEDURAL AND OTHER MATTERS RELATING TO GOODS

Chapter VI.1 Customs Valuation 279
Introduction 279
Discipline 280
Transaction Value 281
Other Methods of Determination of Customs Value 285
Other Provisions 291

Chapter VI.2 Import Licensing 293
Introduction 293
General Disciplines 293
Automatic Licensing 294
Non-Automatic Licensing 295
Other Provisions 296

Chapter VI.3 Rules of Origin 299
Introduction 299
Discipline 300
Main Criteria Applied in the Rules of Origin 300
Disciplines in the Transition Period 302
Harmonisation of Rules of Origin 304
Disciplines After Transition Period 306
Common Declaration on Preferential Rules of Origin 306
Other Matters 307

Chapter VI.4 Preshipment Inspection 309
Introduction 309
Definitions and the Process 309
Disciplines 309
Other Obligations 312

Chapter VI.5 State Trading Enterprises 313
Introduction 313
Definition 313
General Disciplines 314
Institution 316

Chapter VI.6 Part IV of GATT 1994 317
Introduction and Background 317
Article XXXVI 318
Article XXXVII 318
Article XXXVIII 319
The Committee on Trade and Development 319

Chapter VI.7 Plurilateral Agreements 321

PART VII : AREAS OTHER THAN GOODS

Chapter VII.1 Services 325
Introduction 325
Frame of Commitments 325
Modes of Supply 326
Specific Commitments 327
General Obligations and Disciplines 339
Safeguard Measures, Subsidies, Government Procurement 351
Consultation and Dispute Settlement 352
Annexes on Specific Issues and Sectors 353

Chapter VII.2 Trade-Related Aspects of Intellectual Property Rights (TRIPS) 355
Introduction 355
Basic Objectives, Principles and General Obligations 358
Patents 360
Copyright and Related Rights 374
Trademarks 379
Geographical Indications 381
Industrial Designs 382
Layout-Designs of Integrated Circuits 383
Undisclosed Information 387
Anti-Competitive Practices 388
Enforcement of IPRs 388
Dispute Settlement Process 389
Application of the Agreement, Interim Measures 390
Institutional Arrangement, Review, Security Exceptions 393

PART VIII: DISPUTE SETTLEMENT AND INSTITUTIONAL MATTERS

Chapter VIII.1 Dispute Settlement Process 397

Introduction 397

Coverage 398

Articles XXII and XXIII of GATT 1994 399

Procedure for Dispute Settlement Process 406

Cross-Sector and Cross-Agreement Suspension 419

Some Other Provisions 421

Multilateral Process in Dispute Settlement 423

Special Provisions Relating to Dispute Settlement 423

Chapter VIII.2 Institutional Matters 427

Membership 427

Decision-Making 429

Structure of the WTO, Councils, Committees 432

ENDNOTES 435

BIBLIOGRAPHY 439

INDEX 441

PREFACE

THIS book is mainly based on the materials prepared as the training modules for the TRAINFORTRADE course of the United Nations Conference on Trade and Development (UNCTAD). I am grateful to UNCTAD for giving me the opportunity to prepare the course, which was meant to spread the knowledge on the General Agreement on Tariffs and Trade (GATT)/World Trade Organisation(WTO) in the developing countries. This exercise gave me an occasion to study the WTO agreements in some depth. Earlier, while, as the Director of International Trade Programmes of UNCTAD, I was coordinating the work on technical assistance to developing countries for facilitating their participation in the Uruguay Round of Multilateral Trade Negotiations, I had the occasion of following the process of negotiations very closely. This association made me aware of the complexities of the agreements in general and of a large number of formulations in them in particular. I was very much conscious of the grave need for clarification and elaboration of the various provisions of the agreements.

Still earlier, while I was a negotiator in the GATT, I had felt the absence of a book which would have explained to me in simple terms the intricacies of the various articles and concepts of the GATT. Some monumental books had, of course, been written on the GATT in the past, but the GATT had traversed a great distance since then. Particularly, after the conclusion of the Tokyo Round of Multilateral Trade Negotiations in 1979, it had taken a new shape in several important areas. And now, in its new and enhanced incarnation as the WTO, I felt that there was an even more compelling need for a comprehensive book which would explain the intricacies of the agreements in simple terms.

That is how this book has emerged. There have been some serious studies of several WTO agreements from the angles of economics and international law. What was needed was a work for the use of operators and users. This book is essentially targeted at this group, viz., negotiators, senior and high-level trade policy officials, and the executives of industry and trade. Simultaneously, it can be used by students of international trade and of commercial diplomacy to gain a better understanding of the multilateral framework of international trade. It can perhaps be used as reading material for studies in the overlapping domains of international law, international economics and diplomacy.

This book does not give a historical perspective on the various agreements, except a brief historical background of the framework itself in the beginning and also references to predecessor agreements, whenever these are relevant for understanding the new provisions. What it gives is an explanation of the provisions of the agreements as they stand now. Effort has been made to explain the provisions in simple non-technical language, taking care not to detract from legal accuracy. The aim has been to present to the readers an easily readable exposition of the provisions of the agreements.

The following question would naturally arise: what is the value addition in this work? The most authentic form of the agreements is, of course, the original text of the agreements. What, then, is the advantage in having this lengthy exposition which does not give any critical academic analysis, nor any balance sheet of benefits and losses arising out of these agreements? The value addition in this effort lies in its attempt to make the agreements understandable. A simple reading of the original texts would leave most people, except those who have been personally involved in the drafting process, very much perplexed and confused. Legal texts generally do not constitute an easy read for the non-lawyer. And the texts of WTO agreements are particularly complex, because, among other reasons, these are derived, in many cases, as ensembles of disparate texts of the legislation and regulations of several countries.

A plain reading of the original texts of some agreements, particularly those on Agriculture, Subsidies and Anti-dumping, would immediately convince a reader of the relevance of a tool like this book. The text tries to explain technical terms in understandable language, giving examples wherever appropriate. It also tries to link various provisions of an agreement which are connected in their operation and yet lie scattered in the original text of the agreement, perhaps for the reason of legal drafting. Several important provisions can be clear only when one assembles together the texts of some Articles, the relevant annexes and also the connected footnotes. Sometimes one has to go back and forth in some agreements to clarify some terms. This text simplifies matters by engaging in all such exercises. Besides, it also cites examples from actual cases in the GATT to clarify some concepts and illustrate how these have been interpreted in the past.

An attempt has been made to make each chapter complete and understandable in itself, except for some brief references to other places in the book. The aim is to make it useful also for a quick reference on some specific subject, in case one chooses to use it for that purpose.

Some people may raise doubts to the effect that an exercise of this type runs the risk of falling in between two stools. Those who are not familiar with the subject may not understand it; whereas those who are familiar may not need it. In fact, effort has been made in this work to make it useful for both types of readers. Those who are not acquainted with the subject may find it easy to grasp the essentials through this text; and those who are not so new to this area may still find it useful in clarifying certain concepts, ideas and even general provisions.

More discerning ones may question the wisdom of rendering the legal texts in non-technical language on the grounds that any such step is likely to detract from the legal precision. This is, of course, true. A legal text cannot be put in a totally accurate form in any language other than that of the text itself. But one has to take this risk in proceeding to explain a legal text. Efforts have been made here to make the texts understandable while at the same time not detracting from the legal rigour.

The actual utility and relevance of this exercise will be judged only by the users for whom it is meant.

Admittedly there is a need for a thorough understanding of the WTO agreements among trade policy officials, trade negotiators, business executives and students of international economic relations. The WTO is playing a crucial role in the economic life of nations. It is important for countries to know their rights and obligations. It is also important for industry and trade entities to know the parameters within which they can operate. Several major developed countries are continuing with their efforts to deepen and widen the coverage of the WTO. To understand the implications of these new areas, it is necessary to know the existing framework.

Generally, new entrants, and sometimes even those experienced in GATT/WTO work, are overawed by the complexities of some of these agreements. This inhibits them from expressing themselves clearly and firmly on relevant issues. If they are backed by a careful reading of simplified explanations, such as those provided in this text, of any particular agreement, they will be more confident and bold in their presentations. They will also be able to assess their national interest in respect of an issue under consideration and would be able to formulate their national positions more confidently. The book would have served its purpose if those reading it are able to overcome their fear and hesitation in handling the WTO agreements.

In the course of preparing this text, I have had the benefit of several rounds of discussions with a large number of distinguished persons who have intimate technical knowledge of these subjects and also of the political background of the WTO negotiations. These discussions have been extremely useful and I thank all of them. In particular, I wish to thank M.G. Mathur, who was formerly Deputy Director-General of GATT, and Harsha Vardhan Singh of the WTO Secretariat. M.G. Mathur took the trouble to read the entire text of an earlier draft and made a large number of perceptive observations which have helped me to improve the text and also the coverage. He was also a constant source of inspiration and encouragement to me in this exercise. Harsha Vardhan Singh systematically scrutinised the texts on some complex agreements, like those on Safeguards, Subsidies and Anti-dumping, and gave some valuable suggestions on accuracy and presentation of facts. He also provided support in many other ways. In fact, without his support and that of Veena Jha, this work could not have been done.

I immensely benefited from my frequent discussions with Chakravarthi Raghavan, Chief Editor of the *South-North Development Monitor* in Geneva, who has vast direct experience of the happenings in the GATT/WTO and had written on the Uruguay Round on a daily basis over the nine years of its course. I thank him for his advice and ideas. I have also benefited a great deal in the clarification of technical points from my interactions with Richard Eglin, Patrick

Low, Petros Mavroidis and Chris Carson of the WTO Secretariat and Sanjoy Bagchi of the International Textiles and Clothing Bureau Secretariat in Geneva. Murray Gibbs and Xiaobing Tang of the UNCTAD Secretariat helped me with some useful information, materials and ideas. I thank all of them most sincerely for their efforts and interest. Of course, whatever mistakes and inaccuracies that might still be in the text are my own responsibility.

I thank the WTO Secretariat, in particular Anwarul Hoda, Deputy Director-General of the WTO, for the facilities provided to me in using the library and consulting the relevant papers in the WTO.

Finally, I thank UNCTAD and the Third World Network, the former for permitting the publication of this book, and the latter for taking up the work of publication. In particular, I thank Martin Khor Kok Peng, Director of the Third World Network, who took keen interest in this work and encouraged me to accomplish it.

Bhagirath Lal Das

PART I

BACKGROUND AND INTRODUCTION

Chapter I.1

BACKGROUND AND INTRODUCTION

THE World Trade Organisation (WTO) provides the framework for the conduct of international trade in goods and services and for the protection of intellectual property rights. It administers the implementation of a set of agreements, which, for convenience, we may call the WTO agreements. These agreements include the General Agreement on Tariffs and Trade (GATT), some other agreements in the goods sector and, in addition, agreements in two other areas, viz., services and intellectual property rights. Besides, the WTO contains a framework for the enforcement of rights and obligations in these areas. The agreements generally contain disciplines on governments and, in some cases, even on enterprises.

ORIGIN

The multilateral framework of international trade originated from the end of the Second World War. The earlier experience with the Great Depression of the late twenties and early thirties, followed in its wake by the trade protection imposed by major trading nations, made governments aware of the need for a multilateral discipline in the field of international trade. This awareness assumed a new urgency with the devastation caused by the Second World War and with the need for the expansion of international trade as an important tool for development and growth.

All this led to the convening of a United Nations Conference on Trade and Employment in Havana, which resulted in the formulation of the Havana Charter. However, the US, which had been the main proponent along with the UK, failed to ratify it. Without the US participating in the Charter, other countries did not see any advantage in launching it, and thus it remained only a footnote of history. However, the international trade chapter of the Charter was taken out and converted into the GATT in 1947, which was subscribed to by 23 countries, including the US. But the GATT was not an organisation; it was only an agreement. Its implementation was administered by the Interim Commission for the International Trade Organisation (ICITO), which was the formal organisation located in Geneva. But its identity was very much in the background; the GATT continued to be the front, though it had no formal identity as an intergovernmental organisation.

Some important parts of the Havana Charter which were not covered by the GATT and had thus been left out were: commodity prices, competition policy, etc. Besides, the objective of full employment, which was an important part of the Charter, did not find a place in the legal instrument of the GATT.

The GATT has been strengthened and supplemented from time to time. The latest such effort has been in the Uruguay Round of Multilateral Trade Negotiations (MTNs), resulting in the creation of the WTO, which has the formal status of an intergovernmental organisation that had not been available to the GATT.

FURTHER DEVELOPMENTS

The basic approach of the GATT has been that goods, when exported from a country, should generally have free entry into the importing country. Customs duty (tariff) can, however, be imposed at the border. The GATT provides a framework for negotiations on the levels of tariff. It also permits countries to apply, under certain situations, some non-tariff measures (NTMs) to directly restrain imports. Besides, it provides for protection against unfair trade and disguised obstructions to trade. The objective is that such trade-distorting measures should not be permitted to erode the benefit which a country gets by the reduction of tariff levels in other countries.

Up to the beginning of the seventies, the main concern of the GATT had been to reduce the tariff levels in various countries, so that trade in goods was facilitated. Thereafter, the concerns have been wider, as will be explained shortly. Several rounds of MTNs have taken place in the GATT with the objective of facilitating international trade. These MTN rounds were: (i) Geneva (1947); (ii) Annecy (1948); (iii) Torquay (1950); (iv) Geneva (1956); (v) Dillon (1960-1); (vi) Kennedy (1964-7); (vii) Tokyo (1973-9), and (viii) Uruguay (1986-94).

In the first six Rounds, the focus was on the reduction of tariffs. The last two Rounds have covered wider areas, as will be explained later.

DEVELOPMENT DIMENSION

The problems of development came up for consideration in the GATT in the late fifties and early sixties. It was appreciated that the poor countries that did not have much production and trading capacity needed some special consideration within the framework of the GATT. With this problem in view, Part IV was incorporated into the GATT in the early sixties. Later, in the Tokyo Round, differential and more favourable treatment to developing countries as a departure from the normal GATT rules was given formal recognition.

TOKYO ROUND

Up to the sixties, the various Rounds of the MTNs were almost exclusively devoted to the exercise of tariff reduction. Later experience prompted serious consideration of other matters which had an impact on the flow of trade.

Thus, in the Tokyo Round, apart from the reduction of tariffs, a major exercise was undertaken to strengthen disciplines on non-tariff measures, on counter-action against unfair trade and on the prevention of disguised obstructions to trade. That Round resulted in a number of agreements, popularly known as Tokyo Round Codes. These agreements covered the areas of subsidy, dumping, government procurement, technical barriers to trade, customs valuation, import licensing, civil aircraft, dairy products and bovine meat.

The Members of the GATT (called contracting parties) were not obliged to join these new agreements of the Tokyo Round. Only those that were prepared to accept the rights and obligations contained therein, joined them. The final position was that developed countries, with very few exceptions, joined these agreements, but only very few developing countries joined them. Many of them probably thought that the new obligations were too severe, or that the benefit flowing out of them was not great enough.

URUGUAY ROUND

Soon after the conclusion of the Tokyo Round, some major developed countries started feeling that it would be desirable and necessary to expand the coverage of the multilateral trading system so as to include in its folds new issues such as services, intellectual property rights and investment. The growing importance of these issues in the early eighties can be summarised into three points, mentioned below:

- Competitiveness in international trade depends a good deal on the use of developed services and high technology.
- There are new prospects for developed countries in the area of the supply of services and in the export of goods incorporating high technology.
- There is a need for expanding the opportunities and the scope of operation of the investors of developed countries in other countries.

This was the background of the developed countries' rapidly enhancing interest in the trade of knowledge-intensive goods, in services, in the protection of intellectual property rights and in the expansion of their investment opportunities. These new issues were increasingly becoming more important for their economies than the traditional trade of goods.

Besides, some developed and developing countries which were major exporters of agricultural products had been strongly feeling for some time that the normal GATT disciplines should also cover the agriculture sector, an area which had earlier been under soft discipline.

All this led to the launching of the Uruguay Round of MTNs in 1986. It resulted in a comprehensive set of agreements in the areas of goods, services and intellectual property rights. The agreements of the

Uruguay Round came into force on 1 January 1995. In this process, the GATT, which had traditionally been dealing with the trade in goods, got changed into the WTO, with a much wider coverage, including those areas having no direct link with the trade of goods.

GENERAL TRENDS

In the evolution of the process from the beginning of the GATT to the Tokyo Round and finally to the Uruguay Round, certain important trends have evolved which are worth noting.

(i) Various Rounds of MTNs have resulted in the reduction of tariffs. Before the Tokyo Round, the exercise of tariff reduction was mainly done by the developed countries, but in the Tokyo Round, some developing countries also reduced their tariffs. In the Uruguay Round, a large number of developing countries made significant commitments on tariff reduction.
The tariff reduction process in developed countries has been such that their average trade-weighted tariff on imports from developing countries is significantly higher than that on imports from other developed countries.

(ii) In the non-tariff areas, the Tokyo Round tried to improve the disciplines, introduce clarity in concepts and processes, and enhance objectivity. The Uruguay Round carried this process further.

(iii) Through improvements in the dispute settlement process, the Tokyo Round tried to improve the enforcement of rights and obligations. This process was improved significantly in the Uruguay Round, which introduced specific time frames and automaticity.

(iv) Specific attention started being given to some individual sectors in the Tokyo Round through agreements in these sectors. Now, the coverage of sectors has been significantly enhanced by detailed agreements in the agriculture and textile sectors.

(v) The differential and more favourable treatment to developing countries got serious and special attention up to the Tokyo Round, but it suffered a massive dilution in the Uruguay Round. Earlier, such treatment meant a lower degree of obligation for developing countries. Now, with a few exceptions, it largely means only a longer time frame for implementation of the commitments which are generally applicable to all except the least developed countries.

(vi) The Tokyo Round Codes resulted in the weakening of one of the most important pillars of the GATT, viz., the basic principle of most-favoured-nation (MFN) treatment. The rights and obligations of these Codes were not extended to all Members of the GATT, but only to those which accepted them. The Uruguay Round result brought most of these Codes within the folds of the GATT. Yet, even now, plurilateral agreements have been excluded from general application; these are applicable only to the Members that join them. Besides, the Uruguay Round formally acknowledged the abridgement of the basic principles of MFN treatment and national treatment in the field of services. (These terms will be described later.)

(vii) Weaker countries have always been handicapped in the GATT as, ultimately, the only way of enforcing rights and obligations is by taking recourse to retaliation, which is difficult for them. This weakness in the GATT system was not tackled either in the Tokyo Round or even in the Uruguay Round.

(viii) Traditionally, the GATT has been concerned with only the trade in goods. The Uruguay Round agreements brought some other areas, viz., services and intellectual property rights, within the folds of the WTO. All these areas have been linked through the possibility of cross-retaliation in the dispute settlement process. There is continuing pressure for bringing still other areas within the folds of the WTO.

HOW TO READ WTO AGREEMENTS

The WTO agreements, which have all been enumerated in the box on the following page, are contained in the WTO publication, *The Results of the Uruguay Round of Multilateral Trade Negotiations: The Legal Texts.* This is the authentic version of the agreements. On some subjects, it is not sufficient to just read the text of the agreements in order to know the obligations of Members. Some schedules should also be consulted for this purpose. These schedules are contained in separate volumes, which are available as WTO publications. For example, the commitments of Members on tariffs are in their tariff schedules, those in respect of subsidies in agriculture are in their respective schedules on agriculture, and the limitations to their obligations in the services sector are in their services schedules.

Some terms which appear repeatedly need to be properly understood. Some of these are given below.

GATT 1947: It means the original GATT of 1947 along with all its amendments till 31 December 1994. The main text of GATT 1947 is given at the end of the WTO publication, *The Results of the Uruguay Round of Multilateral Trade Negotiations: The Legal Texts.* Wherever an Article in GATT 1947 has an asterisk attached to it, one should consult Annex I, which contains the notes and supplementary provisions relating to all Articles marked with asterisks.

GATT 1994: It means GATT 1947, plus the decisions taken under it till 31 December 1994, plus the Uruguay Round Understandings on various Articles as mentioned in the box below, plus the new Protocol relating to tariff concessions adopted at Marrakesh in April 1994.

Now, merely mentioning the GATT as a legal instrument is not correct; one should mention GATT 1994 to refer to the obligations in the goods sector as mentioned in the General Agreement with all its amendments and decisions until December 1994 and the new Understandings operating since 1 January 1995.

Contracting parties to GATT: A country or a territory which had been a member of GATT 1947 is called a contracting party to the GATT. When a reference is made to the contracting parties acting jointly, they are designated as the "CONTRACTING PARTIES".

THE FAMILY OF WTO AGREEMENTS

(I) Multilateral Agreements on Trade in Goods, with the following components:

(i) GATT 1994, consisting of the following:

- (a) GATT 1947, i.e., the original GATT with its amendments, etc. as it stands up to 31 December 1994;
- (b) Decisions taken under GATT 1947 up to that date;
- (c) Understandings reached in the Uruguay Round in six areas, viz., other duties and charges, state trading enterprises, balance-of-payments provisions, customs unions and free-trade areas, waivers of obligations, and tariff modification; and
- (d) Tariff schedules and the manner of implementation of these schedules as agreed to in the Uruguay Round.

(ii) Other agreements in the area of goods, viz., the 12 agreements covering the areas of:

Agriculture, Sanitary and Phytosanitary Measures, Textiles and Clothing, Technical Barriers to Trade, Trade-Related Investment Measures, Anti-dumping, Customs Valuations, Preshipment Inspections, Rules of Origin, Import Licensing, Subsidies and Safeguards.

(II) General Agreement on Trade in Services

(III) Agreement on Trade-Related Aspects of Intellectual Property Rights

(IV) Trade Policy Review Mechanism

(V) Understanding on the Settlement of Disputes

(VI) Plurilateral agreements in two sectors, viz., Civil Aircraft and Government Procurement. (Those on Dairy and Bovine Meat have been discontinued.)

The agreements listed from (I) to (V) are called the Multilateral Trade Agreements.

Member: The countries or the territories participating in the WTO are called its Members.

Conflict Between GATT 1994 and Other Agreements on Goods

In the case of a conflict between a provision of GATT 1994 and a provision of another agreement on goods in the WTO, the provision of this other agreement will prevail to the extent of the conflict. It means that the new agreements in the goods sector have precedence over the old provisions in case of differences between the two, and, to that extent, the old provisions will be considered to have been modified.

GENERAL SCHEME OF AGREEMENTS

The main elements of the WTO agreements in respect of goods consist of disciplines regarding tariff and non-tariff measures. There is a framework for the reduction of tariffs and commitments on maximum levels of tariff on different products. Unlike tariffs, which are generally allowed, there is no general permission for non-tariff measures. For example, a Member cannot generally prohibit or restrict the import of goods into its territory or the export of goods from its territory. There are specific preconditions for such non-tariff measures, which can be taken only through prescribed procedures.

The WTO agreements lay down these conditions and procedures. For example, a Member may raise tariffs or apply quantitative restrictions on imports to safeguard its industry from a sudden surge of imports. Or it may take measures to reduce its imports if it faces balance-of-payments difficulties. The conditions and procedures for such actions have been specified in the respective agreements.

To ensure continuance of competitive opportunities, these agreements provide for protection against unfair trade practices. For example, if a government grants subsidies for its exports or if a firm adopts a predatory practice by unduly lowering the price of its goods, i.e., by dumping its goods, Members that are put to disadvantage have the possibility of taking measures to offset the effects of these unfair trade practices.

Sometimes, there may be the fear of disguised obstructions to trade, for example, the provision of unnecessarily high standards of quality or performance, or over-valuation of imported goods so as to charge unduly high customs duties. Besides, governments may sometimes be tempted to curtail competitive opportunities by introducing lengthy licensing procedures or by using state trading organisations. Specific protection against such actions and tendencies has been provided in the WTO agreements.

Attention has also been given to special sectors which have been facing special problems, e.g., agriculture and textiles. The former remained outside the scope of general disciplines, while the latter was covered by derogation from the disciplines. A start has been made to bring them into the folds of the general rules outlined above.

Finally, the WTO agreements cover the area of trade in services and also the standards of protection of intellectual property rights.

And all these have been integrated within a common framework of enforcement through the dispute settlement process which is meant to ensure the protection of rights and the discharge of obligations of Members.

These main elements have been elaborated through various provisions of GATT 1994 and other WTO agreements in different areas. These will be explained in detail in the chapters which follow.

PART II

GENERAL PRINCIPLES

There are certain basic principles which are applicable to all multilateral agreements relating to goods. These are, however, not applicable, by themselves, to the areas of services and intellectual property rights, except in so far they have been explicitly stipulated in the agreements relating to these areas. Two general provisions of a very important and basic nature are: most-favoured-nation (MFN) treatment and national treatment. Then, there are some other general provisions which are about (i) the obligations relating to local governments, (ii) the status of laws and regulations not applied and (iii) transparency.

This Part thus covers the following subjects:

1. Most-favoured-nation (MFN) treatment,
2. National treatment,
3. Other general principles:
   - (i) Obligations relating to local governments,
   - (ii) Status of laws and regulations, and
   - (iii) Transparency.

Chapter II.1

MOST-FAVOURED-NATION (MFN) TREATMENT

INTRODUCTION AND BROAD DEFINITION

THE provision of most-favoured-nation (MFN) treatment contained in Article I of GATT 1994 essentially means non-discriminatory treatment among the Members. Quite contrary to its name, this provision does not mean any special favour to any country; in fact, it prohibits special favours even to the most friendly country. What this principle actually means is that any benefit in connection with exporting or importing given to a product of a most favoured nation (whether a Member or not) has to be given to the like product of all Members without discrimination. This basic principle runs through the entire structure of the multilateral WTO agreements related to goods, except where it is modified or curtailed by some specific provisions in these agreements or by specific decisions of Members.[1]

Essentially, it amounts to total non-discrimination as between Members. In fact, the term "MFN treatment", in respect of any subject, has come to mean non-discriminatory treatment among Members regarding that particular subject.

MFN treatment is considered to be the very pillar of the multilateral trading system, as will be explained briefly towards the end of this chapter. This Article is very precisely worded and contains several important concepts and terms which need a lot of elaboration.

No reason whatsoever, other than the exceptions which will be explained later, is sufficient to justify any deviation from MFN treatment.

The principle of MFN treatment applies to both imports and exports, i.e., when a Member:

- imports like products originating in the territories of other Members, and
- exports like products destined for the territories of other Members.

For example, if Member country A has been imposing a customs duty of 10 per cent on steel bars, and if it now starts charging only 6 per cent duty on the steel bars of any particular country (whether a Member or not), it has to reduce the duty to 6 per cent for the steel bars of all Member countries. Similarly, if a Member had earlier banned the export of coal, and now allows its export to a particular country (whether a Member or not), it has to allow export to all Member countries.

Of course, a Member is not bound to give MFN treatment to a country which is not a Member of the WTO. The treatment given to non-Member countries depends on the Member's bilateral agreements with each one of them. However, if a Member gives a certain trade benefit to a non-Member, that benefit has to be extended to all Members in accordance with the principle of MFN treatment.

FORMS OF BENEFIT

The benefits covered by MFN treatment may be in the form of advantages, favours, privileges or immunities granted by a Member in respect of a product. For example, an advantage may be in the form of a reduced tariff level; a favour may be extended by allowing the export of a raw material which was not allowed earlier; a privilege may be in the form of exemption from a tax; and an immunity may be given by exemption from a health hazard test. The obligation on a Member is to give these benefits immediately and unconditionally to the like products of all Members once these have been given to a product of any country.

COVERAGE OF BENEFIT

The benefits which have to be extended to all Members may be with respect to the following items:

- customs duties, i.e., the tariff imposed at the time of importation;

- charges of any kind imposed on importation or exportation, e.g., import surcharge, variable levy, excise duty or export.tax;

- charges of any kind imposed in connection with importation or exportation, e.g., customs fee, consular fee, quality inspection fee; (The phrase "in connection with" has a different connotation to the phrase "on". The latter indicates a direct charge on the transaction, whereas the former involves a charge which is levied on processes connected with the transaction.)

- charges imposed on the international transfer of payments for imports or exports, e.g., some tax or fee charged by governments at the time of these transfers;

- the method of levying such duties and charges, e.g.,the method of assessing the base value on which the duty or charge is calculated, or the type of forms seeking information which will help in calculating the amount to be charged;

- all rules and formalities in connection with importation and exportation, e.g., requirement of giving specific information or declarations at the time of import or export;

- internal taxes or other internal charges (the matters referred to in Article III.2 of GATT 1994), e.g., sales tax, charges imposed by local bodies;

- laws, regulations and requirements affecting internal sale, offering for sale, purchase, transportation, distribution or use of any product (the matters referred to in Article III.4 of GATT 1994), e.g., requirement of quality certificates, restrictions relating to movement, transport, storage or retailing channels, need for particular type of packaging, restriction on use.

The simplest implication of MFN treatment as contained in Article I of GATT 1994 is that a Member cannot apply different rates of customs duty on a product imported from different Member countries. (There are exceptions to this principle of MFN treatment which will be explained later.) Similarly, in any of the matters mentioned above, a Member cannot give different treatment to different Member countries, nor can it give better treatment to a non-Member country.

For example, if a Member charges a 10 per cent import duty on a product, say textile machinery, imported from Member countries, it will not be permissible to charge only a 5 per cent duty on the textile machinery coming from a Member country which has allowed aid to buy this product. Similarly, if a Member charges a 3 per cent customs duty on a product coming from Member countries in general and now wishes to raise it to 5 per cent for an unfriendly Member, it is not permitted to do so. Similar discipline applies to the other matters listed above.

Some specific cases of "charges of any kind imposed on or in connection with importation" are given below.

Cuba applied consular charges at the rate of 5 per cent to some countries, but only at the rate of 2 per cent to other countries. The Chairman of the Contracting Parties gave a ruling in August 1948 that consular charges were "charges of any kind" covered by the MFN treatment obligation.[2]

The US adopted the practice of exemptions from merchandise processing fees. The Panel examining this practice found in February 1988 that this fee was a "charge of any kind" and was thus covered by the MFN treatment obligation.[3]

SOME IMPORTANT CONCEPTS

Two important concepts have emerged above in defining the scope of obligation of MFN treatment. As described above, the obligation of a Member is to give this treatment to the "like product" of all Members "unconditionally". It is important to understand the implications of these terms.

Like Product

The benefits have to be extended to the like product originating in all Member countries or destined for all Member countries. The phrase "like product" has not been specifically defined. This phrase and other similar phrases appear in some other Articles of GATT 1994, for example, in Articles II, III, VI, IX, XI, XIII, XVI and XIX. This term has different meanings in different contexts. At the time of formulation of this term in the context of MFN treatment, it was suggested that the method of tariff classification could be used for determining whether products were "like products". This phrase in this Article has a scope "which more nearly accords" with tariff classifications because the obligations here "are intended as concomitants and reinforcements" of the tariff concessions.[4] A problem arises, however, when a particular tariff classification itself might have been done with discrimination as an objective. This is elaborated later in the section on circumvention.

On several occasions, serious consideration has been given to this phrase as, understandably, it has presented problems of interpretation. Some of the broad points which have been considered while determining whether two products are like products are: listing of products in the tariff schedule, duties applied to the products, process of production, composition and content, chemical and synthetic origin, etc.

Some examples of the consideration of this matter in the past are given below.

- Australia had different treatment for ammonium sulphate and sodium nitrate fertilisers and this was challenged by Chile as being inconsistent with Article I. The Working Party (April 1950) examined this issue and noted that in the Australian tariff schedule, these products were listed separately and enjoyed different treatment. Further, in the tariff schedules of many other countries, these products were also listed separately. The Working Party concluded that these were not like products.[5]

- The Panel on EEC – Measures on Animal Feed Proteins (March 1978) examined whether all products used for the same purpose of adding protein to animal feed should be considered to be like products within the meaning of Article I. The Panel noted such factors as the number of products and tariff items carrying different duty rates and tariff bindings, the varying protein contents, and the different vegetable, animal and synthetic origins of the protein products under consideration. It concluded that these various protein products could not be considered as like products.[6]

- Spain had divided unroasted coffee into five tariff classifications: Colombian mild, other mild, unwashed Arabica, Robusta and other. The first two were duty-free and the other three were subject to a 7 per cent duty. Brazil claimed that all these were like products and that different rates of duty were inconsistent with Article I. The Panel on Spain – Tariff Treatment of Unroasted Coffee (June 1981) noted that the arguments given for differentiation were based on geographical factors, cultivation methods, the processing of the beans and genetic factors. The Panel did not consider such grounds as sufficient for differentiation and noted that no other Member made such a classification. It concluded that these should be considered like products within the meaning of Article I.[7]

Unconditional Application of Benefits

MFN treatment has to be extended to Members immediately and unconditionally. If a Member formulates an improved set of rules on the trade of goods within the framework of GATT 1994, it cannot limit the application of these rules to only those Members that fulfil some conditions. For example, it cannot say that the improved rules will be applicable only to those that undertake to adopt similar rules. Such a limited application will be treated as a conditional application, and will not be allowed.

Some examples of the consideration of this issue are given below.

- Belgium had a system of granting exemption from a levy to products purchased by public bodies only from countries which had a system of family allowance similar to that of Belgium. The Panel on Belgian Family Allowances set up to examine this issue held this practice to be inconsistent with the principle of MFN treatment as, apart from other problems, it introduced an element of conditionality in the application of an advantage (November 1952).[8]

- A Working Party in the GATT in 1952 considered the proposal to insert a reciprocity clause in the International Convention to Facilitate the Importation of Commercial Samples and Advertising Material. It concluded that such a clause will be inconsistent with the MFN principle because of the conditionality involved.[9]

- The Working Party on the accession of Hungary examined in 1973 the practice of providing certain benefits of tariff treatment only to countries which had a cooperation contract with Hungary. During the course of examination of this matter, the GATT Secretariat gave, on request, a legal opinion that the prerequisite of having a cooperative contract in order to get beneficial tariff treatment appeared to imply conditional MFN treatment and would not appear to be compatible with Article I (July 1973).[10]

SOME IMPORTANT CONSIDERATIONS

Over the course of years, some important points have emerged in respect of the application of MFN treatment. Some of the more significant ones are given below.

Coverage of Unbound Duty

The MFN treatment obligation applies to customs duties irrespective of their being bound or unbound. If a Member is committed not to raise the customs duty on a product beyond a particular level, the duty is said to be bound, otherwise the duty is unbound.(The process of the binding of customs duties will be explained later in the chapter on tariffs.) On the unbound duty, there is no obligation to provide a particular level of duty; however, according to the MFN treatment principle, even in such cases, the same duty rate will have to be applied in respect of all Members.

This matter came up for consideration in 1981 in the case of the tariff of Spain on unroasted coffee. The Panel on Spain – Tariff Treatment of Unroasted Coffee (June 1981) took note of the fact that Spain had not bound the tariff rates on this product and came to the conclusion that the MFN obligation under Article I of GATT 1994 applies equally to bound and unbound tariff items.[11]

Balancing of Treatments Not Permissible

Each relevant measure or step has to satisfy the condition of MFN treatment by itself. There cannot be a balancing of the treatment, i.e., a Member is not allowed to give less favourable treatment in one case to balance more favourable treatment in another case.

Goods Transitting Through Several Countries

The benefits apply to products "originating in" the territories of Members. This phrase signifies that even if the product might have passed through some other countries on the way, it has to be given the particular benefit in the importing Member country based on its country of origin. How a product will be considered to have originated in a particular country is determined by the rules of origin, which will be discussed in the relevant chapter.

Possibility of Circumvention

There may be cases where the rules and procedures appear non-discriminatory and yet the application of these rules and procedures causes discrimination in actual practice. Some examples are given below.

- The classification of products may be made in such a way that one class of products gets less favourable treatment, and it may so happen that this class of product is exported by a single country or only a few countries. The case of the unroasted coffee of Spain mentioned above may be an example.

- A Member may prescribe some requirements for the entry of a certain product; for example, it lays down that the product must be accompanied by a quality certificate issued by a particular authority. A particular Member may be specially benefited in this manner if the certifying authority is located in its territory and is not easily available to the exporters in other Member countries.

The Panel report on EEC – Imports of Beef from Canada (March 1981) examined an EEC regulation imposing a levy-free tariff quota on high-quality grain-fed beef. The suspension of import levy was conditional on the production of a certificate of authenticity. The Panel found that the only authorised certifying agency was a US agency authorised to certify only meat from the US. The Panel concluded that the regulation had the effect of preventing access of like products from other countries and was thus inconsistent with Article I.[12]

- A Member may prescribe a significantly higher charge at a particular port. The rules may appear to apply uniformly to all Members, but it may so happen that in actual practice, this port is utilised by only one Member or a limited number of Members for supplying practically all its/their products. These Members may have a genuine complaint that their products are being put at a disadvantage.

EXCEPTIONS

Some provisions of GATT 1994 and some decisions of Members have provided for exceptions to MFN treatment. These are explained below.

Enabling Clause

The Enabling Clause, more formally called the Differential and More Favourable Treatment, Reciprocity and Fuller Participation of Developing Countries, is contained in the Decision of the CONTRACTING PARTIES of 28 November 1979. It allows Members to accord differential and more favourable treatment to developing countries without according such treatment to other Members and, to that extent, it is a relaxation of the MFN clause. The treatments covered by this exception are specified below:

(i) Generalised System of Preferences (GSP), which is a system of tariff preferences accorded by developed countries to developing countries.

(ii) Differential and more favourable treatment in respect of non-tariff measures governed by the provisions of instruments multilaterally negotiated earlier under the auspices of the GATT and now within the framework of the WTO. Through this exception, special treatment was given to developing countries in the various Codes which emerged after the Tokyo Round and in various agreements resulting from the Uruguay Round.

(iii) Arrangements among developing countries as a whole or among a few of them on tariff preferences. In respect of non-tariff preferences, the provision in the Enabling Clause is that these should be in accordance with the criteria or conditions which may be prescribed by the CONTRACTING PARTIES of the GATT (now the Members of the WTO). No such criteria or conditions have been prescribed so far.

(iv) Special treatment of the least developed countries in the context of general or special measures in favour of developing countries.

Free-Trade Area, Customs Union (Article XXIV of GATT 1994)

A group of Members may constitute themselves into a customs union or a free-trade area, and have totally free trade or reduced levels of duties and of other trade-restrictive regulations among themselves without the obligation of extending such treatment to other Members. This is permissible in accordance with Article XXIV.5 of GATT 1994. Regional trading entities have been formed and are in the process of being formed in many areas under this provision.

A free-trade area is a group of two or more countries in which duties and other trade-restrictive regulations are eliminated on substantially all the trade between these countries.

A customs union is a group of countries forming themselves into one customs territory in which duties and other trade-restrictive regulations are eliminated with respect to substantially all the trade between the countries or, at least, with respect to substantially all the trade in products originating in these countries. Further, the Members constituting the customs union should apply substantially the same duties and other trade regulations to the products of countries outside the union.

While forming a free-trade area or a customs union, certain disciplines must be followed in respect of the new trade regime in relation to the previous regime. In particular, these are the following:

(i) At the time of the formation of a customs union, the duties and other trade regulations applied to Members outside the union must not be, on the whole, higher or more restrictive than what were applicable in these countries prior to the formation of the union. It does not mean a restriction on the average tariff for each individual product; it merely means that the whole level of tariffs of a customs union should not be higher than the previous average overall level of the constituent territories.
Here, a comparison is envisaged with respect to the general incidence of the duties "applicable" in the territories. The term "applicable" has given rise to differences of opinion as to whether it refers to the bound levels or to the actual levels applied. This matter has not been conclusively settled.

(ii) In respect of a free-trade area, the duties and other trade regulations in the countries forming the area should not be higher or more restrictive at the time of formation of the area than what they were in these countries prior to the formation of the area.

(iii) Article XXIV.5 of GATT 1994 enables the formation of a customs union or a free-trade area "as between the territories of contracting parties" of the GATT. Various Working Parties in the GATT, while considering this matter, have recorded diverging views as to whether this enabling provision applies in cases when such unions and areas are formed with countries which are not contracting parties (now Members). In practice, several non-Members have been included in such arrangements in the past. Detailed positions on this issue have been recorded in the report of the Working Party on EEC – Agreements on Association with Tunisia and Morocco (September 1970).[13]

Frontier Trade

Advantages accorded by a Member to adjacent countries in order to facilitate frontier traffic are permitted by Article XXIV.3 of GATT 1994.

Government Procurement

The MFN obligation of Article I does not apply to the import of products for immediate or ultimate consumption in government use and not otherwise for resale or use in the production of goods for sale. There is a special plurilateral agreement governing such purchases.

General Exceptions

Article XX of GATT 1994 allows Members to restrict imports or exports from/to specific sources. Such measures can be taken for some specified purposes, for example, for the protection of public morals, protection of human, animal or plant life or health, etc.

Security Exception

Restrictions on imports and exports from/to specific countries can be imposed for security reasons in accordance with Article XXI of GATT 1994.

Measures Permitted by WTO Agreements on Goods

The WTO agreements permit taking specific measures, after following specified procedures, in the form of countervailing duties, anti-dumping duties and retaliatory measures following the dispute settlement process. These can be taken in respect of products originating in specific Member countries.

Plurilateral Agreements

The WTO agreements include two agreements which are called plurilateral agreements. These are: Agreement on Trade in Civil Aircraft and Agreement on Government Procurement. (Those in the areas of Bovine Meat and Dairy have now been discontinued.) These are applicable only to the Members that have accepted them. Hence, the benefits given by a Member in any of these agreements may be limited only to those Members that have accepted that particular agreement.

IMPORTANCE OF MFN PRINCIPLE FOR MULTILATERALISM AND EROSION OF THE PRINCIPLE

The basic objective of the MFN treatment principle is to strengthen the multilateral process in international trade policy. When two countries exchanging tariff concessions between themselves extend these new tariff levels to all Members, the principle that gets emphasised is that all Members have an expectation of sharing the benefits of the system. In the same way, when a Member gets into some difficulty, for example, because of a balance-of-payments problem or increased imports, all Members get prepared to share the burden of reduced export opportunities into the territory of that Member. The underlying presumption in the multilateral process is that two or three Members should not, among themselves, share the benefits, nor should they be called upon to share the strains.

The multilateral nature of the system has, however, been undergoing serious erosion for some time.

The most serious erosion came about during the Tokyo Round when a number of Codes were evolved which did not operate on a non-discriminatory basis across the total Membership of GATT 1947. These Codes were, of course, open for Membership to all, but were applicable only to those Members who joined them. Though within each Code, the principle of non-discrimination was followed, it was not extended to the overall Membership of GATT 1947. In actual practice, very few developing countries joined these Codes.

The Uruguay Round results subsumed most of these Codes into agreements which are now applied universally to Members of the WTO. Some areas are still left, however, where only limited application of the rules holds. For example, there are two plurilateral agreements which are applicable only to those Members which join them. Besides, in the General Agreement on Trade in Services, deviations from the MFN treatment principle have been specifically permitted.

The multilateral process is further eroded by the formation of large regional trading blocs. As has been explained above, the formation of customs unions or free-trade areas is, of course, permitted in GATT 1994, but if the world will be divided into a few very large trading blocs, the relevance of the multilateral system as enshrined in the WTO agreements will be very much reduced. The risks to the system can be lowered and confidence in it retained if the regional trading areas are formed and operated with the objective of enhancing trade among the Members concerned in order to achieve a broader objective of enhancing trade within the multilateral system as a whole.

Yet another risk to the multilateral process comes from unilateral action or the threat of such action from economically strong Members of the system. It reduces the confidence of the weaker Members in the efficacy and effectiveness of the system.

Here, the main responsibility for building up confidence in the system rests with the economically strong Members. They are, of course, capable of extracting concessions bilaterally, but it is better for the functioning of the system if they resist the temptation to do so. They should show patience, exercise moderation and adopt the multilateral process to achieve their objectives.

Chapter II.2

National Treatment

INTRODUCTION

ALONG with MFN treatment, explained in the previous chapter, national treatment is also an important basic principle in the WTO agreements on goods. Whereas the former essentially means non-discrimination as among Members, the latter means non-discrimination as between domestic products and imported products. Basically, the principle of national treatment prescribes the obligation that an imported product, after entering the country of import, should be treated as a national product. Like MFN treatment, this principle is also an important pillar in the foundations of the multilateral trading system.

The main objective of this principle is to ensure that the effects of tariff concessions are not frustrated by providing indirect protection to domestic products. These disciplines aim at establishing competitive conditions for imported products in relation to domestic products and at providing equal opportunities to imported products and domestic products in the domestic market.

The obligation of national treatment is contained in Article III of GATT 1994. Though the concept appears simple, this Article is very complex and has given rise to a large number of problems of interpretation in the course of its application. And as time passes and new features emerge in the international trade of goods, further complexities enter into the operation of this principle.

MAIN ELEMENTS

To understand the basic disciplines, as contained in the various paragraphs of Article III of GATT 1994, one has to understand properly some clarifications and the implications of some terms. A simple reading of this Article may prove somewhat cumbersome.

Basic Discipline

The essential elements of the basic discipline of this Article are given below.

(i) Imported products must not be subject to internal taxes or other internal charges in excess of those applied to like domestic products.
For example, an excise tax which is applicable to a domestic product cannot be applied to an imported product at a rate higher than that applicable to the domestic product. Similarly, an imported product cannot be subject to a charge which, for example, is in the nature of a contribution to a fund meant for facilitating imports, if such a charge is not levied on the like domestic product.

(ii) Imported products must not be accorded treatment less favourable than that accorded to like domestic products with respect to laws, regulations and requirements affecting their sale, purchase, transportation, distribution or use.
For example, it is not permissible to lay down a condition that an imported product must be stored in particular types of godowns or must be transported by particular types of vehicles, when no such conditions apply to a like domestic product.

(iii) A Member cannot have any quantitative regulation requiring compulsory utilisation of a product from a domestic source in preference to using a like imported product.
For example, it cannot be prescribed that in the manufacture of a chemical, a certain quantity or proportion of a constituent must be obtained from domestic sources.

(iv) A Member cannot apply internal taxes or other internal charges or internal quantitative regulations in a manner so as to afford protection to domestic production.

The first three elements described above relate to direct imposition of taxes, other charges and regulations, whereas the fourth element is about "the manner of application" of these taxes, other charges and quantitative regulations. The implication of the difference will be explained briefly later.

Some Clarification

A particular manner of application of taxes, other charges and quantitative regulations is prohibited if it affords protection to domestic production. Here, "domestic production" does not mean only the production of that particular product; it also means the production of directly competitive or substitutable products. This implies that even if the taxes or charges are applied at the same rate on the imported and like domestic products, the manner of application should not be such as to afford protection to domestic production. Similarly, a quantitative regulation also cannot be applied in a manner which affords protection to domestic production.

The notes and supplementary provisions relating to Article III of GATT 1994 provide some clarification and qualification of these disciplines relating to the "manner of application". The relevance of the manner of application of internal taxes or other charges in this connection arises only in cases where competition is involved between directly competitive or substitutable imported and domestic products. There may be cases where the taxes or charges are applied at the same rate on the imported and like domestic products, and yet, the manner of application is such that protection is afforded to the domestic production of a directly competitive or substitutable product. Such a practice is prohibited. Clearly, a distinction is to be drawn between a "like product" and a "directly competitive or substitutable product".

For example, a country may apply a very high internal tax rate on oranges which is, of course, applicable to both imported and domestic products, but if this country does not produce oranges, this tax, in effect, goes to raise the price of only imported oranges. And in this manner, this country may be affording protection to its own production of apples, in so far as oranges are directly competitive or substitutable with apples.[14] Such protection is prohibited by the second sentence of Article III.2 read with Article III.1.

In respect of quantitative regulations, the notes and supplementary provisions clarify that the manner of application of quantitative regulations which do not prescribe compulsory use of like domestic products is not prohibited if all of the products subject to the regulations are produced domestically in substantial quantities.

Further, the manner of application of a quantitative regulation cannot be justified on the grounds that the prescribed proportion or quantity constitutes an equitable relationship between imported and domestic products.

An element of the MFN treatment principle has been introduced in respect of internal quantitative regulations in Article III.7 of GATT 1994. It prohibits the application of any such regulation in a manner so as to allocate specific quantities or proportions among external sources of supply.

Implications of Some Terms

Article III.2 of GATT 1994 prescribes that imported products shall not be subject to, "directly or indirectly", internal taxes in excess of those applied, "directly or indirectly", to like domestic products. Also, in accordance with Article III.5 of GATT 1994, quantitative regulations cannot prescribe, "directly or indirectly", compulsory use of the like domestic product. Further, Article III.4 of GATT 1994 prescribes that imported products must not be accorded less favourable treatment than that accorded to like domestic products in respect of laws, regulations and requirements "affecting" the sale etc. of the products. These terms need elucidation.

Directly or Indirectly

The meaning of "directly" is clear. The term "indirectly" appears to cover even such taxes which are not on the product as such, but on the processing of the product. Besides, it is also considered to imply that taxation methods and rules for tax collection are covered in this discipline. In respect of internal quantitative regulations, this term would seem to imply that the discipline covers not only a regulation specifically laying down the requirement of compulsory use, but also a regulation which, by implication or in the process of application, has the effect of such a requirement.

Affecting

The term "affecting" sale or purchase etc. has been considered to cover not only such laws or regulations which directly regulate sale or purchase, but also those which might adversely modify the conditions of competition between the domestic and imported products. This term implies that not only the substantive provisions, but also the process of enforcement, are relevant. Thus, the term "affecting" has a wide coverage in its interpretation.

The implication of "affecting" has been considered on some occasions, as given below.

- The Panel on Italian Discrimination Against Imported Agricultural Machinery (October 1958) observed that the selection of this word would imply that the discipline covers not only the laws and regulations which directly govern the conditions of sale or purchase, but also any law or regulation which might adversely modify the conditions of competition between the domestic and imported products in the internal market.[15]

- The Panel on US – Section 337 of the Tariff Act of 1930 (November 1989) held the view that the enforcement procedures cannot be separated from the substantive provisions which they seek to enforce.[16]

SOME IMPORTANT CONCEPTS

Two important concepts need elaboration, viz., what constitutes the "like product", and what are the determinants for concluding that "discrimination" against an imported product has taken place or that the domestic product has been "protected".

Like Product

The concept of "like product" is as crucial in the context of national treatment as it is in the context of MFN treatment, which has already been discussed in the preceding chapter. What a like product is has not been specifically defined. Decisions on this matter have been taken on a case-by-case basis.

Principles in Defining This Concept

Over a long course of implementation of this Article, the following principles appear to have emerged in determining whether some products are "like products".

- The concept of "like product" would seem to go beyond the concept of an identical or equal product; it would seem to include also products with similar qualities.

- Product coverage in Article III appears to be wider than that in Article I where also the concept of "like product" is relevant. The latter relates more to classification, whereas the former relates more to competitive conditions.

- The product coverage of Article I is a matter for negotiation between Members, whereas the obligations under Article III relate to interpretation and analysis.

- In examining a product differentiation which has a bearing on the determination of a "like product", the objective of the product differentiation becomes relevant. It has to be examined if such a differentiation is serving any national objective or if it is meant to provide protection to domestic industry.

Some of the factors to be considered are: properties, nature, quality and end use. While deciding whether an imported product is a like product in relation to a domestic product, one has to be guided by the basic objective of Article III that imported products should not be exposed to more rigorous competitive conditions, and domestic products should not enjoy a more favourable situation of competition.

Specific Examples

The process of determining what a like product is can best be explained by taking some specific examples.

- The Panel on Japan – Customs Duties, Taxes and Labelling Practices on Imported Wines and Alcoholic Beverages (November 1987) considered the Japanese system of giving different tax treatment to liqueurs and sparkling wines according to alcoholic and extract content. It found that imported liqueurs and sparkling wines with high raw-material content were subjected to higher internal taxes than those applied to domestic liqueurs and sparkling wines which had lower raw-material content. Keeping in view end uses, properties and classifications, the Panel considered them as like products and concluded that the differential treatment was not consistent with Article III.[17]

- The Working Party on Border Tax Adjustments (December 1970) was of the view that the interpretation of "like product" should be examined on a case-by-case basis. It identified some criteria for the determination of like products. These were: end uses in a given market, consumers' tastes and habits, which differ from country to country, and the properties, nature and quality of products.[18]

- The Panel on Canada – Measures Affecting the Sale of Gold Coins considered the case of Maple Leaf (Canadian) and Krugerrand (South African) gold coins. It appears to have found that these were normally purchased as investment goods, were produced to very similar standards, had the same weight in gold and competed directly with each other in international markets. The Panel considered them as like products.

- The Panel on US – Taxes on Petroleum and Certain Imported Substances (June 1987) examined the differential internal taxation on domestic and imported petroleum and some petroleum products. It found that the domestic products were crude oil, crude oil condensates and natural gasoline, and the imported products were crude oil, crude oil condensates, natural gasoline, refined and residual oil, and certain other liquid hydrocarbon products. It concluded that either the domestic products and imported products were identical or they served substantially identical end uses. The Panel considered them like products.[19]

- The Panel on US – Measures Affecting Alcoholic and Malt Beverages (June 1992) considered the excise tax exemption on wine made from a particular type of grape, viz., scuppernong grapes. On the complaint of Canada that this practice was inconsistent with Article III, the US argued that the tax provision was uniformly applicable to all wines produced from this particular variety of grape. The Panel examined this question based on the usual criteria of end use, consumer tastes and habits, and the properties, nature and quality of the products, and also on the objective of Article III. The Panel found it relevant to consider whether the differentiation of the products was being made so as to afford protection to domestic production. It observed that tariff classification and tax laws in the US did not generally make a distinction between still wines on the basis of the variety of grape used in their production and that the US did not claim any public policy purpose for this tax provision except the purpose of subsidising the small local producers. The Panel concluded that unsweetened still wines were like products and that the differentiation in the tax regulation was affording protection to local products and was therefore inconsistent with Article III.2.[20]

Discrimination Against Imported Products, Protection of Domestic Products

Discrimination against imported products or protection of domestic products can often be easily detected if done through differential internal taxes or differential internal charges. However, it is not easy if the discrimination or protection is alleged in respect of laws, regulations and requirements affecting sale, purchase, transportation, distribution and use. This matter has been the subject of a large number of disputes in the past. Certain principles have evolved in the course of the consideration of this issue by the various panels. Some of these important principles are given below.

(i) Any requirement on the imported product going beyond the obligation to indicate the origin of the product would be considered inconsistent with Article III of GATT 1994 if it does not also apply to the domestic product.
In 1955, there was a Hawaiian regulation that firms which sold imported eggs had to display a placard stating "we sell foreign eggs". Australia complained that this requirement affecting sale was inconsistent with Article III.4. The regulation was later withdrawn.

(ii) Granting financial facilities, e.g., special credit facilities, tax refunds or tax remission or exemption, for the purchase of domestic products would be considered discriminatory against imported products and as protection of domestic products.
The Panel on Italian Discrimination Against Imported Agricultural Machinery (October 1958) examined an Italian law providing special credit facilities to farmers for the purchase of agricultural machinery produced in Italy. It was considered that any favourable treatment granted to the domestic product had to be given to like imported products.[21]
The Panel on US – Measures Affecting Alcoholic and Malt Beverages (June 1992) examined the US tax measure providing excise tax exemption for domestic producers of beer and wine, which was not available for imported products. The Panel found that the tax law operated to create a lower tax rate on domestic beer and wine than on like imported products and that thus it was discriminatory.[22]
The UK had a "utility" system under which goods satisfying certain quality and price criteria were exempt from purchase tax, whereas this facility was not available to like imported products. The Netherlands brought a complaint against this system in 1950. The UK authorities agreed that this discrimination had a protective effect and they modified the system.

(iii) If investors or local industry or importers are obliged to purchase domestic products, there is a denial of opportunity to the like imported products for competing in this particular market. Hence, it would be considered discriminatory againt the imported products.

The Panel on Canada – Administration of Foreign Investment Review Act (June 1983) examined the Canadian system of written undertakings on purchase and export. Investors were required to give an undertaking to purchase goods of domestic origin. The Panel held that such a requirement clearly meant that imported goods were less favourably treated than domestic goods and that hence, this provision was not consistent with Article III. Further, even if the undertaking was conditional on the goods being competitively available in Canada, the less favourable treatment still held as it resulted in giving preference to domestic products when imported and domestic products were available on equivalent terms.[23]

The Panel on EEC – Measures on Animal Feed Proteins (March 1978) examined a regulation requiring domestic producers or importers of oilseeds etc. and importers of corn gluten feed to purchase a certain quantity of surplus skimmed milk powder held by intervention agencies. The Panel found that these agencies held only domestic products and concluded that this regulation protected the domestic product.[24]

(iv) Imported products cannot be subjected to any special processing requirement which is not obligatory for the domestic product. The UK had a regulation that domestic poultry, after slaughter, could be chilled by any method, whereas imported poultry was to be cooled by only the spin-chill method. The US complained about it and a panel was formed, but the matter got settled in the meantime.[25]

(v) If imported products are required to pass through certain specified wholesale or retail channels or some specified means of transport and if this requirement is not applicable to domestic products, such a requirement will be held to be discriminatory against the imported products.

The Panel on US – Measures Affecting Alcoholic and Malt Beverages (June 1992) considered a requirement in some states of the US that imported beer and wine be sold only through in-state wholesalers or other middlemen, while some in-state like products were permitted to be sold directly to retailers. The US argued that in-state breweries and wineries bore the same costs as did the wholesalers in respect of record-keeping, auditing, inspection and tax collection. It also said that most in-state beer and wine producers preferred to use wholesalers rather than to market their products directly to retailers. The Panel held that Article III requires relative competition opportunities in the market, irrespective of the actual choices made by enterprises, and that denial of such opportunities creates less favourable treatment to the imported products.[26]

This Panel also examined the requirement of some states in the US that alcoholic beverages imported into the state be transported by common carriers authorised to operate as such within the state, whereas in-state producers of alcoholic beverages could deliver their products to customers in their own vehicles. The Panel concluded that such a requirement resulted in less favourable treatment to imported products.

(vi) A regulation that domestic products and imported products should both adhere to a minimum-price requirement is not consistent with Article III of GATT 1994, even though the regulation is equally applicable to both domestic and imported products.

This matter was considered by the Panel on Canada – Import, Distribution and Sale of Certain Alcoholic Drinks by Provincial Marketing Agencies (February 1992). The Panel was of the opinion that this practice did not necessarily accord equal conditions of competition to imported and domestic products in the sense that the imported product was prevented from being supplied at a price below that of the domestic product.[27]

(vii) If there are wider choices for punitive action against imported products, or if there are tighter time schedules for disposal of complaints against imported products compared to that available in respect of domestic products, it amounts to discrimination against the imported products.

These matters were examined by the Panel on US – Section 337

> of the Tariff Act of 1930 (November 1989) in respect of products which violate patent provisions. The Panel found that these types of facilitation of legal action against the imported products when such facilities were not available for action against domestic products were discriminatory against the imported products.[28]

An important question which has emerged for some years is the relationship between the "like product" as understood in the context of Article III and the regulatory distinction of products on the basis of the general exceptions (particularly for environmental reasons) contained in Article XX of GATT 1994, for example, whether a distinction could be made between low-alcohol beer and high-alcohol beer. The 1992 Panel on US – Measures Affecting Alcoholic and Malt Beverages considered that even though these two types of beer had similar characteristics, they should not be considered like products, as the relevant US law made a distinction between these two categories for the protection of human health [Article XX(b) of GATT 1994].[29] As countries get subjected to more and more pressures on the grounds of environmental protection, it is likely that there may be a tendency to make finer distinctions between products for the purpose of differential treatment as between an imported product and an "almost like" domestic product. This subject is likely to come up for serious consideration in the near future as the disputes on this subject may multiply, and, in this process, it is likely that there may be some further clarity on the issue.

SOME IMPORTANT CONSIDERATIONS

Products with Unbound Duty

The obligation of national treatment applies irrespective of the fact whether or not the product is covered by tariff binding. (The process of tariff binding is explained in the chapter on tariffs.) A Member cannot justify a higher internal tax rate on an imported product on the grounds that it could, in any case, apply a higher tariff on the product not subject to tariff binding. Some of the instances when this matter has been considered are given below.

- The Working Party on Brazilian Internal Taxes (June 1949) held that a contracting party is bound by the Article III obligation whether or not it has undertaken a tariff commitment in respect of the goods concerned.[30]

- The Panel report on EEC – Regulation on Imports of Parts and Components (adopted on 16 May 1990) held that internal taxes which discriminate against imported products are prohibited, whether or not the items concerned are bound.[31]

Balancing Not Allowed

The obligation of national treatment has to be undertaken as applicable to each individual case of imported products. Balancing is not allowed as between the effects of various measures or the treatment accorded to various products. Thus, less favourable treatment accorded to an imported product cannot be justified on the grounds that it has received more favourable treatment in another way, or that another product from the exporting country has received more favourable treatment.

This principle clearly emerged in the report of the Panel on US – Section 337 of Tariff Act of 1930 (November 1989).[32]

Different Regional Treatment

When a domestic product is given different treatment in different regions of a country, the treatment which is the most favourable among these is to be accorded to the like imported product.

This principle evolved in the course of the examination of differential excise taxes on alcoholic beverages in the US by the Panel on US – Measures Affecting Alcoholic and Malt Beverages (June 1992).[33]

Measures Having Negligible Effect

Some countries, while defending measures which seemingly violate the obligations of national treatment, have argued that the measures had only a negligible effect on trade and that, therefore, they cannot be causing adverse effects on the imported products. In the course of the consideration of this issue in the past, the position which is well established by now is that the actual trade effect is not an important point to be considered; what is crucial to the issue is whether competitive conditions for the imported products in relation to domestic products have been adversely affected. The national treatment principle of Article III obliges Members to establish competitive conditions for imported products in relation to domestic products. A measure is considered inconsistent with Article III of GATT 1994 if it disturbs the competitive conditions of the imported product in relation to domestic products, even though the domestic products getting more favourable treatment compared to the imported product may be negligible in quantity or even if the domestic products might not have effectively received any advantage from the measure. Thus, even in the absence of a trade effect, a case of violation could occur.

Some important cases where this issue has been discussed in the past are described below.

- The Panel on US – Taxes on Petroleum and Certain Imported Substances (June 1987) examined the excise tax in the US which was higher for imported products than for domestic products. The US argued that the tax differential of 3.5 US cents per barrel was so small that it would not nullify or impair the benefits accruing to other Members. (Nullification and impairment are specific concepts in the context of dispute settlement in the WTO agreements. These will be described in detail in the chapter on the dispute settlement process.) The Panel held that the obligation in Article III is to establish certain competitive conditions and that it does not refer to trade effects. The panel held the differential tax to be inconsistent with this obligation.[34]

- In the Working Party on Brazilian Internal Taxes (June 1949), Brazil argued that Article III is not violated in a case where there are no imports of a given product or where imports are small in volume. The majority of members did not agree with this view. They argued that the absence of imports from contracting parties in the past would not necessarily be an indication that they had no interest in the export of that product. In their view, the obligation of Article III is equally applicable whether imports from other contracting parties are substantial, small or non-existent.[35]

- The Panel on US – Measures Affecting Alcoholic and Malt Beverages (June 1992) examined a complaint regarding the reduction of excise duty for some domestic products. In the Panel hearing, the US argued that only 1.5 per cent of domestic beer was eligible for the reduction in the excise tax on beer and less than 1 per cent benefited from the reduction, hence the tax neither discriminated against imported beer nor provided protection to domestic production. The Panel was of the opinion that Article III protects competitive conditions between imported and domestic products and that this protection is not conditional on trade effects.[36]

Risk of Discrimination

An important matter which has come up for consideration in the past is whether a law, regulation or practice which does not necessarily discriminate against imported products but is capable of doing so, is consistent with Article III.4. This question was examined by the Panel on EEC – Payments and Subsidies Paid to Processors and Producers of Oil Seeds and Related Animal Feed Protein (January 1990). The Panel noted that the exposure of particular imported products to a risk of discrimination constitutes, by itself, a form of discrimination. It concluded that the relevant purchase regulation of the EEC creating such a risk must be considered to be according less favourable treatment to the imported products.[37]

EXCEPTIONS

Some exceptions to the general discipline of national treatment have been provided in Article III.8 (a), III.8(b) and III.10 of GATT 1994. An exception also appears in the Agreement on Subsidies and Countervailing Measures. In this connection, the relevant provisions of the Agreement on Trade-Related Investment Measures (TRIMs) should also be considered. A list of important exceptions is given below.

(i) The obligation of national treatment does not apply to laws, regulations or requirements governing government procurement where products are purchased for the use of the government and not for commercial resale nor for use in production of goods for commercial resale.

(ii) The obligation of national treatment does not prevent payment of subsidies exclusively to domestic producers. In this connection, a US tax measure providing credit against excise taxes to domestic producers of beer and wine came up for consideration in the Panel on US – Measures Affecting Alcoholic and Malt Beverages (June 1992). The US argued for exemption from the obligation of national treatment on the grounds that the measure in question was in the nature of a subsidy. The Panel noted that the word "payment" of subsidies in Article III.8(b) refers only to direct subsidies involving payments and not to other measures like tax credits or tax reduction.[38]

(iii) Establishing or maintaining internal quantitative regulations relating to exposed cinematograph films in accordance with Article IV of GATT 1994 is permitted and Article III does not prohibit it.

(iv) A new exception appears in the Uruguay Round Agreement on Subsidies and Countervailing Measures. Subsidies contingent on the use of domestic goods over imported goods are allowed, in the case of developing countries, for five years from the date of the coming into force of the WTO Agreement. For the least developed countries, they are allowed for eight years from that date [Articles 3.1(b) and 27.3 of the Agreement on Subsidies and Countervailing Measures].

(v) The local content requirement (requirement that permission for investment will be conditional on the use of domestic products to some extent) and the limitation on the use of imported products (related to the value or volume of the domestic products that the firm exports) have been declared to be inconsistent with the obligations of Article III of GATT 1994 in the Agreement on

TRIMs. Developed country Members have, however, been given two years from the coming into force of the WTO Agreement to eliminate these measures if they have them. For developing country Members, this period is five years and for least developed country Members, it is seven years. There is a further provision in the Agreement that developing country Members are free to deviate temporarily from the obligation of not imposing these measures to the extent that the rules governing balance-of-payments provisions permit. (These rules will be described in the relevant chapters on TRIMs and balance-of-payments provisions.)

EMERGING PROBLEMS

The emerging problems in the area of national treatment relate to the attempts to link it with health hazards and the environment. So far, the criteria of determining like products have been based on the characteristics of the products; attempts have been initiated to broaden the scope so as to include in the criteria even the method of production of the products. The distinction between the present practice and the attempted broadened scope will be made clear by an example.

Suppose the imported product is produced in factories which pollute the environment by discharging harmful fluids into the neighbouring river. At present, this aspect of the production will be totally irrelevant in comparing this imported product with the domestic product having similar composition, use and other characteristics. The domestic product and the imported product will be considered like products, and, as such, the imported product will have the benefit of national treatment.

Now, attempts are being made to distinguish the imported product from the domestic product on the grounds of whether the production process of the former causes pollution to the environment. If this is accepted as a criterion for determining the like product, the imported product in the example given above will be declared as not being a like product, and, as such, it will not have the benefit of national treatment.

Such attempts have so far met with resistance, and, thus, the criteria continue as before.

Chapter II.3

OTHER GENERAL PRINCIPLES

OBLIGATIONS RELATING TO REGIONAL GOVERNMENTS

Article XXIV.12

THE government at the national level is responsible for the implementation of the WTO agreements. Article XXIV.12 of GATT 1994 prescribes the responsibility relating to the implementation of the relevant provisions of the agreements by regional and local governments, and other authorities in the country. This responsibility is slightly less than that applicable to the implementation by the government at the national level itself. This provision prescribes that a Member shall take "such reasonable measures as may be available to it to ensure observance of the provisions...by the regional and local governments and authorities within its territories". The responsibility is thus limited, in this provision, to taking "reasonable measures as may be available".

Understanding on the Interpretation of Article XXIV.12

The Understanding on the Interpretation of Article XXIV.12 of GATT 1994, which is itself a part of GATT 1994, clarifies the obligation of the Member further. It says that the dispute settlement process may be invoked. If it is found in this process that a provision of GATT 1994 has not been observed, the Member concerned is obliged to take such reasonable measures as may be available to it to ensure observance.

The Understanding goes on to clarify that the provisions of compensation and suspension of concessions apply in cases where it has not been possible to secure such observance.

Thus, a Member is required to compensate for its failure to ensure compliance by regional and local governments and other authorities. This ultimate relief is similar in nature to the one against non-compliance with the provisions by the Member itself.

STATUS OF LAWS AND REGULATIONS

Earlier Consideration

A question which has been examined several times is whether the mere existence of a provision in a national legislation is enough to violate a provision of the agreement with which it conflicts, or whether the violation of the provision will be considered to occur only after certain measures affecting trade have been taken in pursuance of the legislation. The problem reduces itself to the examination of the issue as to whether the legislation itself, or only the application of the legislation, can be challenged.

While considering this matter, a distinction has been made between:

(i) a mandatory provision in the legislation, i.e., one in which the authorities are obliged to take certain measures which, if taken, would violate some provision of the agreement, and

(ii) a discretionary provision in the legislation, where the authorities have the discretion to take such measures, but where there is no mandatory obligation that they must take such measures.

The very existence of the former type of provision is considered to violate the provision of the agreement if it conflicts with it. Therefore, nullification or impairment will be presumed to have been caused by the mere existence of even one mandatory provision in the legislation if it violates the agreement. However, in the latter case, there is no such presumption. The situation of violation will occur only when some measure infringing some provision of the agreement is taken in pursuance of such discretionary legislation. The determinant factor is whether or not there is an absence of discretion in the legislation to take a measure which would violate the provisions of the agreement. If there is an absence of discretion, there is violation of the agreement.

Examples of the relevant observations of some panels are given below:

The Panel on US – Taxes on Petroleum and Certain Imported Substances (June 1987) found that the Superfund Act which directed tax authorities to impose tax on petroleum etc. was inconsistent with Article III of GATT 1994. But the law allowed the possibility of avoiding the need to impose the tax by issuing a regulation. The Panel concluded that in this situation, the legislation did not, by itself, constitute a violation of obligation.[39]

The Panel on EEC– Regulation of Import of Parts and Components (May 1990) examined Japan's complaint about the anti-circumvention provision in the EEC anti-dumping legislation. Japan had argued that the very existence of the provision was violating the EEC's obligation. The Panel noted that the provision was not mandatory – it only authorised the taking of certain measures – and concluded that the mere existence of such legislation did not violate the obligations.[40]

The Panel on Thailand – Restrictions on Importation of and Internal Taxes on Cigarettes (November 1990) concluded, on similar lines, that the possibility that legislation might be applied contrary to obligations was, by itself, not sufficient to make it inconsistent with the agreement.[41]

The absence or existence of discretion is the unifying thread in all such cases.

On similar lines as in the previous type of situation, it has been decided by some panels that a measure or a legislation may be considered to be violating a provision of the agreement even if it is to come into effect only on a later date.

The Panel on US – Taxes on Petroleum and Certain Imported Substances, referred to earlier, considered the argument of the US that its Superfund Tax was not to be effective before 1 January 1989 and that hence it was not causing any immediate effect on trade. As such, the US claimed, it fell outside a dispute. The Panel noted that though the tax authorities had to apply the legislation only after a particular date, the legislation was mandatory, and thus concluded that the complainants were entitled to an investigation as to whether the legislation violated the US' obligation under the GATT.[42] The basis of this principle, perhaps, is that the mere existence of a mandatory provision causes harm to the trade interest of a country, as the operators of trade, i.e., the importers and exporters, will be aware of this mandatory provision and will see the clear possibility of it being operated upon. In the case of discretionary provisions, however, there is scope for the executive authorities not to take action in accordance with the provisions.

New Provision in WTO Agreement

The Marrakesh Agreement Establishing the WTO (WTO Agreement) changes the situation now. Article XVI.4 of this agreement lays down that each Member "shall ensure the conformity of its laws, regulations and administrative procedures with its obligations as provided in the annexed Agreements". The annexed agreements include GATT 1994. This new obligation makes it necessary for Members to bring their laws into conformity with the WTO agreements. If a Member has any law or administrative procedure which is not in conformity with its obligations, it will be violating Article XVI.4 of the WTO Agreement. In such a situation, the consequences will follow as in any case of violation of the WTO agreements. Thus, now, the mere existence of such laws, regulations and procedures is enough to make the Member liable for the consequences of violation of its obligations.

TRANSPARENCY

Article X of GATT 1994 prescribes the need for the publication of official materials in such a manner as to enable governments and traders to become acquainted with them. The method of publication is, of course, for the government to choose; all that is required by this obligation is that governments and traders should have an opportunity to know about these materials. Thus, the publication can be made through well-known government publications or through newspapers etc.

Another aspect of transparency is the notifications which are required to be sent to the WTO. Various agreements prescribe these notifications which help other Members to get acquainted with the policies and measures of a Member.

PART III

MARKET ACCESS

Essentially, GATT 1994 is about the market access of goods. All its provisions relate to the export or import of goods in some way or another. However, there are certain subjects in GATT 1994 which affect market access directly. These subjects are discussed in this Part. They are:

1. Tariffs

2. Safeguards

3. Balance-of-Payments Provisions

4. Technical Barriers to Trade

5. Sanitary and Phytosanitary Measures

6. Trade-Related Investment Measures (TRIMs)

7. General Exceptions – Article XX of GATT 1994Chapter III.1

Chapter III.1

TARIFFS

INTRODUCTION

UNDER normal situations, an imported product is expected to have free entry into the country of importation. However, a Member is authorised to impose a tariff, i.e., customs duty, on an imported product at the time of import. Tariffs serve the following purposes:

(i) Governments get revenue through tariffs. In the case of developing countries, they are an important source of income, and are also convenient to collect, since the number of points of collection is limited.

(ii) Tariffs provide protection to local industry, as like imported products may become more costly after the imposition of tariffs, and therefore, domestic products become relatively cheaper.

(iii) Differential tariffs can be used to bring about a rational allocation of foreign exchange if it is scarce. For example, high tariffs on luxury goods may discourage the import of such products, and low tariffs on industrial machinery or industrial inputs may encourage these imports, thus channelling foreign exchange to preferred directions.

Tariffs affect the competitive position of imported products adversely. Besides, frequent changes in tariffs will cause uncertainty in trade and industry. Hence, detailed disciplines have been introduced on the imposition and raising of tariffs. Further, as mentioned earlier, repeated efforts have been made to reduce tariffs, so that international trade would be liberalised.

MAIN DISCIPLINES

The main disciplines on tariffs are contained in Articles II and XXVIII of GATT 1994. The former prescribes the limits on the imposition of tariffs and the latter contains the procedure for raising tariffs beyond specified levels.

Following a certain procedure, which will be discussed later in this chapter, Members assume an obligation on the maximum levels of tariffs on different products. These tariff levels are recorded in schedules which are maintained in the WTO and which are also available as WTO publications. Each Member has a schedule which contains its tariff ceilings on various products. Article II of GATT 1994 lays down that a Member cannot normally raise the tariff on a particular product above its scheduled level. These levels can be raised only under particular circumstances which will be discussed in later chapters. If a Member wishes to raise the levels without these circumstances having occurred, it has to follow the procedure prescribed in Article XXVIII of GATT 1994 which will be discussed later in this chapter.

A Member need not assume an obligation regarding tariff levels in respect of all products. Those products for which such an obligation has not been taken by a Member, will not feature in the tariff schedule of the Member.

TYPES OF TARIFF

There are three types of tariff:

(i) *Ad valorem*:

A tariff may be levied as a percentage of the value of the imported product. For example, a Member may impose a 12 per cent tariff on a chemical product. If the import value of this product is $1,000 per tonne, the tariff will be $120 per tonne; and the total cost of importing this product will be $1,120 per tonne.

(ii) Specific:

A tariff may be levied on the basis of the quantity of an imported product, i.e., in terms of a rate per unit of the quantity. For example, a Member may impose a tariff of $50 per tonne on an imported product. If the import value of the product is $500 per tonne, the total cost of importing this product will be $550 per tonne.

(iii) Combined:

A tariff may have two components, one *ad valorem* and the other specific. For example, the tariff on a product may be 6 per cent on value and, in addition, $30 per tonne. If the import value per tonne is $1,000, the tariff per tonne will be $90, and the cost of importing this product will be $1,090 per tonne.

Now, mostly *ad valorem* tariffs are used; and wherever there are specific tariffs, the tendency is to convert them to *ad valorem* tariffs.

CLASSIFICATION

A country maintains a list of its tariffs on different products based on a certain classification of products. Earlier, various Members had different systems of tariff nomenclature, which made concordance very difficult. Comparison of tariffs among different countries was difficult. Besides, it was not easy for a country to assess the impact of the tariffs of another country on its own export prospects. There was an obvious need for harmonisation of tariff nomenclatures, which has been provided for now by the adoption of what is commonly called the Harmonised System (HS). Generally, countries are now moving towards adopting this system. More formally, it is called the Harmonised Commodity Description and Coding System. The International Convention on the Harmonised Commodity Description and Coding System, which had been established under the auspices of the Customs Cooperation Council (CCC), entered into force on 1 January 1988. According to this convention, Members are required to convert their customs tariff and statistical nomenclature of products to HS.

A number of technical problems arose along the way to conversion by Members of their own nomenclatures to HS. From time to time procedures and modalities were worked out to make the conversion easier. Now, HS classification is generally being followed.

In HS classification, broad categories of products are assigned numbers going from one to two digits. Thereafter, further divisions and subdivisions are made on the basis of the decimal system. A typical example of HS classification is given below:

85	Electrical machinery and equipment and parts thereof; sound recorders and reproducers, television image and sound recorders and reproducers, and parts and accessories of such articles
8501	Electrical motors and generators (excluding generating sets)
8501.10	Motors of an output not exceeding 37.5 W
8501.10 10	Synchronous motors of an output not exceeding 18 W
8501.10 93	AC motors
8501.20	Universal AC/DC motors of an output exceeding 37.5 W

In this example, "electrical machinery" is the broad group and within that, "electrical motors" is a group, which is further divided into small groups, of which "motors of an output not exceeding 37.5 W" is one, and "universal AC/DC motors of an output exceeding 37.5 W" is another. The first small group, in turn, is divided into finer groups of which "synchronous motors of an output not exceeding 18 W" is one, and "AC motors" is another. In this manner, through the addition of numbers on the right, more and more subdivisions can be made, and the products can be further differentiated.

When a reference is made to six-digit HS nomenclature, say,one is referring to the levels of groups like 8501.10 and 8501.20, which have six digits.

BINDING OF TARIFFS

National Jurisdiction

The determination of tariff rates and the making of changes in the tariff rates on different products are within the jurisdiction of the national policies of Members. They impose tariffs and make changes in them in accordance with their own respective national policies. What is required, however, is that the rates should be published so that other Members and other interested parties, i.e., the trade and industrial sectors in different countries, are fully aware of them. Further, once a tariff is prescribed for a product, it has to be applied uniformly to the particular product coming from different Member countries according to the MFN principle.

The national jurisdiction in tariffs has been reiterated on many occasions. Some of these cases are mentioned below.

The Panel on Canada/Japan – Tariff on Imports of Spruce, Pine, Fir (SPF) Dimension Lumber (July 1989) noted that Members have wide discretion in relation to the structure of national tariffs and the classification of goods in the framework of such a structure. It noted that further tariff differentiation is basically a legitimate means of trade policy. Then, it observed that "a contracting party which claims to be prejudiced by such practice bears the burden of establishing that such tariff arrangement has been diverted from its normal purpose so as to become a means of discriminating in international trade".[43]

Earlier, the Panel on Spain – Tariff Treatment of Unroasted Coffee (June 1981) had also observed that "a contracting party had the right to introduce in its customs tariff new positions or subpositions as appropriate".[44]

Process of Binding

Members engage in the exercise of negotiations with the objective of having an overall reduction of tariffs, particularly on the products of interest to them. Such negotiations take place on two types of occasion. First, the Multilateral Trade Negotiation (MTN) Rounds provide this opportunity. Second, two Members or a group of Members get down to negotiating among themselves for this purpose. Both these types of negotiation result in countries agreeing to "bind" tariffs on some products at particular levels, which means that they undertake the obligation not to raise the tariffs on these products beyond the respective "bound" levels applicable to these products. As mentioned earlier, the bound levels of tariffs of a Member are recorded in a table which is called the "schedule" of the Member. A sample of a schedule is given later.

Implications of Binding

Not all products are covered by "binding" by a Member. Tariffs on products not bound by a Member can be raised at any time without limit. However, in respect of the products covered by the commitment of binding, a Member normally cannot raise the levels of tariffs beyond the bound levels. If a Member desires to do so, it will have to follow a detailed prescribed procedure which will be explained later. A Member, of course, is quite free to apply the tariff on a product at a level lower than the bound level.

Approaches of Binding

In the negotiations for tariff reductions and tariff binding, two broad approaches are followed, viz.:

(i) reduction based on some general formula or principle for an across-the-board tariff cut, commonly called the formula approach;

(ii) product-by-product negotiation based on requests and offers among countries.

Formula Approach

In the MTNs, generally, the first approach is adopted. In the beginning, there are negotiations on the formula or the principle which should be adopted. Some elements of the formula are usually the following:

(i) reducing tariffs across the board by a certain percentage over a period of time;

(ii) laying down a peak level beyond which a Member would not apply tariffs on the bound items;

(iii) prescribing an overall reduction of the average tariff level by a certain percentage, with the conditions that there would be a certain minimum percentage reduction in each tariff line and that the peak tariff would not be above a particular level;

(iv) laying down a minimum percentage of the tariff lines to be covered by binding.

Once the formula is decided, Members work out their charts of reductions, which are examined by other Members and then finalised.

Request-Offer Approach

When negotiations on tariffs take place outside the MTNs on an *ad hoc* basis for particular purposes, generally the second approach is followed.

In this type of negotiation, generally two countries get together to negotiate. Country A has an interest in the export of product P to country B; and country B has an interest in the export of product Q to country A. A will ask B to reduce its tariff on product P; similarly, B will ask A to reduce its tariff on product Q.

In the final agreement between the two countries, an attempt will be made to achieve reciprocity as far as possible. Reciprocity is generally achieved by equalising the reduction of total customs duty on each side. Let us consider that these are *ad valorem* tariffs. The loss of customs revenue to B is calculated by multiplying: (i) the average value of the export of product P from A to B by (ii) the reduction of tariff. If the average value of the export is US$200,000 and the tariff is proposed to be reduced by 3 per cent, the loss of revenue is US$200,000 x 0.03, i.e., US$6,000. This is a measure of the concession which A gets from B. The quantum of concession which B gets from A on the export of product Q will be calculated in a similar manner. An effort will be made to match the two. In this manner, A and B will agree to their mutual new tariffs on products P and Q. Then, these two new tariff levels will get included in their respective schedules, i.e., the new tariff on P will be included in the schedule of B and the new tariff on Q, in the schedule of A. These new levels bound by A and B will not be limited to these two countries; they will be applied to all Members of the WTO, according to the MFN principle.

In actual practice, when two countries sit down to negotiate on tariff reduction, each gives its own request list and offer list to the other. When the request of the one matches the offer of the other, the identification of the products for which the levels of reduction will be negotiated becomes easy. When these do not match, the two countries negotiate on the inclusion of particular additional products in the negotiation.

If country A has to decide on the product to be included in the request list to be presented to country B, A would normally choose a product on the following considerations:

(i) the existing and potential production prospects for this product in country A should be good;

(ii) there should be a good demand or high potential of demand for this product in country B;

(iii) the tariff on this product in country B should be high, adversely affecting the export of country A at present.

Similarly, while choosing a product for inclusion in the offer list which country A will present to country B, the following points will be taken into consideration:

(i) the product should be needed in country A;

(ii) the product should be of export interest to country B;

(iii) the reduction of the tariff on this item should not have the possibility of damaging the prospects of the firms producing the product in country A.

The points mentioned above illustrate the differing interests of the two sides in the tariff negotiation. The process of negotiation involves matching these interests.

INCREASE IN TARIFF BEYOND BINDING

If a Member wishes to raise the tariff on a product above the bound level, it has to offer compensatory concession on some other items. Article XXVIII of GATT 1994 prescribes the procedure for this purpose. The following steps have to be followed:

(i) The Member wishing to raise the tariff informs the Council for Trade in Goods about its proposal, and the Council authorises a negotiation for this purpose.

(ii) The negotiation will take place specifically with the following Members:

(a) The Member with which the concession, i.e., tariff binding, was initially negotiated.
This Member is said to hold initial negotiating rights (INR). Normally, the schedule identifies the Member having INR. There are some cases where a Member has secured an agreement to accord to it the status of INR holder. Such a Member is the holder of a "negotiated INR". It is also likely that the tariff on an item might have been reduced in several negotiations. In such cases, there will be different Members holding INR for different rates of tariff.
A complexity has emerged because the tariff reductions in recent Rounds have generally been done on the basis of the formula approach and not on the basis of the request-offer approach between two Members. Hence, it is not possible to identify the Member having INR. Now, the practice is that the INR remains "floating", and when a question on INR arises, the INR is deemed to rest with the Member which had, during a representative period prior to the time when the question arose, a principal supplying interest in the product concerned. (The term "principal supplying interest" is explained immediately hereafter.)
However, if a Member has INR as a result of bilateral negotiations, such a right will continue.

(b) The Member having principal supplying interest.
Such a Member is the one which had a larger share in the market of the modifying Member than the holder of INR over a reasonable period of time prior to the negotiation for the modification of the tariff. Generally, only one Member will have this right of negotiation. In exceptional cases of near equality of share, at the most, two Members may be declared to have principal supplying interest. The identification of the Member having principal supplying interest will be done in the Council for Trade in Goods.

(c) The Member having the highest ratio of export of the product in question into the modifying Member country compared to its total export of that product.
This item has been included through the Understanding on the Interpretation of Article XXVIII of GATT 1994 (Decision in the Ministerial Meeting in Marrakesh) with a view to redistributing the negotiating rights in favour of small and medium exporting Members.

Besides, consultation will take place with any other Member determined as having substantial interest. This term is not precisely defined, but it has been prescribed that it will cover only those Members which have a significant share in the market of the modifying Member.

(iii) Negotiations will take place to decide on the product(s) which will be subjected to tariff reduction and the depth of the reduction, in order that the concession offered in this manner is almost equivalent to the proposed withdrawal or modification of the concession in question.

(iv) If agreement is reached in these negotiations and consultations, the revised tariff levels on the products covered by the negotiations and consultations will be applied. Even though the negotiations and consultations have taken place only among a limited number of Members, the tariff levels agreed upon will be applicable, in this country, to the particular product of all Members, based on the MFN principle.

SCHEDULE

Tariff item number	Description of products	Base rate of duty	Bound rate of duty	INR	Other duties and charges
7415 10 00	Nails and tacks, drawing pins, staples and similar articles	6.5	4.0		
7906 00 00	Zinc tubes, pipes and tube or pipe fittings	8.0	5.0		
7907 10 00	Gutters, roof capping, sky-light frames and other fabricated building components	7.0	5.0		

(v) If agreement is not reached, the modifying Member will be free to take the action as proposed by it, and the Members having INR and principal supplying interest or substantial interest will be free to withdraw substantially equivalent concessions initially negotiated with the modifying Member. The withdrawal has to take place within six months of the action of the modifying Member. A notice of withdrawal has to be given and withdrawal can be effected after 30 days of the notice.

SCHEDULE

A sample of a typical tariff schedule is given on page 65. This is a tariff schedule emerging after the Uruguay Round of MTNs. The first column gives the HS number of the product and the second column gives the description of the product as occurring in the HS classification against that number. Though there are places for eight digits in column 1, actually only a six-digit-level classification has been utilised.

The third column gives the rate of duty as it was applicable before the negotiations started. According to the Marrakesh Protocol, the tariff reduction will generally be implemented in five equal rate reductions. The first reduction was effective from 1 January 1995, each successive reduction will be made on the 1st of January of each of the following years, and the final bound rate will be effective by the end of 1998.

The fifth column gives the names of Members which have INR. The sixth column gives the "other duties and charges". These "other duties and charges" are those levied on imported products over and above the customs duties. With their being recorded in the schedule, there is an assurance of transparency and a commitment that these will not be raised, and also that new such duties and charges will not be imposed unilaterally by any Member. Earlier, these were not recorded in the schedule, but with the Understanding on the Interpretation of Article II.1(b) of GATT 1994 in the Ministerial Meeting in Marrakesh, these have been brought under this discipline.

TARIFF QUOTA

The tariff schedule also includes the tariff quota on a product, if it exists in the case of the particular Member. The tariff quota is the quantity of import up to which a lower level of tariff is applied; beyond that limit of quantity, the normal tariff in the schedule applies. The tariff quotas included in the schedule are binding on a Member, and these cannot be modified without following the procedure for modifying the tariff schedule.

An important principle regarding the modification of the tariff quota was laid down in the report of the Panel on Newsprint (November 1984). This Panel examined a complaint of Canada's about the modification of the tariff quota on newsprint by the EC. The schedule of the EC had provided for an annual tariff quota of 1.5 million tonnes of duty-free import; beyond that quantity, a duty of 7 per cent was applicable. Meanwhile, the EC had an agreement with European Free Trade Association (EFTA) countries, according to which the imports of newsprint from EFTA countries into the EC became duty-free. EFTA countries were important suppliers of newsprint to the EC. Since after the agreement, the import from EFTA countries would automatically be duty-free, the EC thought that it need not continue with the previous level of the tariff quota. It modified the tariff quota for newsprint to 50,000 tonnes a year. The Panel concluded that the EC, in unilaterally establishing a reduced tariff quota, had not acted in conformity with its obligations under Article II of GATT 1994. The Panel suggested that the EC should promptly engage in negotiations under Article XXVIII of GATT 1994, and, pending that process, continue with the tariff quota of 1.5 million tonnes.[45]

PREFERENTIAL TARIFF

The general tariff listed in the tariff schedule is to be applied to all Members without discrimination. Besides, Members sometimes apply concessional rates of tariff to some products of some specified Members. These "preferential tariffs" are also recorded in the tariff schedule, specifically mentioning the names of the Members for whom these are applicable. There are generally two situations in which preferential tariffs are applied, viz.:

(i) preferential tariffs applied by developed countries to the products of developing countries under the Generalised System of Preferences (GSP); and

(ii) preferential tariffs among some countries as a result of their forming a regional trading area or a free-trade area, for example, the countries of the Association of South-East Asian Nations (ASEAN), the countries of the North American Free Trade Agreement (NAFTA), etc.

These preferences are possible as exceptions to the MFN treatment principle, as explained in the chapter on MFN.

OTHER MATTERS

Other Concessions in the Schedule

The schedule of a Member may contain concessions other than tariffs, and these concessions will also be considered binding. Hence, any withdrawal or modification of these concessions can be done only through the procedure prescribed by Article XXVIII of GATT 1994. These concessions could be in the form of minimum import quotas, or commitments for elimination of import licensing schemes, import permit requirements, import prohibitions, etc.

Tariff Escalation

The term "tariff escalation" is used to indicate that the rate of tariff in a country is higher on a product with a higher level of processing than on one with a lower level of processing or on the basic raw material in a product chain. For example, in the case of hides and skins, the tariffs on products with different levels of processing, as applied by some major Members, are given in the following table:

Products	Canada	EU	Japan	US
Raw material	0.0	0.0	0.0	0.0
Leather	6.6	3.7	7.0	3.1
Leather products	12.6	4.3	9.4	9.0

Tariff escalation has an important implication for the development of the processing of raw materials in developing countries. A large number of developing countries depend on the processing of raw materials for their industrialisation, as they do not have much prospects for more sophisticated manufacturing production. The processing of raw materials in developing countries can be encouraged if major developed countries do not apply tariff escalation, i.e., if they do not impose higher tariffs on products with a higher level of processing.

This has been the subject of multilateral discussions and negotiations over several decades, but it still continues to be an important problem faced by developing countries.

Importance of Tariffs in Market Access

Now, with the reduction of tariffs all around, the importance of tariffs as a hindrance to market access has been considerably reduced. Developed countries have significantly reduced their tariffs on products of their mutual interest, though tariffs in these markets are still comparatively high on products of interest to developing countries.

Developing countries had very high tariffs, but in the Uruguay Round, there were significant commitments by them to reduce their tariffs. However, tariffs do continue to be high in most of these countries. Within the programme of the Global System of Tariff Preferences (GSTP), in the framework of Economic Cooperation among Developing Countries (ECDC), developing countries have carried out some tariff reductions in respect of trade among themselves.

The importance of tariffs, particularly in developed countries, will now lie more in their use as a weapon for trade retaliation than as a normal trade protection measure.

Chapter III.2

SAFEGUARDS

INTRODUCTION

NORMALLY, a Member is not permitted to restrict imports into its territory or exports from its territory. Article XI of GATT 1994 contains disciplines in this regard and prohibits quantitative restraints on imports or exports. The provision of safeguard measures is an important exception to the general prohibition of quantitative restraints on imports.

Safeguard measures are emergency trade measures taken temporarily by a Member to provide relief to its domestic industry in the situation of its getting hurt from an increase in imports. Under certain conditions, a Member may take recourse to trade measures restricting its imports of a product so as to "safeguard" its domestic industry. Sometimes, safeguard measures have also been called an "escape clause" as they enable a Member to "escape" its obligations in specified situations. The disciplines on safeguard measures were initially contained in Article XIX of GATT 1994; now, these have been clarified, augmented and reinforced in the Agreement on Safeguards which forms part of the WTO agreements. In order to understand fully the rights and obligations in the area of safeguards, one must consult both Article XIX of GATT 1994 and the Agreement on Safeguards together.

The purpose of such a provision in the international trading system is to lighten the burden on the country whose domestic industry is facing acute problems due to imports. The objective is to disperse the burden over all the Members to enable the affected Member to adjust smoothly to the new situation of international competition in that particular product line. By its very nature, a safeguard measure has to be temporary and in support of the adjustment process. Since it is meant to provide temporary protection to the domestic industry to facilitate its adjustment, it is not expected to be used as an instrument of long-term protection.

Like MFN treatment, it is also an important feature of the multilateralism in international trade. The former results in the sharing of the benefits of multilateralism, while the latter is about sharing the burdens.

NATURE OF SAFEGUARD MEASURES

Taking safeguard measures means withdrawing or modifying the concessions which a Member has given under the WTO agreements in respect of goods; or suspending, wholly or partly, other obligations undertaken in the WTO agreements in respect of goods.

Examples of the former are:

(i) withdrawal of concession by raising the tariff on a product above the bound level; or

(ii) modification of the concession by raising the tariff level for imports beyond a particular value or volume.

An example of the latter may be the imposition of quantitative restrictions to limit the import of a product in suspension of the obligation not to restrict its import.

In respect of the tariff example given above, it is important to note that if the tariff is not bound, a Member is fully within its rights to raise the level without going through the process of the safeguard measure. Also, if the tariff on the particular product is bound and the actual applicable tariff is lower, a Member can raise the tariff up to the level of binding, without following the safeguard procedure. It is only when the tariff is to be raised above the bound level that there is a need to adopt the prescribed procedure of the safeguard measure.

PRECONDITIONS FOR TAKING SAFEGUARD MEASURES

Safeguard measures are taken to provide temporary protection for the producers of a specific product. Certain preconditions must exist before any such measure can be taken. These are described below.

Main Element

The main elements of the preconditions are the following:

(i) Imports of the product should have increased. There should have been either an absolute increase or an increase relative to domestic production.

(ii) The imports should be in such quantities and under such conditions as to cause or threaten to cause serious injury to domestic producers of like or directly competitive products.

The various terms used here will be explained later.

Article XIX of GATT 1994 Modified

Article XIX of GATT 1994 mentions two other factors in this connection, viz.:

(i) The increased imports should be the result of unforeseen developments.

(ii) The increased imports should be the effect of the obligations of the Member in GATT 1994, e.g., they could be the result of a tariff concession given by the Member in respect of that product.

These have, however, not been included in Article 2 of the Agreement on Safeguards which appears to be comprehensive and complete in itself in laying down the conditions for taking safeguard action. These two additional provisions of Article XIX of GATT 1994 are in the nature of qualifying the preconditions, but have been left out of the Agreement on Safeguards. In such a situation, according to the general interpretative note to Annex 1A of the WTO Agreement, the provisions of the Agreement on Safeguards will prevail. Thus, the conditions given in Article 2 of the Agreement on Safeguards will be operative without having to be qualified or modified by the relevant provision of Article XIX of GATT 1994. It will mean that, even if increased imports causing serious injury could have been foreseen, or even if these were caused by factors other than the undertaking of obligations, applying safeguard measures will be justified, if the main elements as mentioned above are present.

Clarification of Some Terms

Some terms occurring in the main elements of the preconditions need clarification. These are: "relative increase", "serious injury", "like" or "directly competitive" product, and "domestic industry" .

Relative Increase

"Increase in import relative to domestic production" can best be explained by an example. Let us suppose that the domestic production and import of a product in the past were, respectively, 9,000 and 1,000 units, and now, these are, respectively, 4,000 and 800 units. Therefore, earlier, the import was 11 per cent of domestic production, and now, it has risen to 20 per cent. This is a situation in which the import relative to domestic production has increased, even though there has actually been a decrease in the volume of import.[46]

Serious Injury

No specific criteria have been laid down in the Agreement or in GATT 1994 to determine the existence of serious injury. All that has been said is that serious injury means "a significant overall impairment" in the position of the domestic industry.

Thus, the existence of serious injury has to be examined on a case-by-case basis. Some guidelines have, however, been provided. One has to evaluate some relevant factors, like:

(i) the rate and amount of the increase in imports of the product, in absolute terms or relative to domestic production;

(ii) the share of the domestic market taken by increased imports; and

(iii) changes in the levels of sales, production, productivity, capacity utilisation, profits and losses, and employment.

A useful input in this process may be the consideration of relevant cases of countervailing duties for subsidies and anti-dumping duties where the precondition is the existence of material injury. Serious injury should generally be considered to be a higher degree of injury than material injury. A large number of cases have come up recently on anti-dumping duties and countervailing duties, and the existence of material injury has been examined in most of these cases. One may see what effects and consequences have qualified to be classed as material injury in these cases. This may provide some guidance for examining the existence of serious injury.

The threat of serious injury means serious injury being clearly imminent. The existence of imminence is to be decided on the basis of facts and not merely on allegation, conjecture or remote possibility.

Like Product, Directly Competitive Product

The phrases "like" and "directly competitive" products have not been specifically defined here. They are determined on a case-by-case basis. Some guidelines on this matter were given in the chapters on MFN treatment and national treatment.

Domestic Industry

"Domestic industry", in the current context, means all the producers of like or directly competitive products in the country, or, at least, those whose collective production of like or directly competitive products forms a major proportion of the total domestic production of those products. It would mean that while determining whether there is a serious injury to the domestic industry, one has to examine the condition of all the producers of the product or, at least, of those whose production forms a major proportion of the total domestic production of that product. Thus, if only a small number of producers having a small share in domestic production have suffered serious injury, the cause of action would not arise.

PROCEDURE FOR TAKING SAFEGUARD MEASURES

A procedure has been clearly laid down which has to be meticulously followed by a Member before taking safeguard measures. The various important steps in the procedure have been listed below.

Competent Authority

A Member has to designate competent authorities that will hold investigations on the existence of the preconditions for taking safeguard measures. It also has to formulate the procedures for such investigations. These procedures have to be published in such a manner as to enable governments and traders to become acquainted with them. It is presumed that all Members would have designated their respective competent authorities and formulated the procedures by now. If, however, a Member has not done so, it must be done before the process for the first safeguard action is initiated.

Investigation

The investigation as to whether or not the preconditions exist for taking a safeguard measure has to be entrusted to the designated competent authority which has to conduct the investigation according to the prescribed procedure.

Notification and Public Notice and Public Hearing

At the time of initiating an investigation process, a Member has to notify the Committee on Safeguards about it, giving reasons for initiating the process. Besides, public notice has to be given to all interested parties, viz., importers, exporters and others.

The competent authority has to conduct public hearings or adopt other appropriate alternative means so that the interested parties are able to:

(i) present evidence and their views on:

    (a) the existence of preconditions, and

    (b) whether or not the application of a safeguard measure would be in the public interest, and

(ii) respond to the evidence, and the views and arguments of other parties.

If any party provides confidential information, it will be required to furnish a non-confidential summary of it which could be made public. The original information will, of course, be treated as confidential. If a summary is not provided, the reasons for not providing it will have to be given.

The competent authority may disregard the information for which confidentiality has been claimed, if:

(i) it finds that the request for confidentiality is not warranted,

(ii) the party is not willing to authorise its disclosure in generalised or summary form, or

(iii) there is no demonstration from other appropriate sources that the information is correct.

Determination of Facts, Findings and Conclusions

The competent authority has to determine the following facts:

(i) whether there has been an absolute or relative increase in the import of the product,

(ii) whether serious injury or the threat of serious injury has been caused to the domestic industry, and

(iii) whether there is a causal linkage between the increased imports and the serious injury or its threat. (If factors other than increased imports are causing injury to the domestic industry at the same time, the injury must not be attributed to increased imports.)

At the conclusion of the investigation, the competent authority has to publish a report giving its findings and conclusions on all pertinent issues of fact and law. The report should include a detailed analysis of the case, a demonstration of the relevance of the factors examined and the reasons for reaching particular conclusions. All these have to be specifically included in the report; it is not enough to say that these are available in the records of the investigating authority.

Application of Safeguard Measures

Once there is a finding of serious injury or threat of serious injury caused by increased imports, the Member has to notify the Committee on Safeguards about it. Before actually taking a safeguard measure, the Member has to follow a specific procedure which is described below.

Consultation

Before applying or extending a safeguard measure, a Member has to give notice to all those Members that have a substantial export interest in the product and invite them for consultation. The obligation on the Member is to give them an adequate opportunity to enter into consultation. In spite of the notice, if a Member does not take part in the consultation, the responsibility of the Member seeking consultation ceases in this regard.

The consultation will be carried out with the objectives of reviewing the information provided by the Member proposing safeguard action, exchanging views on the proposed measure and reaching an agreement regarding compensation (explained later) in order to maintain the level of concession and other obligations.

Types of Safeguard Measures

After the consultation, if the Member finally decides to take a safeguard measure, it may do so. The measure may be in the form of:

(i) a tariff measure, e.g., increase in import duty beyond the bound level, imposition of surcharges or surtaxes, compensatory taxes on the product, or introduction of a tariff quota, i.e., a quota for imports at a lower tariff and imposition of a higher tariff for imports above the quota; or

(ii) a non-tariff measure, e.g., fixing global quotas for import, introducing discretionary licensing, import authorisation and other similar measures to control imports, or introducing import deposit schemes.

On some occasions, a Member has taken both tariff and non-tariff measures at the same time on a product.

The Member has to notify the Committee on Safeguards about its decision to apply the safeguard measure.

Provisional Measure

There may be a situation in which a Member finds that safeguard measures must be taken urgently. In such a situation, it has to consider if a delay would cause damage which would be difficult to repair. Such a situation may occur, for example, when there has been a sudden surge of imports, or when the domestic industry needs immediate relief because of a rapidly emerging adverse situation as a result of the increased imports. Once the Member is satisfied about the critical nature of the situation and the need for urgent action, it has to hold a preliminary enquiry to determine if there is clear evidence that increased imports have caused or are threatening to cause serious injury. This enquiry, by its very nature, need not be very detailed. If the result of the determination is positive, the Member may apply provisional safeguard measures.

Such measures should be in the form of a tariff increase, which should be promptly refunded if the final investigation determines that there is no evidence of serious injury or its threat or that there is no link between the imports and such injury.

The provisional measure can be applied for a maximum duration of 200 days, and by then, the investigation and subsequent consultation with the Members concerned must be completed.

SPECIAL DISCIPLINES REGARDING QUANTITATIVE RESTRICTIONS

If the safeguard measure is in the nature of a quantitative restriction on imports, a Member has to follow a certain special procedure. It has to enter into consultations with the Members having substantial interest in the export of the product and decide on the global quota as well as on the shares of individual Members having substantial interest.

Consultation

Which Members should be considered as having "substantial interest" has not been specified in the Agreement on Safeguards, nor in Article XIII of GATT 1994, which lays down the procedure for fixation of the quotas and shares. This concept, however, occurs prominently in connection with negotiations on the modification of tariffs in Article XXVIII of GATT 1994, explained in the chapter on tariffs. But here, again, it is not defined except to the extent that it covers only those Members that have a significant share in the market of the importing Member. However, in a meeting of the Committee on Tariff Concessions in July 1985, it was stated that the "10 per cent share" rule is generally applied for the definition of a "substantial" supplier.[47] Of course, Members having principal supplying interest (explained in the chapter on tariffs) will naturally be invited for consultation.

In deciding which Members to invite for consultation, one important additional point which should be kept in view is that the definition of a Member having principal supplying interest has been expanded by the Understanding on the Interpretation of Article XXVIII of GATT 1994 (explained in the chapter on tariffs). According to this Understanding, the group of such Members will include a Member which has the highest ratio of exports of the product in question to its total exports.

Quota and Shares

General Discipline in Fixing Quota and Shares

While applying quantitative restrictions as safeguard measures, a Member has to ensure that the quantity of imports is not reduced below the average level of imports in the last three representative years for which statistics are available. The level of imports can be kept lower only if clear justification is given that a different level is necessary to prevent serious injury or to remedy serious injury.

One effective way of applying quantitative restrictions is to decide on a global quota for imports and then allocate this quota among supplying countries. As mentioned above, the Member has to hold consultations on fixing the global quota and the shares of individual countries having substantial interest in the export of the product. If agreement on the quota and the shares is not possible, the Member may allocate shares among those Members that have a substantial interest in supplying the product, based on their proportions of the total quantity or value of imports of that product in the country during a previous representative period. While doing so, due account should be taken of any special factors affecting the trade of the product.

Clarification of Some Terms

Several concepts mentioned here need explanation and elucidation. This provision of quota allocation has been lifted from Article XIII of GATT 1994 and thus would bear elucidation relevant to that Article.

Previous Representative Period

The "previous representative period" in connection with Article XIII of GATT 1994 has been usually considered to be the previous three years. The Panel on EEC – Restrictions on Imports of Apples from Chile (November 1980)[48] and The Panel on EEC – Restrictions on Imports of Dessert Apples (June 1989)[49] have both considered the previous-three-years period as relevant. The stipulation of "representative years" is made in order to exclude from the average the imports of a year which is abnormal for some reason or another. For example, the former Panel mentioned above, while considering representative years prior to 1979, left out 1976 as there were some restrictions in that year. Hence, the Panel chose the years 1975, 1977 and 1978.

Special Factors

The term "special factor" includes changes in relative productive efficiency as between domestic and foreign producers, or as between different foreign producers. In the Panels mentioned above, it was noted that Chile's increased export capacity and its relative productive efficiency should have been taken into account in determining its share.

Thus, the determination of the shares has to be done on the basis of the past performance of the Members concerned, duly modified by any special factors.

Departure from Normal Allocation of Shares, Quota Modulation

Departure from the allocation of shares based on past imports has been stipulated in Article 5.2(b) of the Agreement on Safeguards, the so-called "quota modulation" clause. The mode of departure or the quantitative limits on departure have not been specified. It would appear that the quota of some Members may be kept higher or lower compared to what would be required on the basis of the criteria of representative years mentioned above. The preconditions for such departure are that:

(i) the Member should have held consultations under the auspices of the Committee on Safeguards with the Members having substantial interest, and

(ii) the Member clearly demonstrates the following points:

(a) imports from certain Members have increased by a disproportionate percentage in relation to the total increase of imports of the product concerned in the representative period,

(b) the reasons for the departure from the system of allocating shares based on past proportions of imports are justified, and

(c) the conditions of such departure are equitable to all suppliers of the product concerned.

LIMITATIONS AND GENERAL DISCIPLINES

Intensity of Safeguard Measure

A basic limitation on safeguard measures is that they have to be applied only to the extent necessary to prevent or remedy serious injury and should only be applied in order to facilitate adjustment of the industry. However, in the past, it has not been easy to establish what is the appropriate level of intensity of such measures in a particular case. This consideration has to be made on a case-by-case basis.

Duration of Safeguard Measure

A safeguard measure is supposed to be of a temporary nature and taken primarily to afford opportunity to the domestic industry to adjust itself to the competition from imports.

General Guidelines on Duration

There are specific limitations regarding the maximum duration of safeguard measures. There is a general provision that safeguard measures will apply only for the period which is necessary to remedy or prevent serious injury, and to facilitate adjustment of the domestic industry.

Specific Limitations

The specific limitations on the duration of safeguard measures are the following:

(i) When a safeguard measure is in the form of a modulated quota, described above, the maximum duration of the measure will be four years. This maximum duration would include the period of the provisional measure, if the measure had been applied on a provisional basis.

(ii) The duration of a provisional measure must not exceed 200 days.

(iii) In other cases, the duration will initially be up to four years, but it can be extended (total overall duration cannot exceed eight years), if the competent authority of the Member country has determined that:

   (a) the safeguard measure continues to be necessary to remedy or prevent serious injury; and

   (b) there is evidence that the domestic industry is adjusting.

   In this determination, the competent authority has to follow a procedure similar to that for the initial investigation on taking the safeguard measure.
   The Member extending the duration has to notify this to the Committee on Safeguards. Besides, it also has to hold consultations with other Members having substantial interest as exporters of that product.
   The initial maximum period of four years would include the period of the provisional measure, if the measure had been taken provisionally.

(iv) The total period of the measure, including the duration of the provisional measure, must not exceed eight years.

A developing country Member has the flexibility of extending a measure for an additional duration of two years, beyond the general limit of eight years.

Repeated Application of Measures

Once a safeguard measure has been applied on a product, there are limitations on applying it again on that product. These limitations are the following:

(i) A safeguard measure cannot be applied again to the import of a product for a period of time equal to that during which the measure had previously been applied. For example, if a Member had applied a safeguard measure on certain basic chemicals and had continued it for a total period of five years, it cannot again take safeguard measures against these products for at least five years from the date of discontinuance of the initial measure.
A developing country Member may, however, apply a safeguard measure again after a time equal to half of the earlier duration of the measure.
The period of non-application will, however, be at least two years in both the cases mentioned above.

(ii) A safeguard measure taken for a duration of up to 180 days can be applied again if:

(a) a period of at least one year has elapsed since the introduction of the measure, and

(b) such a measure has not been applied on the product more than twice in the five years immediately preceding the introduction of the measure.

For re-application of the measure, all procedures will have to be followed as if it were a new measure.

Review and Progressive Liberalisation

There are provisions for review and progressive liberalisation as follows:

(i) If the duration of the safeguard measure exceeds one year, the measure will be progressively liberalised at regular intervals during the period of application.
For example, if the measure is applied for two years, the intensity of the measure has to be reduced at regular intervals. For example, there could be a lessening of intensity at intervals of six months, or at any other intervals during the two-year period.

(ii) If the measure exceeds three years, the Member applying it has to review it during the period of application, at the latest, by the mid-term of the measure. After such a review, either the measure will be withdrawn or its liberalisation will be accelerated, if appropriate. It is not clear in the Agreement how appropriateness will be determined. Perhaps initially, the Member applying the measure will decide on the appropriateness at its own discretion and then, if another Member has any problem with it, the matter may come up before the Committee on Safeguards.
Let us suppose that the measure is to be applied for four years. By virtue of its continuing beyond one year, there has to be a provision of progressive liberalisation at regular intervals as mentioned above. Besides, at the latest, by the end of two years, there will be a review; following that review, either the measure will be withdrawn, or the pace of liberalisation which had been decided on earlier will be increased, if considered appropriate.

(iii) If, after the initial period of the application of a measure (which cannot exceed four years), it is extended, it cannot be more restrictive than what it was at the end of the initial period of application.

Compensation and Retaliation

Main Elements

When a Member introduces a safeguard measure, it, in effect, reduces the level of the concessions given by it to other Members and/or the level of obligations undertaken by it. Article 8.1 of the Agreement on Safeguards stipulates that the Member has to endeavour to maintain a substantially equivalent level of concessions and other obligations existing between itself and the exporting Members. This would require giving trade compensation to the exporting Members.

Consultation

For this purpose, the Member has to enter into consultation with the Members having substantial interest in the export of the product. The compensation usually offered is in terms of a reduction of tariffs on some other products in which these Members may have an export interest. The extent of the compensation has to be substantially equivalent to that of the reduction in concessions and other obligations.

In the case of a safeguard measure in the form of a tariff increase, it may be easy to evaluate equivalence. Usually, the amount of additional tariff income from the tariff increase is taken as a measure of the concession withdrawn or obligation reduced. This should be compensated for by a generally equal decrease in tariff income from the reduction of tariffs on other products. For the purpose of this calculation, the average annual import of the product in the last three years is considered.

If, however, the safeguard measure is in the nature of a quantitative restriction, equivalence may be calculated based on an approximate estimate of the imports foregone as a result of the restriction. In actual practice, it is not easy to arrive at a precise equivalence and, as such, Members approach this problem in a practical and pragmatic way.

As the export profiles of the various Members having export interest in the product in the market of the Member proposing to apply the safeguard measure may be different, generally it is not easy for this Member to select the product(s) on which it would offer to reduce its tariff. The selection of products and the extent of the tariff reduction on each of these products will have to be worked out in detailed consultations with the affected Members. The interest of one exporting Member may not coincide with that of another; hence, a pragmatic balance is worked out which generally satisfies all the substantial exporters and which is, at the same time, equivalent to the quantum of the concession and the obligation which this Member has reduced by the application of the safeguard measure.

If an agreement is reached, the Member applying the safeguard measure will implement it.

Agreement Not Reached

The Agreement on Safeguards and Article XIX of GATT 1994 provide for a situation when no agreement is reached in these consultations. Article 8.2 of the Agreement on Safeguards mentions a situation when an agreement is not reached in these consultations in 30 days, but it does not clearly specify that the Member proposing to take the safeguard measure will be entitled to take the measure after the expiry of this period. It is, however, reasonable to infer that the Member will be free to apply the safeguard measure and also to give the compensation contemplated by it, if no agreement is reached in the consultations within 30 days.

From which reference date the 30-day period is to be calculated is also not specified in Article 8.2 of the Agreement on Safeguards. It could be either from the date the notice for consultation is given or from the date the consultation is started. Considering the urgency of the matter relating to safeguards and following some other such time limits, it may be reasonable to infer that the 30-day period should be counted from the date of giving notice for consultation.

Retaliation

Main Element

If the affected Members are not satisfied with the measures taken or the compensation given, they have the option to suspend substantially equivalent concessions or other obligations under GATT 1994 in respect of the trade of the Member applying the measure.

No criteria have been specifically laid down to determine what will be considered as substantially equivalent concessions or other obligations. This matter has come up for consideration several times, but Members have differed. For example, in 1982, Australia raised the issue of the equivalence of the EEC's retaliation measures against Australian restrictions on imports of motor vehicles. In 1985, Canada raised a similar issue of the equivalence of the EEC's proposal for compensatory measures in response to Canadian restrictions on the imports of footwear. Members have been expressing their opinions in this regard, but the matter has been generally left for settlement between the parties concerned.

Moratorium

The right to such suspension cannot be exercised for the first three years of the safeguard measure, provided that:

(i) the safeguard measure had been taken as a result of an absolute increase in imports,

(ii) the safeguard measure conforms to the provisions of the Agreement on Safeguards.

Before applying the suspension, a Member has to give notice to the Committee on Safeguards and the suspension may be applied upon the expiration of 30 days from the day the notice is received by the Committee on Safeguards.

In other cases, i.e., the cases in which the conditions mentioned above are not fulfilled (for example, if the measure had been taken without an investigation and thus does not conform to the provisions of the Agreement), the stipulation of deferment for three years does not apply. In such cases, suspension can be effected on the expiry of 30 days after the notice of suspension has been received by the Committee on Safeguards.

Time Bar

There is another time constraint that the suspension, in cases where the conditions for the three-year moratorium are not fulfilled, should be applied not later than 90 days after the safeguard measure is applied. But this provision of 90 days has been waived on a number of occasions in the past.

The Role of the Council

There is an additional condition in respect of the retaliatory suspension of concessions and obligations. It stipulates that such a suspension can be applied if the Council for Trade in Goods does not disapprove of it. This provision is similar to a provision in Article XIX of GATT 1994. It does not mean that a Member will have to obtain prior approval for the suspension. So far, only in one case was a specific decision taken not to disapprove of the action. (This decision related to the action of Turkey against the US in 1952.)[50] The Review Session Working Party on Quantitative Restrictions (March 1955) noted that "it is clear, both from the text itself and from the practice followed so far by the CONTRACTING PARTIES, that the contracting party affected is not obliged to obtain prior approval from the CONTRACTING PARTIES and that the object of the phrase... is merely to indicate that the CONTRACTING PARTIES have the right to require adjustments in the action taken if they consider that the action goes beyond what is necessary to restore the balance of benefits".[51]

TERMINATION OF PRE-EXISTING MEASURES

A Member has to notify all safeguard measures taken in accordance with Article XIX of GATT 1994, which were existing on 1 January 1995.

A Member must terminate a pre-existing measure within eight years of the date on which it was first applied or within five years of 1 January 1995, whichever comes later.

GREY-AREA MEASURES

Nature of Measures

A major problem of the GATT has been with respect to what came to be known as grey-area measures. Over a course of time, several countries have taken trade-restrictive measures which were not in accordance with GATT 1994. Sometimes these were unilateral actions; but more often, these were taken in pursuance of agreements among countries. The most common examples are voluntary export restraints (VER) and orderly marketing arrangements (OMA). Because of their doubtful legality, these measures have been called "grey-area" measures.

Grey-area measures were taken mainly to circumvent the process of Article XIX of GATT 1994.

Process of Application

The process would start with an increase in imports of a certain product which would be perceived as affecting the domestic producers in the country adversely. The normal procedure would be to initiate action in accordance with Article XIX of GATT 1994. But this process would have required taking restrictive action globally and providing for compensation. Some major trading partners might be annoyed by this process and contemplate retaliation. Hence, the country concerned about the increasing imports would limit the restrictive action only to those exporting countries which are relatively weak and would not be able to offer much resistance. Naturally, the targets in almost all cases would be the developing countries.

The affected country would normally start consultations with the exporting developing countries and would persuade them to limit their export of the product to a specified quantity or value. The anticipated threat, in case of disagreement, would be a unilateral import restraint by the importing country. Under such circumstances, the exporting countries would generally agree to restrain their exports of the particular product to that particular importing country. This is what is called a voluntary export restraint though, as explained above, there is nothing voluntary about it.

Then there are cases when several importing and exporting countries would arrive at arrangements of the same nature together, under almost similar situations. These multilateral arrangements are called orderly marketing arrangements. One example of OMA is the Arrangement Regarding International Trade in Textiles, commonly known as the Multi-Fibre Arrangement (MFA).

New Disciplines

Article 11.1(b) of the Agreement on Safeguards now clearly prohibits resorting to such measures. Thus, new measures of the nature of VER, OMA, etc. cannot be taken now.

Measures of this type which existed on 1 January 1995 must either be brought into conformity with the Agreement on Safeguards or be phased out. The process of phasing out has been prescribed as follows:

(i) All these measures have to be notified to the Committee on Safeguards within 60 days of 1 January 1995.

(ii) A timetable for the elimination of these measures will be provided by the Members maintaining these measures within 180 days of 1 January 1995.

(iii) This timetable must provide for eliminating these measures or bringing them into conformity with the Agreement on Safeguards within four years of 1 January 1995.

(iv) A Member can continue to have not more than one measure beyond the period of four years, but even this measure will have to be eliminated by the end of 1999. Such exceptions are possible only if they have been mutually agreed to between the Members directly concerned. These measures have to be notified to the Committee on Safeguards within 90 days of 1 January 1995. The Committee on Safeguards will have the role of reviewing and accepting these measures.

Sometimes, enterprises of two countries enter into their own agreements resulting in restrictions on exports or imports. Members are required not to encourage or support the adoption or continuance of such non-governmental measures.

NON-DISCRIMINATION OR SELECTIVITY

The question of whether safeguard measures should be applied on the basis of non-discrimination or whether there can be selective application of safeguard measures against only some selected exporting countries has been a matter of serious consideration in the GATT for a long time.

The Agreement on Safeguards appears to have settled this issue.

The raising of tariffs or the use of other tariff-type charges as a safeguard measure had, in any case, to be applied to all Members, even in the past. The question of selectivity arises only while applying quantitative restrictions. Article 2 of the Agreement on Safeguards provides that "safeguard measures shall be applied to a product being imported irrespective of its source". Hence, safeguard measures cannot target only a few selected Members supplying the product. Besides, new grey-area measures have been totally prohibited. Hence, there is no provision now for selecting specific countries for safeguard action or safeguard-type action.

Some element of discrimination comes up only in the matter of the allocation of shares in the quota. The quota modulation provision contained in Article 5.2(b) allows departure from the practice of taking past performance as the basis for the allocation of shares. A Member may depart from this practice if certain conditions are fulfilled, particularly the condition of disproportionate increase in the import shares of some Members.

Following this process, there can be some modification in the normal practice of the allocation of shares, but selective targeting of only a limited number of exporting countries for the application of a safeguard measure appears to have been stopped by the Agreement on Safeguards. Hence, if a quantitative restriction is to be resorted to, it has to be applied globally, i.e., to all exporting countries, but under certain conditions, the shares of the quota may be reduced in the case of some countries and increased in the case of others.

In the past, some safeguard measures linked to the price of the products have been taken. For example, restraints have been applied to the import of products below a particular price level. Though apparently the measures were applied on a non-discriminatory basis, in actual practice, these measures might have had a selective impact on low-cost suppliers. This matter has come up in discussions on safeguard measures on several occasions but a decisive view has not yet emerged as to whether or not measures linked to prices are in conformity with Article XIX of GATT 1994.

NOTIFICATION

Members have an obligation to send some notifications to the Committee on Safeguards. Some of these notifications are of a general nature, while others relate to specific safeguard or grey-area measures. Most of these have been mentioned earlier while discussing specific topics, but these are being summarised again in a consolidated way.

The general obligations on notification are the following:

(i) A Member has to notify its laws, regulations and administrative procedures regarding safeguard measures. Whenever any modification is made in them, such modification also has to be notified.

(ii) Pre-existing safeguard measures have to be notified within 60 days of 1 January 1995.

(iii) Grey-area measures also have to be notified within 60 days of 1 January 1995.

(iv) Reverse notification on all these matters may also be made. Thus, a Member may send a notification relating to some measure taken by another Member, if it finds that the other Member has not fulfilled its obligations regarding the notification of its existing measures.

The obligations regarding notification in respect of specific safeguard measures are the following:

(i) Notifications have to be sent when:

(a) an investigation is started,

(b) existence of serious injury or its threat is determined, and

(c) a decision is taken to apply or extend a safeguard measure.

The notification on injury must contain evidence of serious injury and the precise nature of the product involved. The notification on the application of a safeguard measure must contain, in addition, the proposed measure, the proposed date of introduction, the expected duration and a timetable for progressive liberalisation. The notification on the extension of a measure must also contain evidence that the domestic industry is adjusting.

(ii) Notification has to be sent before taking a provisional safeguard measure.

(iii) The results of consultations, the results of mid-term reviews, the information on compensation and the information on the suspension of concessions and other obligations have to be notified to the Council for Trade in Goods through the Committee on Safeguards.

PROVISIONS FOR DEVELOPING COUNTRIES

There is a *de minimis* provision regarding safeguard action against products from developing countries. No safeguard action will be taken against a product originating in a developing country Member as long as its share of imports of the product in the importing country concerned does not exceed 3 per cent. If several developing country Members are exporting the product to this particular Member country and their individual shares are less than 3 per cent each, safeguard measures will not be taken against the product concerned from these developing country Members so long as their shares collectively account for not more than 9 per cent of the total import of the product in the importing Member country proposing to take safeguard measures.

The method of application of this provision has not been clearly laid down. However, it should be correct to presume that the developing countries will be excluded from tariff-type safeguard actions or quantitative restrictions up to the *de minimis* level. In the latter case, it would mean that the imports from such developing countries will not be adjusted against the global quota, and that, therefore, their exports of the product covered by the quantitative restriction will be beyond the global quota.

There are special provisions regarding developing countries in respect of the duration of safeguard actions and also relating to the taking of repeated action, which have been described in the relevant sections above.

DISPUTE SETTLEMENT

The settlement of any dispute regarding the provisions of the Agreement on Safeguards will be done in accordance with the Dispute Settlement Understanding (described in the chapter on the Dispute Settlement Understanding).

SPECIAL SAFEGUARD PROVISIONS

There is a general prohibition in Article 11.1(a) of the Agreement on Safeguards that a Member must not take any type of safeguard measure unless it is applied in accordance with the Agreement on Safeguards.

There are certain exceptions to this general rule. In certain cases, special safeguard provisions are applicable. These differ from the Agreement on Safeguards in important ways. These measures are permitted in accordance with Article 11.1(c) of the Agreement on Safeguards, which says that this Agreement does not apply to measures taken in pursuance of some specific provisions of GATT 1994 (other than Article XIX), Uruguay Round Agreements contained in Annex 1A of the WTO Agreement (other than the Agreement on Safeguards), and agreements, arrangements or protocols concluded within the framework of GATT 1994. Some important cases are given below.

(i) In the Agreement on Agriculture, special safeguard measures have been provided under certain conditions. They will be explained in detail in the chapter on agriculture.

(ii) In the Agreement on Textiles, there are special transitional safeguard measures which will be explained in detail in the chapter on textiles.

(iii) In some protocols of accession, there are special safeguard provisions. For example, the protocol of accession of Poland has a provision for Poland to limit its exports or for a Member to restrict its imports from Poland in cases of serious injury or the threat of serious injury caused by the imports from Poland. The provision is special as it deals with the injury caused or threatened by products from a particular source and the consequent restraint on imports from that source.

The protocols of accession of Hungary and Romania also contain special safeguard provisions. These cases again deal with injury caused or threatened by products from particular sources and the restraint on imports from those sources, but the difference is that the rights and obligations of these countries and those of other Members are reciprocal in these protocols.

Chapter III.3

BALANCE-OF-PAYMENTS PROVISIONS (ARTICLE XVIIIB OF GATT 1994)

INTRODUCTION

DEVELOPING country Members have the flexibility to deviate temporarily from specific obligations of the WTO agreements if they face balance-of-payments (BOP) problems. There are similar (but not exactly the same) provisions for Members in general, i.e., including developed countries, in Article XII of GATT 1994, but developed countries now generally do not take recourse to these measures..

The BOP provisions for developing countries are contained in Article XVIIIB of GATT 1994 and are further clarified and elaborated by:

(i) the 1979 Declaration on Trade Measures Taken for Balance-of-Payments Purposes (1979 Declaration), adopted on 28 November 1979[52], and

(ii) the Understanding on Balance-of-Payments Provisions, contained in Annex 1A of the WTO Agreement.

The main purpose of these special provisions for developing countries is to provide them with some relief and flexibility when they face problems of low inflow and small reserves of foreign exchange. It is recognised that they need foreign exchange for their development. As such, they should have the flexibility of departing from their normal obligations under GATT 1994 in order to conserve their forcign exchange and also to put the available foreign exchange to the best use in pursuit of their development objectives.

The BOP provisions in GATT 1994 prescribe the conditions under which a developing country can take specific measures and the related disciplines on notification and consultation as well as the limitations on this flexibility.

GENERAL CONDITIONS FOR USE OF ARTICLE XVIII OF GATT 1994

Main Elements

Even though only Article XVIIIB of GATT 1994 contains provisions about the measures to be taken in the event of BOP difficulties, it will be useful to consider briefly the contents of the other parts of Article XVIII of GATT 1994 as well.

Article XVIII contains four types of provisions:

(i) Article XVIIIA permits the modification or withdrawal of a committed concession in order to promote the establishment of a particular industry. Such measures can be taken for: (i) the development of new production structures, or (ii) the modification or extension of existing production structures with a view to achieving fuller and more efficient use of resources in accordance with the priorities of the developing countries' economic development (1979 Decision on Safeguard Action for Development Purposes, adopted on 28 November 1979).[53]

(ii) Article XVIIIB permits limiting the quantity or value of imports in order to:

   (a) safeguard the country's external financial position, and

   (b) ensure a level of reserves needed for economic development programmes.

(iii) Article XVIIIC permits taking measures affecting imports, if government assistance is required to promote the establishment of a particular industry. The purposes mentioned in Article XVIIIA also apply here.

(iv) Article XVIIID permits taking similar measures as in Article XVIIIC, but its applicability is limited, as will be mentioned later.

Developing countries have utilised the flexibility provided by Articles XVIIIA and XVIIIC only on very few occasions, presumably because these involve giving compensatory concessions to other Members who may be adversely affected by the measures taken. Article XVIIID has never been utilised. Article XVIIIB, however, has been very widely used by developing countries.

In order to be eligible to utilise the flexibility provided by Articles XVIIIA and XVIIIC, it is necessary that a developing country satisfy the following two conditions:

(i) It has a weak economy, so that it can only support low standards of living.

(ii) It is in the early stages of development.

The eligibility conditions for using Article XVIIIB are somewhat more stringent. They are the following:

(i) The developing country has a weak economy, so that it can only support low standards of living.

(ii) It is in the early stages of development.

(iii) It is experiencing BOP difficulties arising mainly from:

(a) its efforts to expand its internal markets, and

(b) instability of its terms of trade.

Article XVIIID applies to those Members that do not satisfy these conditions, but are still in the process of development.

Clarification of Some Terms

Low Standard of Living, Early Stage of Development

The criteria for determining whether an economy can support only a low standard of living or whether a country is in the early stages of development have not been laid down. It has, however, been clarified that the Member countries in the early stages of development will include not only those which have just started their economic development, but also those which are undergoing a process of industrialisation in order to be free from excessive dependence on primary production. Further, in determining the weakness of the economy, only the normal position of the economy has to be taken into account, and not any abnormal situation resulting from the temporary existence of exceptionally favourable conditions for the main export product of the country (Interpretative Notes to Article XVIII of GATT 1994).

In this connection, the Panel on Article XVIII Applications (November 1957), while examining eligibility, used the criteria of per capita gross national product and the share of manufacturing, mining and construction in the gross national product.[54]

BOP Difficulties

There are no specific criteria for determining whether BOP problems exist. As will be explained later, Members take into account the facts and information provided by the International Monetary Fund (IMF) for this purpose. In examining the eligibility of the Republic of Korea for the benefits of the BOP provisions, a detailed consideration of this issue took place in 1989. The Panel on Republic of Korea – Restrictions on Imports of Beef (November 1989) found that the country's reserves were increasing and that the Committee on Balance-of-Payments Restrictions (BOP Committee) had earlier held the prevailing view that import restrictions were no longer justified. The Panel concluded that the Republic of Korea did not have BOP difficulties justifying the utilisation of Article XVIIIB.[55]

PERMISSIBLE ACTION UNDER ARTICLE XVIIIB

While taking recourse to Article XVIIIB, a Member may resort to:

(i) price-based measures, i.e., import surcharges, import deposit requirements or similar measures having an impact on the price of goods, or

(ii) quantitative restrictions, i.e., restrictions on the quantity or the value of imports.

The Understanding on BOP Provisions puts a qualification on the choice of measures by Members. It says that Members shall seek to avoid the imposition of new quantitative restrictions unless price-based measures cannot arrest a sharp deterioration in the external payments position. While applying quantitative restrictions on imports, Members have to justify why price-based measures are not adequate to deal with the problem. Though the phrase "seek to avoid" provides a strong guidance in this regard, it does not amount to a mandatory obligation.

Price-Based Measures

Price-based measures may be applied by a Member in excess of the bound levels of duties inscribed in its schedule. If the duty on a product is not bound, a Member is free to raise the duty without going through the process prescribed by the BOP provisions. (The binding of duty and inscription in the schedule were explained in the chapter on tariffs.)

Quantitative Restrictions

While resorting to quantitative restrictions, a Member may apply restrictions on a particular product or class of product. It may totally stop the import of a particular product or class of product, or it may limit the import of a product to a specified volume or value.

A Member resorting to quantitative restrictions has to provide justification for the criteria used to determine the maximum level of quantity or value allowed for import. In implementing such measures, a Member may use the instrument of discretionary licensing (described in the chapter on import licensing) only when it is unavoidable and must phase it out progressively. Thus, discretionary licensing is not totally prohibited, but there have to be strong reasons for using it.

Choice of Products

While selecting products for applying measures for BOP reasons (either price-based measures or quantitative restrictions), a Member has to give justification for the criteria used to determine which products should be covered by such measures.

A Member may choose the products in such a way as to give priority to the import of more essential products in the light of its policy of economic development. In this respect, the Understanding on BOP Provisions specifically mentions that Members applying these measures may limit the application of the restrictive measures in the case of essential products, such as basic consumption goods, capital goods or inputs needed for production.

LIMITATIONS ON ACTION UNDER ARTICLE XVIIIB

Though a Member is allowed discretion regarding the choice of products and the choice of restrictive measures, subject to what has been said above, it has to impose these measures within certain limitations. These are the following:

(i) Not more than one type of restrictive measure may be applied on the same product.

(ii) The restrictions on imports should not be excessive; they should be commensurate with the BOP difficulties faced. Restrictions imposed by a Member with inadequate monetary reserves should be just enough to enable it to achieve a reasonable rate of increase in its reserves. If there is a decline or the threat of a decline in the monetary reserves, the restrictions should be just enough to stop a serious decline or to forestall the threat of a serious decline.

(iii) The measures for BOP reasons should not be taken to protect domestic production. In order to minimise any incidental protective effect, the restrictions have to be administered in a transparent manner.

(iv) The restrictions should be applied in such a way as to avoid unnecessary damage to the commercial or economic interests of any other Member.

(v) A Member applying the restrictions should not unreasonably prevent the import of any product in minimum commercial quantities.

(vi) The restrictions should not be applied in such a way as to prevent the import of commercial samples.

(vii) The restrictions should not prevent compliance with patent, trademark and copyright or similar procedures.

(viii) A Member must progressively relax the restrictions as conditions improve and must eliminate the measures when conditions no longer justify their existence. Of course, a Member will not be called upon to relax or eliminate the measures only on the grounds that a change in its development policy would make these measures unnecessary.

NOTIFICATION

A Member applying measures because of BOP difficulties has to send notifications to the WTO Secretariat on the measures.

Every year, it has to send a notification to the Secretariat indicating:

(i) the types of measure applied,
(ii) the criteria used for their application,

(iii) the product coverage of these measures, and
(iv) the trade flows affected by these measures.

This information has to be sent in a consolidated way for each tariff line to which the measure applies. Along with this notification, a Member also has to send information on changes in laws, regulations, policy statements or public notices.

Besides, a Member also has to send notification on a specific measure to the General Council of the WTO when:

(i) a new measure is introduced, or

(ii) any change is made in the application of existing measures, or

(iii) any modification is made in the time schedule for the elimination of the measures taken to address BOP difficulties.

Normally, a Member should endeavour to send the notification in advance of implementation. In other cases, where prior notification has not been possible, the notification should be sent promptly after the implementation. The Understanding on BOP Provisions lays down that significant changes must be notified prior to or not later than 30 days after their announcement. What will constitute significant changes has not been specified; it will evolve over the course of time.

There is also a provision for reverse notification. If any Member believes that another Member has taken some measures for BOP reasons and has not sent a notification, it may bring the matter to the attention of the BOP Committee, and the chairman of the committee will have the information on the measures collected and made available to all Members.

CONSULTATIONS

A Member taking measures for BOP reasons has to have consultations with other Members. Such consultations take place in the BOP Committee. The broad process of the consultation is that the Member explains, in the BOP Committee, the details of the measures and the justification for taking these measures. Other Members ask questions, seek clarifications and make comments. Finally, the BOP Committee comes to its conclusions regarding the desirability of applying the measures, the programme of relaxation or elimination of measures, etc.

The BOP Committee consists of Members of the WTO which have expressed their desire to be its members. Hence, all active WTO Members are on it.

Schedule of Consultation

Consultation with a Member in the BOP Committee is held on two types of occasion:

(i) when a new measure is taken, when there is a change in the application of an existing measure or when there is any modification in the time schedule for the elimination of a measure, or

(ii) when the slot of consultation with the Member comes up during the programme of consultations.

When a Member applies a new measure or substantially intensifies an existing measure, it has to enter into consultation in the BOP Committee within four months of the introduction or intensification of the measure. For this purpose, it has to make a request. If it fails to make such a request, the chairman of the BOP Committee will invite the Member to hold such consultations.

Types of Consultation

Details of the procedure for consultations have been laid down in the 1979 Declaration, referred to earlier. These consultations are of two types:

(i) "Simplified consultations", following the procedure approved on 19 December 1972[56], which are much less detailed, and

(ii) "Full consultations", following the procedure approved on 28 April 1970[57], which involve a detailed examination of the BOP measures and the related policies of the Member applying the measures.

Simplified Consultation

Circumstances

The simplified consultation process may be applied in the following cases:

(i) when least developed country Members are involved;

(ii) when other developing country Members are pursuing liberalisation efforts in conformity with the schedule presented in previous consultations, and

(iii) when the trade policy review of a developing country Member is scheduled for the same calendar year in which the consultation is fixed.

Documents

The basic documents to be prepared are: a written statement prepared by the consulting Member, a Background Paper prepared by the WTO Secretariat and a Document on Recent Economic Developments prepared by the IMF.

Result of Consultation

In this type of consultation, the BOP Committee is called upon to recommend whether full consultation is desirable. If the Committee is satisfied with the steps taken by the consulting Member, full consultation will not be recommended.

In such cases, the decision as to whether the full consultation procedure should be recommended is made on the basis of the criteria given in the 1979 Declaration, which are the following:

(i) the time elapsed since the last full consultation,

(ii) the steps the consulting Member has taken in the light of the conclusions reached on the occasion of previous consultations,

(iii) the changes in the overall level or nature of the trade measures taken for BOP purposes,

(iv) whether the BOP problems are structural or temporary in nature.

Except in the case of least developed country Members, no more than two successive consultations will be held for a Member under the simplified consultation procedure.

All cases not covered by the "simplified consultation" procedure as mentioned above will be covered by the "full consultation" procedure.

Full Consultation

Programme

The programme for full consultation is drawn in January every year in consultation with the Members that are to be covered by the procedure in that year. Since the contribution of the IMF is important in these consultations, the schedules of consultations of the IMF with the Member governments are also kept in view while making the annual programme.

Once the programme has been established, a consultation can be postponed only with the consent of the BOP Committee.

Documents

Three main documents are prepared for the consultation:

(i) Basic Document prepared by the consulting Member which covers the following points:

(a) an overview of the BOP situation and prospects, the internal and external factors having a bearing on the BOP situation, and the domestic policy measures taken in order to restore equilibrium on a sound and lasting basis,

(b) a full description of the restrictions applied, their legal basis and steps taken to reduce incidental protective effects,

(c) measures taken since the last consultation to liberalise import restrictions in the light of the conclusions of the BOP Committee,

(d) a plan for the elimination and progressive liberalisation of the existing BOP measures.

In addition, if the consulting Member wishes to have particular attention paid to the external trading environment, it will give detailed information on the external factors which it considers relevant and indicate specific measures and products on which it considers action to be of particular importance. It is in pursuance of the provisions in the full consultation procedure of 1970 and also in the 1979 Declaration that "particular attention should be given to the possibilities for alleviating and correcting these problems through measures that contracting parties might take to facilitate an expansion of the export earnings of (developing) countries".[58]

(ii) Background Paper prepared by the WTO Secretariat: It is expected to be a factual paper dealing with the different aspects of the Plan of Consultations (described below). It must also include material on the incidence of the external trading environment on the BOP situation and the prospects of the consulting Member.

(iii) Document on Recent Economic Developments prepared by the IMF: It contains a picture of the economy of the consulting Member. It is expected to help the BOP Committee in assessing the extent of the BOP problems of the consulting country.

Plan of Consultations

The full consultation procedure has a detailed Plan of Consultations with four main elements:

(i) BOP position and prospects, covering:

BOP situation and monetary reserves; BOP prospects and expected movements in reserves; special factors affecting the availability of or the need for monetary reserves; factors, either external or internal, affecting the various elements of the BOP; effects of the restrictions on the BOP and expected duration of the restrictions; and prospects of relaxation or elimination and likely effects of such action on the BOP.

(ii) alternative methods to restore equilibrium, covering:

internal monetary and fiscal situation and other relevant matters which may affect the BOP; internal action to preserve or restore equilibrium, including long-term measures such as those designed to raise productivity and export capacity or to reduce structural disequilibrium or rigidities; and other measures which may help to restore the Member's BOP.

(iii) system and methods of restriction, covering:

legal and administrative basis of the restrictions; methods used in restricting imports; treatment of imports from different countries or currency areas; and the use of state trading or governmental monopolies in imports and the restrictive operation, if any, of such regimes.

(iv) effects of the restrictions, covering:

protective effects of the restrictions on domestic production; difficulties or hardships that may be expected upon relaxation or elimination of the restrictions; steps taken to reduce incidental protective effects of the restrictions; steps taken to minimise the difficulties of transition to the stage where the restrictions may be eliminated; and steps taken in relation to damage to the interests of other Members, imports in minimum commercial quantities, import of samples and protection of patents, trademarks, copyright or similar procedures.

In addition, if a developing country consulting Member so requests, the BOP Committee has to give particular attention to the possibilities for alleviating and correcting the BOP problem through measures that Members might take to facilitate an expansion of the export earnings of the consulting Member (1979 Declaration).

The Plan of Consultations above is not to be rigid; it is subject to suitable adaptation in individual cases.

Report

The report of the BOP Committee on full consultation contains the following:

(i) conclusions on the different elements of the Plan of Consultations and the facts and reasons on which these are based,

(ii) the steps taken by the consulting Member on the conclusions reached in earlier consultations,

(iii) in the case of developing country Members, which is normally the case, the facts and reasons on which the BOP Committee based its decision on the procedure followed.

The BOP Committee has to endeavour to include in its conclusions proposals for recommendations aimed at promoting the implementation of Articles XII and XVIIIB of GATT 1994, the 1979 Declaration and the Understanding on BOP Provisions. The BOP Committee is thus expected to make proposals for recommendations to the General Council if it finds that a restrictive measure taken by a consulting Member is inconsistent with any provision of these instruments. If the General Council decides to make specific recommendations to any Member in this regard, it will operate as an obligation on the Member.

EMERGING ISSUES

Recently, a large number of developing countries have been persuaded in the WTO to "disinvoke" Article XVIIIB. It implies an understanding that they would not be taking trade-restrictive measures under this Article. Though they have not lost their right to take the measures if the preconditions are present, they will need to make a very strong case for taking these measures. In fact, some developing countries which have lately faced BOP difficulties have thought of taking these measures, but have met with severe resistance in the WTO. However, the situation of the stability of foreign exchange income and reserves in the developing countries is such that the use of Article XVIIIB may continue to be necessary.

Chapter III.4

TECHNICAL BARRIERS TO TRADE

INTRODUCTION

SOMETIMES, governments lay down mandatory technical regulations on products for reasons of security, health or the environment. They also often formulate or encourage the formulation of non-mandatory standards for products in order to facilitate their utilisation. In the absence of standards, producers will have to design their production to suit the needs of individual consumers, which will be cumbersome and costly. Widely accepted standards make it possible to have uniform designs, machinery, tools and inputs, resulting in economy of production and an assurance of quality. They also help the consumers, who have more confidence in buying a product if standards for the product have been laid down and the producer is known to adhere to the standards.

However, these regulations and standards may sometimes operate as barriers to imports, and thereby distort international trade. Hence, detailed disciplines have been prescribed in this regard. Earlier, these were inscribed in the Tokyo Round Code on Technical Barriers to Trade (TBT), and now, these are contained in the Agreement on Technical Barriers to Trade which forms a part of the WTO agreements. Annex 1 of this Agreement contains some important provisions for fully understanding the provisions of the Agreement; hence, this Annex should be read along with the Agreement.

To bring about uniformity in respect of the product regulations and standards and to reduce the possibility of their being used for trade-restrictive purposes, governments are encouraged to adopt international standards wherever these are available. They are also encouraged to participate fully in the formulation of international standards.

The disciplines in the field of technical regulations and standards cover three main topics, viz., those relating to:

(i) Formulation of technical regulations
These are formulated by governments. It is mandatory to observe them.

(ii) Formulation of standards
These are formulated by the standardising bodies of governments. Adherence to standards is voluntary.

(iii) Determination of conformity with these regulations and standards

DEFINITIONS AND PROCEDURE

The definitions of technical regulation, standard and the procedure for conformity assessment are given in Annex 1 of the Agreement which also contains some other definitions and explanatory notes on the definitions. Hence, it is necessary to consult this Annex to understand various concepts and terms.

Technical Regulations

Technical regulations are a set of rules which lay down:

(i) the characteristics of a product;

(ii) related processes and production methods; and

(iii) applicable administrative provisions, compliance with which is obligatory.

These also may cover: (i) terminology, (ii) symbols, and (iii) requirements for packaging, marking or labelling, applicable to (i) the product and (ii) the process or production method.

What a "related" process and production method is, has not been specifically defined, but, in practice, it is generally understood that the process or production method will be considered "related" if it has an effect on the quality or characteristics of the product.

To clarify, let us take the example of the food processing industry. If a factory does not have an adequate standard of cleanliness or if it uses some hazardous chemicals, the dirt or the chemicals may affect the quality of the processed food. Let us now consider the problem of the chimney of a factory which emits smoke, adding to the pollution in the surrounding area, though it does not affect the quality or the characteristics of the processed food produced in the factory. The technical regulations under the Agreement on TBT will be formulated for the standard of cleanliness or for the chemicals used in the processing, but not for the chimney emission.

Standards

Standards are formulations approved by a recognised body, providing for rules and guidelines on characteristics of products and related processes and production methods. These may also cover terminology, symbols, packaging, marking or labelling applicable to a product or process or production method. Standards are not mandatory, but their importance lies in the fact that products conforming to them are often accepted by consumers as being of assured quality.

Conformity Assessment Procedure

The conformity assessment procedure is used, directly or indirectly, to determine that relevant requirements in technical regulations or standards are fulfilled. These may include procedures for (i) sampling, testing and inspection; (ii) evaluation, verification and assurance of conformity; and (iii) registration, accreditation and approval.

EXCLUSION OF COVERAGE

All products, whether industrial or agricultural, are covered by the disciplines of the Agreement, with the following two exceptions:

(i) The procedures of government procurement are not subject to this Agreement. They are covered by the Agreement on Government Procurement.

(ii) The Agreement does not apply to sanitary and phytosanitary measures which are covered by the Agreement on the Application of Sanitary and Phytosanitary Measures.

DISCIPLINES ON TECHNICAL REGULATIONS

Use of International Standards for Technical Regulations

The Agreement on TBT clearly lays down the primacy of international standards. If there are international standards for regulations in a specific field, Members are obliged to use them as a basis for their own technical regulations. Exceptions have been provided for situations when the international standards will be ineffective or inappropriate. Such situations may arise because of fundamental climatic or geographical factors or fundamental technological problems.

These obligations also apply when the completion of a relevant international standard is imminent, even though it may not yet be operational.

An incentive for using international standards has been provided by the presumption that a national regulation will not be considered to be creating an unnecessary obstacle to international trade if: (i) it is based on international standards, and (ii) it is meant to fulfil certain legitimate objectives, which will be mentioned later. Such a presumption will be rebuttable by affected Members, i.e., they may adduce evidence to prove that despite the international standards having been followed, the regulation does create unnecessary obstacles to international trade.

The Agreement on TBT expects Members to participate fully in the preparation of international standards by appropriate international bodies.

Regulations of Central Government Bodies

If any country wishes to adopt its own regulations, certain disciplines have to be followed. There are different sets of disciplines for the technical regulations of central government bodies and those of local government and non-governmental bodies. This sub-section discusses the regulations of central government bodies.

Legitimate Objectives

An illustrative list of the legitimate objectives for which technical regulations may be prepared, adopted or applied has been given in the Agreement on TBT. These objectives include: (i) national security requirements; (ii) prevention of deceptive practices; (iii) protection of human health or safety; (iv) protection of animal life or health; (v) protection of plant life or health; and (vi) protection of the environment.

This is not an exhaustive list as Members may lay down other objectives which have not been specified.

Requirements

Main Elements

The disciplines on the regulations are the following:

(i) Imported products must receive national treatment, i.e., they must be accorded treatment no less favourable than that accorded to like products of national origin. In practice, it would mean that an imported product cannot be subjected to more severe regulation than what is required of the like domestic product.

(ii) Most-favoured-nation (MFN) treatment is applicable, i.e., there must be no discrimination between the like products of different Member countries. It would mean that there cannot be a specific regulation for the product of a particular Member country which is not applied to the like product coming from other Member countries.

(iii) The regulations must not create unnecessary obstacles to international trade.

Clarification of Some Terms

Though the precise definition of "unnecessary obstacles to international trade" has not been given, there are the following guidelines in this regard in the Agreement on TBT.

(i) The regulations must not be more trade-restrictive than what is necessary to fulfil a legitimate objective. That there will be some trade-restrictive effect is thus recognised, but there has to be specific effort and care to ensure that the effect is limited to what is absolutely necessary.

(ii) The risks involved in not having these regulations will have to be weighed against the effects on trade, to determine whether the regulations are disproportionate in the light of the risks.[59]

(iii) The assessment of the risks should be based on some rational considerations, e.g., (a) available scientific and technical information, (b) related processing technology, and (c) intended end-uses of the product.

Some guidance on this issue is provided by past experience with the implementation of Article XX of GATT 1994 relating to the general exceptions wherein the opposite term "necessary" occurs in relation to measures inconsistent with GATT 1994 taken in certain situations, like protecting human life or health etc. The criteria which should determine whether certain measures are "necessary" have been considered several times by a number of panels. In particular, the Panel on US – Section 337 of Tariff Act 1930 (November 1989)[60], the Panel on Thailand – Restrictions on Importation of and Internal Taxes on Cigarettes (November 1990)[61] and the Panel on US – Restrictions on Imports of Tuna (not adopted)[62] laid down clear criteria.

These panels held the view that a measure would not be considered "necessary" if an alternative measure consistent with GATT 1994 could be employed to meet the same objective. Further, where a choice has to be made among measures inconsistent with GATT 1994, the measure which entails the least degree of inconsistency with GATT 1994 would be considered as a necessary measure.

Based on this principle, a technical regulation would be considered as creating "unnecessary" obstacles to international trade if:

(i) it causes obstacles to international trade; and, at the same time;

(ii) an alternative measure is available which:

(a) would meet the same objectives, and

(b) would not be obstructing international trade, or

(c) would be causing less obstruction.

There are considerable differences of opinion on this matter. The interpretation of the phrases "unnecessary obstacles to international trade", "more trade-restrictive" and "less trade-restrictive" will evolve further in the course of the implementation of the Agreement on TBT.

Limitations

A regulation must not be continued, if:

(i) the need for it no longer exists, or

(ii) adequate results can be had in an alternative manner which is less trade-restrictive.

Procedure for Formulation of Regulations

Preconditions

If a Member wants to formulate a technical regulation, a prescribed procedure regarding prior publication has to be followed if:

(i) the technical regulation has a significant effect on the trade of other Members; and

(ii) a relevant international standard does not exist; or

(iii) the technical regulation is not in accordance with the relevant international standards.

What will constitute "significant effect" has not been specified. It may perhaps be elaborated further during the course of operation of the Agreement on TBT.

Notices and Prior Publication

The Member wishing to introduce the regulation has to take the following steps:

(i) send notice to the WTO Secretariat giving the details of the regulation, the products covered, the objectives to be fulfilled and the rationale of the regulation;

(ii) publish a notice indicating that it proposes to introduce the regulation, so that interested parties in other Member countries are able to know about it;

(iii) allow reasonable time for other Members to make comments, discuss these comments if so requested and take the written comments and results of discussions into account while finalising the regulation.

There is, however, an exception for situations where urgent problems of safety, health, environment or national security might arise or where there may be a threat of such problems arising. In such a situation of urgency, the Member need not go through the process of prior notification, discussion, etc. The regulation may be introduced, but the Member must notify the Secretariat of the relevant details, provide copies of the regulation to other Members on request, allow other Members to make comments and discuss the issues, and take into account these comments and results of discussions.

What would constitute urgency or threat has not been specified.

Some Other Obligations

Some other obligations are the following:

(i) The Member introducing a regulation must allow a reasonable interval to elapse between the publication of the regulation and its actual entry into force, so that the producers in exporting countries will have time to adapt themselves to the new requirements. This is particularly relevant for developing exporting countries.

(ii) Members should specify technical regulations based on product requirements in terms of performance rather than design or descriptive characteristics.

(iii) Members should consider accepting the technical regulations of other Members as equivalent, if they adequately fulfil the objectives of their own regulations.

Regulations of Local Government Bodies and Non-Government Bodies

In respect of the obligation regarding notification of regulations to the Secretariat, it is obligatory on a Member to ensure that the regulations of local governments at the level directly below the central government are notified to the Secretariat.

For all other matters, the obligation of a Member is limited to taking reasonable measures as may be available to ensure compliance by local government and non-government bodies.

Besides, a Member is prohibited from taking measures which require or encourage such bodies to act in a manner inconsistent with the obligations which have been enumerated in respect of central government bodies.

Also, a Member must formulate and implement positive measures and mechanisms which are supportive of the observance of these obligations by other such bodies.

A Member is fully responsible for the observance of the disciplines by its local government and non-government bodies. The obligation of the Member is guided by the general provisions in this regard which have been discussed in the chapter on other general principles.

FORMULATION OF STANDARDS

The guidelines for standards are given in the Code of Good Practice for the Preparation, Adoption and Application of Standards (the Code of

Good Practice), which is contained in Annex 3 of the Agreement on TBT.

Code of Good Practice

The main provisions of the Code of Good Practice are:

(i) MFN treatment has to be ensured, i.e., there must not be any discrimination in the treatment of like products originating in different Member countries.

(ii) National treatment must also be ensured, i.e., the treatment given to a product of another Member cannot be inferior to that accorded to a like domestic product.

(iii) Standards must not create unnecessary obstacles to international trade. Though this provision has not been further elaborated in the Code, it is reasonable to presume that the same considerations will appropriately apply here as are applicable to technical regulations, explained earlier.

(iv) International standards, either existing or imminent, must be utilised by the standardising body while developing its own standards, except where these are ineffective or inappropriate, for example, because of insufficient level of protection, fundamental geographical or climatic factors, or fundamental technological problems.

(v) There should be full participation by the body in the work of international standardising bodies while they are engaged in preparing international standards relating to products which are of interest to it.

(vi) There should be no duplication of the work being done by international standardising bodies or by other bodies in the country.

(vii) The standardising body in the country should make efforts to achieve a national consensus on the standards being developed by it.

(viii) At least once every six months, the standardising body in the country must issue a publication indicating the standards it has adopted in the period since the last publication and also its future work programme on standards, giving details of the standards it has decided to develop and, as far as practicable, proposed deviations from relevant international standards.

(ix) At least 60 days will be made available for comments. The comments must be taken into account and only then should the proposed standard be adopted. Immediately on adoption, it should be published.

(x) The standardising body must afford adequate opportunity to other bodies that have accepted the Code for consultation on their representations regarding the operation of the Code.

Obligation of Members

Members have to ensure that their central government standardising bodies adopt the Code of Good Practice and implement it.

As in the case of technical regulations, the obligation of Members in respect of adoption and implementation of the Code by local government bodies or non-government bodies is limited to taking such reasonable measures as are available to ensure that they adopt and implement it.

Members also cannot take measures which have the effect of requiring or encouraging these bodies to act in a manner inconsistent with the Code.

The obligations of Members in respect of compliance with the provisions of the Code by the standardising bodies are applicable, whether or not the standardising body has accepted the Code.

ASSESSMENT OF CONFORMITY

The obligations regarding the procedures for the assessment of conformity with technical regulations or standards are along similar lines to those for the regulations and standards themselves, particularly in respect of: MFN treatment, national treatment, not creating unnecessary obstruction to international trade, full participation in the work of international standardising bodies, prior publication of the procedures, prompt publication on adoption, allowing reasonable time between adoption of the procedure and its entry into force, and enforcement of the disciplines in respect of local government and non-government bodies.

In addition:

(i) these procedures must be completed expeditiously;

(ii) fees must be equitable in relation to those chargeable in respect of like domestic products or like products of other Member countries (it is implied that fees may be different on account of communication, transportation and other costs);

(iii) the location of the facilities which are used in conformity assessment and selection of samples for this purpose must not cause unnecessary inconvenience;

(iv) the flexibility for not following the guidelines and recommendations of international standardising bodies is there only for such reasons as national security, prevention of deceptive practices, protection of human health or safety, protection of animal or plant life or health, protection of the environment, fundamental geographical or climatic factors and fundamental technological or infrastructural problems; and

(v) the central government standardising bodies should rely on the conformity assessment procedure of non-government bodies only if the latter adhere to the disciplines which have been laid down.

DEVELOPING COUNTRIES

The Committee on Technical Barriers to Trade is authorised to grant specified time-limited exceptions from obligations in the case of developing countries. While considering this, the Committee will take into account:

(i) special problems regarding the formulation and application of technical regulations, standards and conformity procedures;

(ii) special development and trade needs of the developing country Member; and

(iii) the stage of technological development of the Member which may have an impact on its ability to discharge fully the obligations under the Agreement.

Besides, there are certain other relevant provisions for special consideration in respect of developing country Members, e.g.:

(i) While preparing and applying the regulations, standards and conformity assessment procedures, Members must ensure that unnecessary obstacles to exports from developing country Members are not created.

(ii) It is recognised that developing country Members should not be expected to use international standards as a basis for their own technical regulations, standards and conformity assessment procedures.

(iii) Special problems of developing countries in participation in international standardising bodies should be taken into account to facilitate their participation in such bodies.

(iv) Technical assistance should be provided to these countries to discharge their obligations under the Agreement.

OTHER PROVISIONS

Institutions

The Committee on Technical Barriers to Trade has been established with representatives from all Members. It carries out its functions assigned under the Agreement and as may be assigned by Members.

Enquiry Points

A Member must establish an enquiry point which is able to respond to enquiries from other Members and interested parties and provide relevant documents relating to central government bodies, local government bodies and such non-government bodies which have legal powers to enforce a technical regulation. The role also extends to regional bodies of which the bodies in the Member countries are members or participants.

Preferably, only one such enquiry point should be established, but if more than one is established for legal or administrative reasons, the scope of the responsibility of each of them must be clearly laid down and information on it sent to all Members.

In respect of the other non-government bodies, the obligation of the Member is limited to taking such reasonable measures as may be available to it.

Dispute Settlement

The dispute settlement process as set out in the Dispute Settlement Understanding will apply. (It will be explained in the chapter on the DSU.)

There is a special provision for cause for action in this regard. A Member may invoke the dispute settlement process if it considers that its trade interests are significantly affected by another Member not achieving satisfactory results with respect to:

(i) formulation of regulations and standards by local government and non-government bodies;

(ii) adoption of disciplines by local government and non-government bodies regarding conformity assessment; and

(iii) adoption of international systems for conformity assessment and compliance by international and regional systems (of which it is a member) with the disciplines on conformity assessment.

There is a provision for the dispute settlement panel to establish a technical expert group to assist it on questions of a technical nature. The procedures for the formation of the group and its deliberations are given in Annex 2 of the Agreement on TBT.

EMERGING ISSUES

There are two important emerging issues in the area of technical regulations. These are explained below.

Related Process and Production Method

Often, proposals are made to widen the coverage of the term "related" process and production method (PPM). The current connotation of the term has been explained in the relevant section. Efforts are being made to include in it even such areas which are considered "not related" at present. Mostly, they are sponsored on the grounds of protection of the environment. The idea is to include in the disciplines PPMs which, while not affecting the composition or characteristics of a product, pollute the environment at the place of production.

The implication from the angle of international trade is that this will enable a country to have an extra-territorial role in taking trade-restrictive measures. This needs some elaboration. At present, a country can take trade measures for some effects of the actions of some other countries which occur in its own jurisdiction, whereas the proposal is to enlarge this role to cover even the effects, e.g., pollution of the environment, which occur in other countries.

Besides, this expansion of coverage may constitute a new weapon for protectionist lobbies in the developed countries.

Implication of International Standards

The formulation of international standards is essentially a technical exercise, but it has important implications for the market access of a country's products. As explained earlier, international standards have a certain primacy in the formulation of technical regulations in a country. If these standards are set on the basis of practices prevalent in highly developed countries, the market access of the goods of countries with much less rigid practices will be adversely affected. International standards are in the process of formulation. Hence, it is important for countries at different levels of development and standards to participate fully in the formulation process, so that the standards set will be reasonable and balanced.

Chapter III.5

SANITARY AND PHYTOSANITARY MEASURES

INTRODUCTION

A MEMBER may apply trade-restrictive measures for the protection of human life or health and of plant or animal life or health. Earlier, such action could generally be taken under the general exception provision contained in Article XX of GATT 1994. But now, the Uruguay Round of MTNs has evolved a detailed discipline in this area which is contained in the Agreement on the Application of Sanitary and Phytosanitary Measures (Agreement on SPSM).

DEFINITIONS

Sanitary and phytosanitary (SPS) measures are those which are applied in order to:

(i) protect (a) human life or health, or (b) animal life or health, from risks arising from:

> additives, contaminants, toxins or disease-causing organisms in foods, beverages or feedstuffs;

(ii) protect (a) animal life or health, or (b) plant life or health, from risks arising from:

> the entry, establishment or spread of pests, diseases, disease-carrying organisms or disease-causing organisms;

(iii) protect human life or health from the risks arising from:

diseases carried by animals, plants or their products, or the entry, establishment or spread of pests;

(iv) prevent or limit other damage from:

the entry, establishment or spread of pests.

NATURE OF SPS MEASURES

SPS measures may be in the form of laws, regulations, requirements, procedures or decrees. Some illustrative items which these may cover are:

(i) end-product criteria;

(ii) processes and production methods (PPMs);

(iii) testing, inspection, certification and approval procedures;

(iv) quarantine treatment, including requirements for transport of animals or plants, or requirements for materials necessary for their survival during transport;

(v) statistical methods, sampling procedures and methods of risk assessment;

(vi) packaging and labelling requirements directly related to food safety.

LIMITATIONS ON SPS MEASURES

Members applying SPS measures must follow the following disciplines regarding the conditions and limitations:

(i) A measure must be applied only to the extent necessary to protect human life or health, animal life or health, or plant life or health.

(ii) A measure must be based on scientific principles, and must not be maintained without sufficient scientific evidence.

(iii) A measure must not be used in a manner constituting a disguised restriction on international trade.

(iv) There must not be any discrimination between Members with similar or identical conditions. This is a modified form of the most-favoured-nation (MFN) principle. It allows discrimination among countries where different conditions prevail.

(v) There must not be any discrimination between the territory of the applying Member and that of other Members.

(vi) Measures must not be more trade-restrictive than required to achieve an appropriate level of protection, taking into account technical and economic feasibility.

CONFORMITY WITH INTERNATIONAL STANDARDS

Generally, Members must base their SPS measures on international standards, guidelines and recommendations if these exist.

A higher level of protection is permitted if a Member has conducted an examination and evaluation of available scientific information and determined that the international standards are not sufficient to achieve an appropriate level of protection.

If a Member has taken an SPS measure conforming to international standards, it will be presumed to be acting in accordance with the Agreement and with GATT 1994. Thus, if another Member has a grievance, it has to adduce evidence to show that the measure is not necessary.

Members should participate fully in the work of relevant international organisations relating to the development of standards, guidelines and recommendations.

ASSESSMENT OF RISK

Measures must be based on the assessment of risks, taking into account risk assessment techniques developed by the relevant international organisations.

The assessment of risk must take into account available scientific evidence, relevant PPMs, relevant inspection, sampling and testing methods, prevalence of specific diseases or pests, existence of pest-free or disease-free areas, relevant ecological and environmental conditions, and quarantine or other treatment.

In determining appropriate levels of protection, Members must take into account relevant economic factors, e.g., potential damage in terms of loss of production or sales in the event of the entry, establishment or spread of a pest or disease, the cost of control or eradication of a pest or disease, and the relevant cost-effectiveness of alternative approaches for limiting the risk.

In determining the levels of protection, the objective of minimising the negative trade effects must be taken into account.

PROVISIONAL MEASURES

If scientific information is not sufficient, provisional measures may be applied. But in such a case, a Member must try to obtain additional information and must review the situation within a reasonable period of time.

This provision for provisional measures gives considerable discretion to Members in applying SPS measures for short periods.

If a Member has a grievance against the application of an SPS measure by another Member, it may seek an explanation from the latter who must provide the explanation.

TRANSPARENCY, PUBLICATION, NOTIFICATION, ENQUIRY POINT

Procedure for Introducing SPS Measures

A procedure has been prescribed in the Agreement on SPSM for introducing SPS measures in certain situations.

The Situations

(i) International standards, guidelines or recommendations on the relevant subject do not exist, or

(ii) When these exist, the proposed regulation of the Member is not substantially the same as the relevant international regulation, guideline or recommendation; and

(iii) The proposed regulation may have a significant effect on the trade of other Members.

Notices, Discussions, Comments

In such situations, the Member has to adopt the following procedure:

(i) a notice has to be published so that interested Members are able to become acquainted with the proposal;

(ii) a notice has to be given to the WTO Secretariat giving a brief description of the proposal and also its objective and rationale, so that the Secretariat is able to notify other Members about it;

(iii) reasonable time must be allowed to other Members to make comments and have discussions;

(iv) the comments and the results of the discussions must be taken into account.

In urgent situations, a Member may proceed with the introduction of the measure without following this procedure, but immediately after the measure is introduced, the actions mentioned above have to be taken. Besides, the notification to the Secretariat must also state the nature of the urgency.

Publication, Enquiry Point

SPS measures must be published by Members so that interested Members can become acquainted with them.

A Member must establish an enquiry point which will be responsible for providing answers to questions relating to the measures, various procedures regarding control, inspection, risk assessment, etc., and participation of the Member in international and regional organisations, bilateral or multilateral arrangements, etc.

OTHER PROVISIONS

Control, Inspection and Approval Procedures

The procedures for control, inspection and approval must be completed without undue delay, and the approximate time taken in this process should be made known to interested persons.

The requirement of information and that of control, inspection and approval of individual specimens of a product must be limited to what is necessary.

The criteria for the siting of facilities for testing etc. for imported products must be the same as those applicable to domestic products.

If a control on production is to be exercised, the Member in whose territory the production takes place must provide assistance to facilitate such control.

Equivalence

Members must accept the measures of another Member as equivalent to their own even if these measures are different, if the other Member demonstrates that its measures are sufficient to meet the objectives of the importing Member.

Consultations should take place with the aim of having bilateral or multilateral agreements on the recognition of equivalents.

Consultation and Dispute Settlement

The provisions of Articles XXII and XXIII of GATT 1994 as elaborated and applied by the Dispute Settlement Understanding apply to this Agreement. It means that the normal dispute settlement process as contained in the DSU will be applicable.

Committee

A Committee on Sanitary and Phytosanitary Measures has been established to carry out the functions necessary to implement the provisions of the Agreement.

Chapter III.6

TRADE-RELATED INVESTMENT MEASURES (TRIMs)

INTRODUCTION

SOMETIMES, governments impose conditions on investment, some of which are trade-related, others are not. For example, a government may prescribe that investment can only be made in a firm which is owned by resident nationals, or it may impose restrictions on the repatriation of profits or on the import of raw materials or the export of products. The restrictions on import and export relate to trade in goods, whereas the others, viz., the restrictions in respect of firm ownership or the transfer of funds from the country, relate to non-trade matters. The Agreement on Trade-Related Investment Measures (TRIMs) covers conditions on investment which are related to trade in goods. Measures which are outside the domain of trade in goods are not covered by it.

The Agreement on TRIMs prohibits investment restrictions which conflict with the obligations of a Member in the WTO agreements. Specifically, it prohibits measures which are in conflict with Articles III.4 or XI.1 of GATT 1994. Since these measures are inconsistent with the obligations of GATT 1994, they are, in any case, prohibited. The Agreement on TRIMs reasserts this prohibition and prescribes procedures for monitoring the obligations.

As mentioned in the chapter on national treatment, Article III.4 of GATT 1994 prescribes that the treatment accorded to an imported product must not be less favourable than that accorded to a like domestic product in respect of laws and regulations affecting sale, purchase, transportation, distribution or use. Hence, for example, it cannot be prescribed that for a particular purpose, the use of the domestic product should be preferred to the use of the like imported product.

Article XI.1 of GATT 1994 prohibits non-tariff restrictions on the import or export of goods. In particular, it says that no quantitative restrictions can be applied by any Member on the export or import of goods.

PROHIBITED MEASURES

In order to specify the types of investment measure which are in conflict with these two provisions of GATT 1994, an illustrative list has been given in the annex to the Agreement describing these measures. For the measures to be covered by the prohibition, the general condition is that:

(i) these are mandatory or enforceable under a domestic law or under administrative rulings, or

(ii) compliance with these is necessary to obtain an advantage.

Measures Inconsistent with Article III.4 of GATT 1994

Measures mentioned in the Agreement on TRIMs as violating Article III.4 of GATT 1994 are the following:

(i) specifying that particular products of domestic origin must be purchased or used by an enterprise, or

(ii) specifying that a particular volume or value of some products of domestic origin must be purchased or used by an enterprise, or

(iii) specifying that an enterprise must purchase or use domestic products at least up to a particular proportion of the volume or value of the local production of the enterprise, or

(iv) restricting the purchase or use of an imported product by an enterprise to an amount related to the export of its (the enterprise's) local production.

The first three are local-content requirements and the fourth is an indirect requirement of partial balancing of foreign exchange outflows and inflows.

These will be more clear if we take an example. Let us take the case of an investment to manufacture steel. In accordance with this Agreement, a government is prohibited from laying down conditions that:

(i) the coking coal or the iron ore required by the firm must be supplied only from domestic sources, or

(ii) one million tonnes of coking coal or iron ore worth $1 million must be obtained from domestic sources, or

(iii) this factory must obtain domestic inputs for its use for at least up to 15 per cent of the volume of its local production or 20 per cent of the value of its local production, or

(iv) this factory can use imported coking coal only to the extent of 10 per cent of the volume of the export of its local production or 15 per cent of the value of the export of its local production.

Measures Inconsistent with Article XI.1 of GATT 1994

Measures inconsistent with Article XI.1 of GATT 1994 are specified in the Agreement on TRIMs as the following:

(i) imposing a general restriction on the import of inputs by an enterprise or restricting the import of inputs to an amount related to the export of its local production,

(ii) restricting the foreign exchange for the import of inputs by an enterprise to an amount related to the foreign exchange inflow attributable to the enterprise,

(iii) restricting export by an enterprise by specifying the products so restricted, the volume or value of products so restricted, or the proportion of its local production so restricted.

The first two are requirements of a partial balancing of foreign exchange, and the third is an export-restraint requirement for ensuring the domestic availability of the product.

Let us again take the illustration of the investment for the steel factory. A Member is not permitted to put the following conditions on the investment:

(i) the factory must not import coking coal, or the value of the import of coking coal must be limited to 75 per cent of the value of the export of the local production of the firm, or

(ii) the foreign exchange for the import of coking coal and iron ore will be limited to 50 per cent of the foreign exchange that the firm gets from abroad, or

(iii) the firm must not export speciality steel, or one million tonnes of hot rolled strip must be kept for domestic use, or only 50 per cent of the local production will be allowed to be exported.

FLEXIBILITY FOR DEVELOPING COUNTRY MEMBERS

A developing country Member is allowed temporary deviation from this obligation in so far as it is covered by the flexibility provided under Article XVIIIB of GATT 1994 as clarified and elaborated by the Understanding on Balance-of-Payments Provisions (explained in the chapter on BOP provisions).

The BOP provision allows flexibility in respect of restraining the import of a product, but once a product is imported, it will have to be given national treatment. There can be no discrimination between the imported product and the like domestic product in respect of their use.

For example, if the BOP situation of a Member satisfies the conditions of Article XVIIIB of GATT 1994 and the Understanding on BOP Provisions, the import of the coking coal or iron ore may be totally prohibited, or the imports of these raw materials may be limited to particular quantities or values. This would automatically mean that these raw materials must be fully or at least partially supplied from domestic sources. But in the absence of such restraints on imports under these provisions, trade measures of the type covered by the Agreement on TRIMs cannot be taken. The Agreement on TRIMs also refers, in this connection, to the flexibility permitted to developing countries in the Declaration on Trade Measures Taken for BOP Purposes adopted on 28 November 1979 (BISD 26S/205-209), but this Declaration has essentially been subsumed under the Understanding on BOP Provisions mentioned above.

ELIMINATION OF EXISTING MEASURES

The Agreement prescribes a time schedule of elimination of all measures which are covered by it. These measures will be eliminated within:

(i) two years of 1 January 1995, by a developed country Member,

(ii) five years of 1 January 1995, by a developing country Member, and

(iii) seven years of 1 January 1995, by a least developed country Member.

If a developing country Member or a least developed country Member faces particular difficulties in eliminating these measures according to this schedule, it may request for an extension of the time. The Council for Trade in Goods will consider this request, taking into account the individual development, financial and trade needs of the Member, and may extend the time.

Measures which were introduced within 180 days prior to the coming into force of the WTO Agreement will have to be eliminated immediately, as a Member does not have the benefit of the time schedule mentioned above in respect of these measures.

During the period of elimination, the terms of any existing measure must not be modified in such a manner as to make it more inconsistent with the Agreement.

INTRODUCTION OF NEW MEASURES

There is a provision in the Agreement for protecting the interests of existing enterprises which are subjected to some investment measures. A Member may apply such measures during the time schedule mentioned above to new enterprises which would produce like products if it is necessary to avoid a distortion to the condition of competition between the new enterprises and the existing enterprises. The measures applied to these two sets of enterprises will be eliminated at the same time.

The term "like products" has been explained in detail in the chapter on national treatment.

NOTIFICATION AND TRANSPARENCY

Members have to notify all TRIMs not in conformity with the Agreement to the Council for Trade in Goods within 90 days of 1 January 1995. The principal features of these measures will be described in this notification.

A Member will also notify the WTO Secretariat about the publications in which its TRIMs may be found. This will also include information about the measures applied by regional and local governments and authorities.

A Member must accord sympathetic consideration to requests for information and provide adequate opportunity for consultation if such a matter is raised by another Member.

COMMITTEE, CONSULTATION AND DISPUTE SETTLEMENT

The Committee on TRIMs, which is open to all Members, is responsible for monitoring the operation and implementation of the Agreement.

The provisions of Articles XXII and XXIII of GATT 1994, as elaborated and applied by the Dispute Settlement Understanding, will be applicable to the consultation and settlement of disputes under this Agreement.

REVIEW

The Council for Trade in Goods has to review the operation of the Agreement on TRIMs with a view to suggesting amendments as considered appropriate. In particular, the review will consider whether the Agreement should be complemented with provisions on investment policy and competition policy.

Chapter III.7

General Exceptions

INTRODUCTION

GENERAL exceptions contained in Article XX of GATT 1994 enable Members to take measures for certain specified purposes and specified reasons, even if such measures are inconsistent with the provisions of GATT 1994. Though all the other Articles of GATT 1994 are covered by these general exceptions, it is generally market access which gets affected by this provision. Members sometimes resort to this enabling provision to stop the import of certain products from a particular country(ies). Lately, this provision has assumed special importance, as will be explained at the end of this chapter.

MAIN ELEMENTS

There are 10 circumstances in Article XX covering the general exceptions. We may put them into five groups for the sake of convenience, though no such grouping actually occurs in the Article.

Environment

There are two provisions relating to the environment, as given below.

- Article XX(b) permits action which is necessary to protect the life or health of human beings, animals or plants. Recently, this provision has been the subject of a great deal of discussion and even controversy. It will be discussed in detail later in the chapter.

- Article XX(g) permits action relating to the conservation of exhaustible natural resources. The condition is that the measures restraining imports for this reason can be taken only in conjunction with restrictions on domestic production and consumption. This provision has also attracted a great deal of attention recently, as will be explained later.

Social and Cultural Matters

The following three circumstances may be grouped into this category.

- Article XX(a) provides for action necessary to protect public morals.

- Article XX(e) permits action relating to the products of prison labour.

- Article XX(f) provides for actions imposed for the protection of national treasures of artistic, historical or archaeological value.

Discharge of Obligations

There are two provisions relating to actions in pursuance of certain obligations.

- Article XX(d) allows action necessary to secure compliance with laws and regulations which are not inconsistent with GATT 1994, e.g., actions imposed for the protection of patents, trademarks and copyrights or for the prevention of deceptive practices.

- Article XX(h) permits action undertaken in pursuance of obligations under intergovernmental commodity agreements.

Domestic Needs

Articles XX(i) and XX(j) provide for export restrictions on materials which are essential for the domestic processing industry and for essential domestic consumption respectively.

Bullion

Article XX(c) permits action relating to the importation or exportation of gold or silver.

RECENT ISSUES

As mentioned earlier, some of these points have lately become important in international trade, as there has been a rising tendency to use the general exceptions for protection of the environment.

Two important cases on Article XX(b) have been in respect of the so-called tuna-dolphin problem in disputes between the US and Canada and between the US and Mexico. The US stopped the import of tuna from Canada and Mexico on two different occasions on the grounds that the mechanism which was used for catching the tuna also caught dolphins whose existence was threatened in this manner. The panels which considered this problem were of the opinion that the prohibition was not correct. One important ground for this finding was that the prohibition had been imposed on a production method which was not related to the product, in the sense that the method of catching the tuna was not in any way affecting its characteristics.

In another case, commonly known as the shrimp-turtle case, the Appellate Body has recently decided that the import of shrimp could be restrained on the grounds that turtles were endangered in the process of catching shrimp.

One important clarification has emerged recently regarding the operation of Article XX(g) in the course of the US-Venezuela dispute on gasoline. The Appellate Body of the WTO has drawn a distinction between the circumstances justifying action under clause (b) for the protection of life or health and those justifying action under clause (g) for the conservation of exhaustible natural resources. It has been held by the Appellate Body that in the former case, the test of necessity of the action is compulsory, whereas in the latter case, it is not so; what is needed here is just to establish a nexus between the trade restriction and the conservation of the particular resource.

Recently, the implementation of the Multilateral Environment Agreements (MEAs) has also been linked to the use of the general exceptions. There are some proposals that a Member should have the flexibility to use the general exceptions as an automatic means of enforcing the decisions taken in the MEAs. These proposals are under discussion in the WTO and have met with considerable opposition, particularly from the developing countries.

PART IV

MEASURES AGAINST UNFAIR TRADE

Certain practices of governments may give unfair competitive advantage to their firms in international trade. Sometimes, even firms resort to unfair measures for improving their export prospects. The WTO agreements provide for remedies against such unfair practices. In particular, two practices are covered, viz., subsidies provided by governments and dumping resorted to by firms. These two subjects are covered by two separate agreements which will be discussed in this Part. These subjects are:

1. Subsidies and countervailing measures, and

2. Anti-dumping.

Chapter IV.1

Subsidies and Countervailing Measures

INTRODUCTION

Unfair Practice

SUBSIDIES are benefits provided by governments to producers and exporters of products which improve their competitiveness in international trade and thereby distort competition. Hence, a subsidy is generally considered to be an unfair practice. However, some of the assistance and facilities provided by governments may be of a general nature, e.g., infrastructure facilities including roads, communication, etc., which are not in the nature of specific assistance for producers and exporters, and therefore are not considered unfair practices. In order to guard against unfair practices, clear rules have been laid down defining what would be considered a subsidy, what types of discipline have to be observed and what the relief is if some Member does not adhere to the discipline.

Governments sometimes provide subsidies for exports; for example, an outright cash payment based on the volume or value of the export of a product or payment of a part of the freight charges. Sometimes, subsidies are provided for domestic production; for example, provision of raw materials at subsidised prices for the production of a particular product or exemption from the payment of some tax or provision of cheap loans. The rules laying down restrictions on subsidies apply to domestic-production subsidies as well, even though the particular product may not be meant for export. The underlying idea is that such a subsidy hampers the competitive prospects of a prospective or possible exporter of another country who could have exported the product in the absence of the domestic subsidy in the importing country. However, the export subsidy is viewed with greater seriousness than the domestic-production subsidy.

Subsidies of Developing Countries

In this connection, it has been appreciated that the producers and exporters of developing countries which are at low levels of development suffer from some natural handicaps, and that exposing them to totally free competition with very strong trading partners may itself appear to be unfair. Hence, a certain degree of assistance and support to them by their governments may be desirable so that they are able to overcome their handicaps, at least partially. Besides, developing countries use subsidies as an important policy instrument for the diversification of their industrial structure and exports, for technological development of their industries and for higher value addition in their industries and exports. For these reasons, some special dispensation for developing countries has been considered necessary.

Differing Effects of Subsidies

In respect of subsidies, it is worth noting that there are differing effects in the importing country. Imports of subsidised products may harm the domestic producer industry, but may benefit the consumers and user industries as they have, in the process, the possibility of buying the product at lower prices and also a wider choice of sources from which to buy. The subsidy is likely to have a positive effect on the prices and quality of products available in the importing country. But the dominant pressure in importing countries is often exerted by the producer industries, rather than by the consumers or industrial users. Hence, there is a stronger push for action against subsidies than for the opposite.

DISCIPLINES

The provisions regarding disciplines on subsidies and countervailing measures are contained in the Uruguay Round Agreement on Subsidies and Countervailing Measures (Agreement on SCM). Subsidies were earlier covered by Article XVI of GATT 1994 and countervailing duties by Article VI of GATT 1994. Some concepts of Article XVI of GATT 1994 have been referred to in the Agreement on SCM and some of the concepts and terms of Article VI of GATT 1994 have been used in it. In respect of those concepts and terms, the operation of these two Articles is relevant. Besides, the provisions of these Articles of GATT 1994, in general, will be valid in respect of subsidies in so far as these do not come into conflict with the Agreement on SCM. Hence, the Agreement on SCM should be read along with these Articles of GATT 1994. There is a separate discipline on subsidies in the agriculture sector; hence, the discussion in this chapter relates only to non-agricultural products.

In the discipline on subsidies, certain policy instruments and measures of Members are allowed even though these may be in the nature of subsidies (non-actionable or permissible subsidies), certain policies and measures are totally prohibited (prohibited subsidies) and certain others are allowed under some conditions up to certain limits (actionable subsidies). When a Member continues with a subsidy which is not permissible or introduces such a subsidy, action against it can be taken by another Member following the procedure prescribed in this Agreement. The action may be in the form of a countervailing duty (under certain circumstances) to offset the effect of the subsidy or may be undertaken through the dispute settlement process.

The relevant points to understand in this field are: the criteria determining which policies and measures are considered subsidies and which among them are allowed or prohibited or restricted, the conditions under which action can be taken against a Member for maintaining or introducing a subsidy, and the procedures to be followed in taking action against subsidies or in defending oneself against such action.

WHAT IS A SUBSIDY?

If there is a financial contribution by the government, or if there is income or price support, and if either of these confers a benefit to production or export, a subsidy is deemed to exist.

Even if a public body, and not the government directly, confers such benefit, it will be deemed to be a subsidy.

Some common examples are: cash support for exports, lower rate of interest on credit, lower freight, etc.

The types of financial contribution by governments or public bodies have been further specified in the Agreement on SCM. This could take the following forms:

(i) direct transfer of funds, e.g., grants, loans and infusion of equity, or potential direct transfer of funds or liabilities, e.g., loan guarantees;

(ii) revenue foregone or not collected, e.g., tax credits;

(iii) provision of goods and services (other than general infrastructure), or purchase of goods.

These measures will be treated as subsidies, even if the government does not undertake them directly but makes payments to a funding mechanism to carry out any of these functions, or directs a private party to undertake them.

There is, however, an exception. If loans, equity and guarantees are given according to usual and normal commercial practice, such measures will not be considered as conferring a benefit and, as such, will not be treated as subsidies. Similarly, if goods or services are provided or if purchases are made at adequate remunerations, keeping in view the prevailing market conditions, such measures will also not be treated as subsidies (Article 14).

The subsidies can be quantified either in terms of benefits accorded to the recipient or in terms of the cost to the granting government, depending on the purpose for which they are calculated. For example, for the purpose of determining the possible quantum of countervailing duty (to be explained later), the subsidy is calculated in terms of the benefits to the recipient, whereas for examining whether there should be a presumption of the existence of serious prejudice as mentioned in Article 6.1 (to be explained later), the subsidy is calculated in terms of the cost to government.

PERMISSIBLE (NON-ACTIONABLE) SUBSIDIES

Main Elements

Two types of subsidy are permitted in the sense that no counteraction against them is normally allowed. These are:

(i) subsidies which are of a general nature, i.e., those subsidies which are not specific to particular enterprises (industrial units) or industries (various industrial sectors); and

(ii) subsidies which, though specific, are meant for (a) research or (b) development of disadvantaged regions or (c) environmental purposes, as will be elaborated later.

These non-actionable subsidies do not, however, have absolute immunity against countermeasures. They may be subjected to actions in the event of serious adverse effects resulting from them. This will be explained later.

Certain types of subsidy are prohibited or actionable, as will be explained later. While considering whether a subsidy is permissible, it should be determined whether it falls under the category of prohibited or actionable subsidy. If it does not, it will be considered as permissible.

Clarification of Some Terms

Specificity

Specificity is defined both in positive terms and in negative terms.

A subsidy is specific if access to it is explicitly limited to specific enterprises or specific industries.

For a subsidy not to be specific, the following conditions have to be fulfilled:

(i) Objective criteria or conditions have been established for the eligibility of enterprises or industries to obtain the subsidy and also for the quantum of the subsidy;

(ii) The criteria or conditions so established are:

(a) neutral, i.e., they do not favour certain enterprises over others;

(b) economic in nature;

(c) horizontal in application, e.g., number of employees, size of the enterprise;

(iii) Eligibility is thereby made automatic; and

(iv) The criteria or conditions are clearly laid down in laws, regulations or other official instruments and are capable of verification.

Permissible Specific Subsidies for Research

Subsidies may be given for scientific research and for helping to adapt the results of research to an industrial process. Detailed limitations have, however, been laid down (Article 8.2) for such subsidies to be non-actionable:

(i) The subsidy should not exceed 75 per cent of the cost of industrial research.

(ii) If it is meant for post-research development, it should not exceed 50 per cent of the cost of pre-competitive development activity, which is an intermediate stage between the research phase and commercial utilisation of the research finding. For example, the preparation of blueprints and designs for new or improved products and the making of first prototypes come under this category of activity.

(iii) The subsidy should be limited to personnel, instruments, equipment, land, buildings, consultancy services and other overhead and running costs which are all incurred directly for the research activity.

It is useful to consult the footnotes to Article 8.2 which contain details of the limitations based on past experiences in respect of subsidy practices.

Permissible Specific Subsidies for Disadvantaged Regions

Subsidies as assistance to disadvantaged regions are permissible if:

(i) these are given pursuant to a general framework of regional development; and

(ii) these are non-specific within the region.

Further, the region itself must satisfy the following conditions:

(i) The region must be a contiguous geographical area with a definable economic and administrative identity.

(ii) The difficulties of the region should be arising out of more than just temporary circumstances.

(iii) The selection of disadvantaged regions must be based on neutral and objective criteria which should be clearly spelled out, so that verification is possible.

(iv) The criteria must be related to the economic development of the region in comparison with the average development of the country, and must include at least one of the following factors:

   (a) per capita income, per capita household income or per capita gross domestic product (GDP) must not be above 85 per cent of the average for the Member territory;

   (b) the unemployment rate must be at least 110 per cent of the average for the Member territory.

Permissible Specific Subsidies for Environmental Purposes

A subsidy in the form of assistance to promote adaptation of existing facilities to new obligatory environmental requirements is permissible. However, there are some conditions attached to it:

(i) The facilities should have been in operation for at least two years at the time when the new environmental requirements were imposed.

(ii) The subsidy should be a one-time non-recurring measure.

(iii) It should be limited to 20 per cent of the cost of adaptation.

(iv) It should not cover the cost of replacing and operating the new machinery.

(v) It should be directly linked to the firm's own planned reduction of pollution.

(vi) It should be available to all firms which have to adapt to the new environmental requirements.

Protection, Consultation and Countermeasures

A Member wishing to provide permissible subsidies for any of these three purposes has to notify the measures in advance of their implementation to the Committee on Subsidies.

Normally, permissible subsidies are immune from countermeasures. However, these can be challenged by other Members on two grounds, viz.:

(i) the measure does not satisfy the conditions and criteria which would qualify it for being treated as a permissible subsidy;

(ii) even if the conditions and criteria are satisfied, the measure is causing serious adverse effects to the domestic industry of another Member, such as to cause damage that is difficult to repair.

Scrutiny of Conformity with Conditions and Criteria

If a Member finds that the measure of another Member does not satisfy the conditions and criteria on permissible subsidies, it may take up the matter in the Committee on Subsidies. The Committee will then determine whether or not the measure satisfies the conditions and criteria. If it is found to be inconsistent with the conditions and criteria, naturally the Member will be asked to withdraw it or bring it into conformity with the conditions and criteria.

A Member dissatisfied with the findings of the Committee in this regard may ask for a binding arbitration on this matter after which it will be subjected to arbitration. The normal arbitration process of the dispute settlement process will apply in this case also. This step can be taken even if the Committee fails to come to a finding regarding the consistency of the measure with the conditions and criteria.

Remedy Against Severe Adverse Effect

If a Member finds that the implementation of a non-actionable subsidy programme by another Member has resulted in "serious adverse effects" to the domestic industry of the former, and if the damage is difficult to repair, it may initiate action for countermeasures. It will first have consultations with the subsidising Member, and if a mutually acceptable solution is not found in 60 days, the matter will be referred to the Committee. If the Committee determines that serious adverse effects do exist and that these cause damage which is difficult to repair, it will recommend the subsidising Member to modify its programme to remove these effects. If the recommendation is not implemented within six months, the Committee will authorise the complaining Member to take appropriate countermeasures commensurate with the nature and degree of the adverse effects. Normally such countermeasures are in the form of the withdrawal of some concessions to the Member or the reduction of obligations benefitting the Member.

What will constitute "serious adverse effects" has not been spelt out. "Adverse effects" have, however, been defined in connection with actionable subsidies. The presumption, naturally, is that for action against non-actionable subsidies, the severity of the effects has to be much higher compared to that in the case of actionable subsidies. The precise definition may emerge during the course of the operation of the Agreement.

Review

The provisions relating to non-actionable subsidies will be applicable only for five years with effect from 1 January 1995. Six months before the end of this period, the Committee must review the operation of these provisions to determine whether they should or should not be extended or whether there should be any modifications (Article 31).

PROHIBITED SUBSIDIES

Main Elements

Two types of subsidy are prohibited. These are:

(i) subsidies contingent on export performance [export subsidies, Article 3.1(a)]; and

(ii) subsidies contingent on the use of domestic goods over imported goods [import-substitution subsidies, Article 3.1(b)].

Even if a subsidy is not formally dependent on export performance, but is in fact tied to actual or anticipated exports or export earnings, it will still fall under the first type of prohibited subsidy.

Annex I to the Agreement on SCM has an illustrative list, and all the items contained therein come within the purview of the first type.

Some Examples

Some typical examples in the illustrative list are the following:

(i) direct payment of subsidy to a firm or an industry based on export performance;

(ii) provision of bonus on exports through currency retention schemes or similar practices;

(iii) internal transport and freight charges on export shipments on terms more favourable than for domestic shipments;

(iv) exemption, remission or deferral of direct taxes, if such a step is specifically related to exports;
(There is an important exception that a deferral will not be a subsidy if appropriate interest charges are collected.)

(v) exemption or remission of indirect taxes in respect of the production and distribution of exported products in excess of those levied on such products for domestic consumption;

(vi) exemption, remission or deferral of prior-stage cumulative indirect taxes on goods or services used in the production of exported products in excess of those levied on such production for domestic consumption;

(vii) remission or drawback of import charges in excess of those levied on imported inputs consumed in the production of the exported product;

(viii) in calculating the base for direct taxes, special deductions directly related to exports in excess of those granted to production for domestic consumption;

(ix) provision of export credit guarantees or insurance at premium rates inadequate to cover the long-term operating costs or losses of such programmes;

(x) grant of export credit at rates below those which are actually paid for getting the funds or would have been paid if the funds had been borrowed in international capital markets;

(xi) full or partial payment of the costs incurred by exporters or financial institutions in obtaining credit if there is a material advantage in export credit terms.

Provisions for Developing Country Members

Export Subsidy

LDCs and Countries in Annex VII

Least developed country (LDC) Members and other developing country Members having gross national product (GNP) per capita less than US$1,000 per annum[63] are placed in a special category in respect of export subsidies [Article 3.1(a) and Annex VII]. For them, the prohibition does not apply. The LDCs can provide export subsidies, and these other developing country Members can also provide export subsidies until their GNP per capita reaches the critical level.

Other Developing Countries

Other developing country Members not included in Annex VII to the Agreement have the following obligations:

(i) they will not increase the level of their export subsidies;

(ii) they will phase out their export subsidies within eight years of 1 January 1995.

Export Competitiveness

There is an obligation for the quicker phasing-out of export subsidies if a developing country Member has attained export competitiveness in a product. The level of export competitiveness is deemed to have been reached if a developing country Member has a share of at least 3.25 per cent of world trade in that product and such share continues for two consecutive years. On reaching this level, LDCs and other developing country Members mentioned in Annex VII will have to phase out export subsidies on this product over a period of eight years. For other developing country Members not included in Annex VII, the obligation is to phase out the subsidies over a period of two years after attaining export competitiveness in that product.

The calculation of the percentage share of world trade will depend critically on the definition of "product". The "product" is, here, defined as a section heading in the Harmonised System nomenclature (described in the chapter on tariffs).

Import-Substitution Subsidy

The disciplines for import-substitution subsidies are more rigorous than those for export subsidies.

The prohibition on import-substitution subsidies [Article 3.1(b)] does not apply to:

(i) LDC Members for a period of eight years from 1 January 1995; and

(ii) all other developing country Members for a period of five years from 1 January 1995.

ACTIONABLE SUBSIDIES

If a subsidy of a Member causes adverse effects to the interests of other Members, action can be taken against the Member. The term "adverse effect" has three alternative elements, any one of which, if present, may be enough to get the action initiated. These are:

(i) material injury or threat of material injury;

(ii) nullification or impairment of benefits under GATT 1994;

(iii) serious prejudice to the interests of another Member, or the threat of serious prejudice.

Injury will be discussed in detail in the section on countervailing duties. Nullification or impairment will be discussed in detail in the chapter on the Dispute Settlement Understanding. Here, we discuss the details of serious prejudice.

Serious Prejudice

Presumption

There is a presumption of the existence of serious prejudice if any of the following four situations exists:

(i) the subsidy on a product exceeds 5 per cent of the value of production;
(For start-up situations, i.e., where new investments have been made for product development or for new production lines for products covered by subsidy, this condition is considered to be fulfilled only if the subsidy exceeds 15 per cent of the funds invested.)
(For this purpose, the amount of subsidy is calculated in terms of the cost to the government, and not the benefit to the recipient.) (Annex IV)

(ii) the subsidy is given to cover the operating losses of an industry;
(Here, the reference is to an industrial sector covering different enterprises.)

(iii) repeating subsidy to cover the operating losses of an enterprise beyond a one-time subsidy for this purpose;

(iv) direct forgiveness of debt, including grants to cover debt repayment.

The presumption of the existence of serious prejudice in these situations is rebuttable. The burden of proof lies on the subsidising Member to demonstrate that in spite of the existence of these situations, the elements of serious prejudice as detailed below do not exist.

In the case of developing country Members, however, there is no presumption of serious prejudice in these circumstances. Thus, serious prejudice will have to be proved by the complaining Member through positive evidence by demonstrating the existence of the conditions given below.

The provision regarding the presumption of serious prejudice is applicable only for five years from 1 January 1995. Six months before the expiry date, a review must be undertaken by the Committee to determine whether this provision should or should not be extended or whether some modifications should be made (Article 31).

Criteria for Serious Prejudice

Main Elements

Serious prejudice is considered to exist if at least one of the following conditions is fulfilled:

(i) The subsidy displaces or impedes the import of a like product of another Member into the market of the subsidising Member. This is a case where the subsidy is given by an importing Member, and the adverse effect is on an exporting Member.

(ii) The subsidy displaces or impedes the export of a like product of another exporting Member in a third country market.
This is a case where the subsidy is given by an exporting Member, and the adverse effect is on another exporting Member, as its exports to a market common to both these exporting countries get displaced or impeded.

(iii) The subsidy results in significant price undercutting, significant price suppression or price depression, or lost sales in a market. Here, price depression means lowering of prices and price suppression means creating a situation in which prices are prevented from rising though normally they would have risen. This is a case where:

(a) the subsidy is given by an exporting Member, and the adverse effect is on the importing Member in its market; or

(b) the subsidy is given by an importing Member, and the adverse effect is on an exporting Member in the market of the importing Member; or

(c) the subsidy is given by an exporting Member, and the adverse effect is on another exporting Member in a third country market.

(iv) The subsidy on a particular primary product or commodity results in an increase in the world market share of the subsidising Member in that product or commodity as compared to the average share it had during the previous three years, and the increase follows a consistent trend over the period in which the subsidy has been granted.

Clarification of Terms

Some of the terms used here have been further explained in the Agreement.

The displacement or impeding of exports mentioned in (ii) above will include cases in which it is demonstrated that there has been a change in the relative shares of the market to the disadvantage of a non-subsidised product, following a clear trend for at least one year.

A change in the relative shares of the market as mentioned above will include any of the following cases: (i) there has been an increase in the market share of the subsidised product; (ii) the market share of the product remains constant though in the given circumstances, it should have declined in the absence of the subsidy; or (iii) the market share actually declines, but at a rate lower than what would normally have occurred in the absence of the subsidy.

What will constitute "significant" price undercutting, price depression, price suppression or lost sales has not been clearly spelt out. It will depend on future interpretations while considering specific cases. However, the method of comparison has been specified. Prices at the same level of trade and at comparable times should be compared. Here, the level of trade refers to the stage of transaction, e.g., retail sale, sale to regional distributor, ex-factory sale, etc.

Some Exceptions

Displacement or impediment cannot be claimed by a Member if the reduction in its export is for reasons totally unrelated to subsidies. For example, the decrease in export may be due to some trade actions of the affected Member or some other Member outside the purview of subsidies, or due to *force majeure*. In particular, the following circumstances have been cited in the Agreement, the presence of which will mean that displacement or impediment does not exist:

(i) prohibition of or restriction on the exports of the product from the complaining Member;

(ii) prohibition of or restriction on the imports from the complaining Member into the relevant third country market;

(iii) in case a monopoly of trade or state trading is operated by a Member, the decision of the Member to shift imports, for non-commercial reasons, from the complaining Member to other sources of supply;

(iv) existence of arrangements limiting exports from the complaining Member;

(v) decrease in the availability of the product for export by some voluntary action of the complaining Member;

(vi) failure to conform to standards and other regulatory requirements in the importing country;

(vii) natural disasters, strikes, transport disruptions or other *force majeure* substantially affecting the production, quality, quantity or price of the export product.

Some examples of serious prejudice or the threat of serious prejudice considered in the past are given below as illustrations.

The Panel on European Community – Refunds on Exports of Sugar – Complaint by Brazil (November 1980) considered the quantity of European Community sugar made available for export with maximum refunds and also the fact that the funds for export refunds did not have a limit. It concluded that the manner of application of the system of granting export refunds contributed to depress sugar prices in the world market, and this constituted a serious prejudice to Brazil.[64]

The Panel on European Community – Refunds on Exports of Sugar – Complaint by Australia (November 1979) had also noted that the European Community export refunds for sugar did not have any effective limitations in respect of production, price or the amount of refunds and thus caused uncertainty in the world sugar markets. The Panel concluded that the refunds constituted a threat of prejudice.[65]

The Panel on European Community – Refunds on Exports of Sugar – Complaint by Brazil mentioned above also held a similar view relating to the threat of serious prejudice.

REMEDIES

For prohibited and actionable subsidies, two types of remedy are possible, viz.:

(i) Remedy through the dispute settlement process, and

(ii) Remedy by imposing countervailing duty.

The route of countervailing duty can be taken only if material injury or a threat of material injury exists. It will be discussed in detail later. There is no such restriction in the case of the dispute settlement process route.

In cases where material injury or its threat exists, both options for a remedy are available. Action along both the routes may be undertaken in parallel, but only one form of relief will be available with regard to the effects of a subsidy in the domestic market of the importing Member (Footnote 35, Article 10).

Hence, in the case of a prohibited subsidy, remedial action through the dispute settlement route is available if such subsidy exists. The route of countervailing duty is also available in such a case if the subsidy has caused material injury or its threat.

In the case of an actionable subsidy, remedial action through the dispute settlement route is available if the subsidy has caused: (i) material injury or its threat, or (ii) nullification or impairment of benefits, or (iii) serious prejudice.

In such a case, remedial action in the form of countervailing duty is available if the subsidy has caused material injury or its threat.

Dispute Settlement Route

These provisions do not apply to products covered by the Agreement on Agriculture, for which there are separate specific provisions as will be explained in the chapter on agriculture.

The procedure is generally similar to the normal dispute settlement process (explained in the chapter on the Dispute Settlement Understanding), except that the time frame is tighter for many stages.

Consultation

For both prohibited and actionable subsidies, the first step towards the remedy is consultation. A Member initiating the action must request consultation with the other Member believed to be maintaining the subsidy. The request for consultation must give:

(i) in the case of a prohibited subsidy, the evidence regarding the existence of such subsidy; and

(ii) in the case of an actionable subsidy, the evidence of: (a) the existence of such subsidy, and (b) the existence of at least one of the three adverse effects, i.e., injury, nullification or impairment of benefits, or serious prejudice.

The consultation will take place immediately, with the objective of arriving at a mutually agreed solution. In the case of a prohibited subsidy, 30 days are allowed for this purpose. In the case of an actionable subsidy, the time allowed is 60 days.

Panel Process

Thereafter, any party to the consultation may refer the matter to the Dispute Settlement Body(DSB), requesting the establishment of a panel. In a normal situation, the panel will certainly be established, since any decision to the contrary would need the consent even of the complaining Member.

The composition of the panel and the terms of reference, in the case of an actionable subsidy, must be finalised within 15 days of the date of establishment of the panel. In the case of a prohibited subsidy, there is no such special time limit; hence, the normal time limit of 20 days as applicable in the normal dispute settlement process will be halved (Article 4.12 of the Agreement), i.e., the time limit for this purpose will be 10 days.

There is a special provision, in the case of a prohibited subsidy, that the panel may request the assistance of the Permanent Group of Experts (PGE) in determining whether a particular measure is a prohibited subsidy. The discretion to enlist the assistance of the PGE lies with the panel. However, once the matter has been referred to the PGE by the panel, the conclusion of the PGE will be binding on the panel. There is no provision for the PGE in the case of an actionable subsidy.

The final report of the panel must be circulated to all Members within 90 days in the case of a prohibited subsidy and within 120 days in the case of an actionable subsidy, counted from the date of finalisation of the panel membership and the terms of reference. (The normal time limit in the dispute settlement process is six months for submission of the report to the parties to the dispute and another three weeks for circulation to all Members.)

In the case of a prohibited subsidy, the panel must specify in its recommendation the time period within which the measure must be withdrawn.

Action on the Panel Report

The report of the panel shall be adopted by the DSB within 30 days of the date the report is issued to all Members. The only exceptions are situations when the DSB decides by consensus not to adopt the report (this is almost impossible as it requires the agreement of even the complaining Member) or when one of the parties notifies its decision to appeal.

The Appellate Body has to issue its report, in the case of a prohibited subsidy, normally within 30 days of the notification of a party's decision to appeal, and, in any case, within 60 days. In the case of an actionable subsidy, these time limits are respectively 60 days and 90 days.

The report of the Appellate Body must be adopted by the DSB within 20 days of the issuance of the report to Members. The adoption of the report is certain, since any decision to the contrary will need the consent of even that Member which benefits from it.

Final Remedy

In the case of a prohibited subsidy, if it has not been withdrawn by the Member concerned within the time period specified by the panel, the DSB will authorise the complaining Member to take appropriate countermeasures, e.g., by withdrawal of concessions or reduction of obligations in respect of the other Member, commensurate with the adverse effects of the subsidy.

It has been clarified in the Agreement that the countermeasure in the case of a prohibited subsidy will not be disproportionate to the loss on the grounds that the subsidy is prohibited.

In the case of an actionable subsidy, such authorisation will be given by the DSB if:

(i) the Member concerned has neither withdrawn the subsidy nor removed its adverse effects within six months of the adoption of the report by the DSB, or

(ii) there has been no agreement on compensation.

The countermeasures should be commensurate with the degree and nature of the adverse effects of the subsidy.

The provisions regarding arbitration, as explained in the chapter on the Dispute Settlement Understanding, are also applicable.

Countervailing Duty Process

Countervailing duty on the subsidised product can be levied only after a detailed process of investigation which has been laid down in the Agreement. The investigation is carried out in order to determine:

(i) the existence of a subsidy which is prohibited or actionable,

(ii) the amount of the subsidy,

(iii) the existence of injury to the domestic industry of the affected Member, and

(iv) the existence of a causal link between the subsidy and the injury.

The remedy of countervailing duty also applies to the agriculture sector, but with certain specific preconditions which will be described in detail in the chapter on agriculture.

A Member has to designate authorities to initiate and conduct investigations. The domestic procedures for the initiation and conduct of investigations also have to be formulated. These have to be notified to the Committee on Subsidies. If a Member has not taken these steps, it has to do so before initiating the first investigation.

Application by Industry

An investigation can be initiated by the authorities in two ways:

(i) on receiving a written application given by or on behalf of the domestic industry; or

(ii) if there is sufficient evidence of the existence of a subsidy, injury and a causal linkage between the subsidy and the injury, even without a written application (but only under special circumstances).

Criteria for Domestic Industry in Respect of Application

It is important to note that the criteria for the domestic industry in respect of the filing of an application are different from those in respect of determining injury to the domestic industry. The latter will be discussed in detail later while discussing injury.

For the purpose of determining whether an application has been filed by or on behalf of the domestic industry, the authorities have to find out the support for and opposition to the application among the domestic producers of the like product. If those supporting the application account for more than half of the total production of both the supporting and opposing groups, the application is deemed to have been made by or on behalf of the domestic industry. In other words, the application will be considered to be filed by the domestic industry or on its behalf, if those supporting it account for a higher level of production of the product than those opposing it.

The following facts should be noted in this connection:

(i) the number of producers is not relevant, but the proportion of production is;

(ii) those who do not express their preference either way are left out of the calculation;

(iii) there is no provision for excluding those producers who are related to exporters or importers, as is the case while determining injury (to be explained later).

There is an important condition that the application will not be considered as being given by or on behalf of the domestic industry if those supporting it account for less than 25 per cent of the total domestic production of the product (Article 11.4).

It is not clear why some of the producers would oppose the application as generally, the countervailing duty on imports should be of benefit to all of them. However, this practice has been taken into account in the Agreement following similar practice in some major importing countries.

If the number of producers is exceptionally large, support and opposition may be determined using statistically valid sampling techniques.

There is a specific recognition that in some countries, even the employees of the domestic producers or their representatives may participate in making or supporting an application (Footnote 39, Article 11.4). A Member is not obliged to take into account the opinions of the employees; however, if some Member adopts such a practice, it will not be objected to. A problem may arise if the producers and their employees hold mutually differing views on support for the application, but such a situation is unlikely to occur in actual practice.

Content of the Application

The application should contain the names of the producers and their volume and value of production, a description of the subsidised product, the country(ies) of origin, the names of known exporters and importers of the product, evidence regarding the existence and quantum of subsidy, and evidence on the existence of injury and its being caused by the subsidised product. (Injury will be discussed in detail later.)

The application must contain such information as is reasonably available to the applicant.

Preliminary Examination

There is a mandatory provision for a preliminary examination of the application. The accuracy and adequacy of the evidence given in the application must be reviewed by the authorities to determine at this very stage whether the evidence is sufficient to justify the initiation of an investigation.

The application must be rejected and investigation terminated in the circumstances given below:

(i) The application is not supported by the stipulated minimum proportion of the domestic producers.

(ii) Sufficient evidence indicating the existence of subsidy and injury is absent.

(iii) The amount of subsidy is *de minimis*, i.e.,

    (a) less than 1 per cent in general cases,

    (b) less than 3 per cent in the case of Annex VII developing countries and those other developing countries which have eliminated export subsidies before the expiry of the permissible period of eight years, and

(c) less than 2 per cent in the case of the rest of the developing countries.

(Articles 11.9, 27.10, 27.11)

(iv) The volume of the subsidised import or the injury is negligible. What will be considered negligible injury has not been specified. What will be considered negligible import in general cases has also not been specified.
However, in the case of a developing country under investigation, the subsidised import will be considered negligible if its volume is less than 4 per cent of the total import of the product in the importing country.
In case more than one developing country is under investigation and individually, they do not account for 4 per cent of the import, action can still be taken if collectively, they account for more than 9 per cent of the total import.
In respect of determining whether the subsidised import volume is negligible, there is no difference between Annex VII countries and other developing countries.

(Articles 11.9, 27.10)

Consultation

After an application is accepted and before initiating the investigation, the initiating Member must give an opportunity to the Member(s) whose products are the subject of the application for consultation aimed at clarifying the facts in the application and arriving at a mutually agreed solution. Such consultation is to be held between governments, and not between the government initiating investigation and the exporting firms (Article 13).

Investigation

If no agreement is reached in the consultation, the investigation may start. The time allowed for the investigation is normally one year, but in no case should it exceed 18 months, except in special circumstances.

Public Notice

When it is decided to initiate the investigation, a public notice of the initiation will be given which should contain the following information:

> the name(s) of the exporting country(ies), the date of initiation of the investigation, a description of the subsidy measure(s) to be investigated, a summary of the factors which form the basis for the allegation of injury, the address to which the representations of the interested Members and interested parties should be sent, and the time limits within which the interested Members and interested parties may make their representations.

Notice to Interested Members and Parties

The interested Members are those whose products are the subject of investigation. The interested parties are: foreign producers, exporters, importers, domestic producers and trade or business associations having among their members a majority of such producers or exporters or importers. This is not an exhaustive list. The investigating Member may include other parties as interested parties (Article 12.9).

Immediately on starting the investigation, the authorities conducting the investigation must provide the application to the responding Member and to the known exporters. Notice will be given to interested Members and interested parties to provide information relevant to the investigation.

Response to Notice

The responding Member and foreign producers or exporters should generally provide the information to the investigating authorities in written form, but it is also permissible to make oral presentations, if justified. Subsequently, such presentations should be made available in written form.

Confidential information should be accompanied by a non confidential summary which can be made public. If such a summary is not provided, the information may be ignored by the investigating authorities, except if it is demonstrated that the information is correct.

If interested Members and interested parties do not cooperate in the investigation and do not provide relevant facts, the authorities may make their determination on the basis of the facts available to them.

Verification of Information in Other Countries

The investigation may also be carried out in other countries, provided the Member concerned has been informed and has not objected. It may also be conducted on the premises of a firm, provided the firm agrees and the Member concerned has been informed and has not objected. Such an investigation may sometimes be required to verify the information provided to the authorities. The procedures to be followed while conducting the investigation on the premises of a firm have been laid down in Annex VI to the Agreement.

Opportunity to Users and Consumers

Opportunity will be provided to industrial users of the product and to consumer organisations (in case the product is commonly sold at the retail level) to supply information which may be relevant to the investigation in respect of subsidisation, injury and causal relationship.

Facts to be Determined

In considering all matters before it, the authorities will determine: whether subsidy and injury exist, and whether the injury is caused by the subsidy. They will have to examine :

(i) whether the measure in question is a subsidy against which action can be taken;

(ii) the extent of the subsidy;

(iii) whether material injury to the domestic industry has been caused or whether there is a threat of material injury to the domestic industry;

(iv) whether there is a causal link between the subsidy and the injury, i.e., whether the injury or the threat of it has been caused by the subsidy.

What constitutes a subsidy was elaborately described earlier.

In respect of the amount of the subsidy, i.e., the extent of benefit to the recipient, a Member must provide the method of calculation in its legislation or regulations.

Some specific types of subsidy have been described in Annexes II and III of the Agreement.

The method of determination of injury and establishment of a causal linkage between the subsidy and the injury will be given later.

Provisional Duty

During the course of the investigation, 60 days after its initiation, a Member may impose provisional countervailing duty. The details of this provision and the related conditions and limitations will be given in a later section.

Undertakings

There is a provision for undertakings in the course of the investigation. These may be either about removing or limiting the subsidy or about raising the price of the product. On receiving a satisfactory undertaking, the Member conducting the investigation may drop it. The details of the process of undertakings and the related limitations will be given in a later section.

Final Report

The authorities conducting the investigation have to give their findings on all the aforementioned points which were to be determined. They have to ensure the accuracy of the facts which form the basis of their conclusions. It is necessary to provide full reasons for the conclusions. It is not enough just to say that the facts and reasons are in the records of the authorities.

Before a final determination is made, the investigating authorities must inform interested Members and interested parties about the facts which form the basis of the determination.

On receiving the report of the investigating authorities, the Member has to take a decision on the imposition of countervailing duty. This step will be discussed later.

DETERMINATION OF INJURY

Main Elements

Injury, in this Agreement, means:

(i) material injury to a domestic industry, or

(ii) threat of material injury to a domestic industry, or

(iii) material retardation of the establishment of a domestic industry.

Hence, injury is related not only to an existing industry, but also to the future establishment of an industry.

Factors Relevant to Injury

The determination of injury involves an objective examination of three factors, viz.:

(i) the volume of the subsidised imports;

(ii) the effect of the subsidised imports on the prices of like products in the domestic market;

(iii) the consequent impact of the imports on the domestic producers of these products.

Volume

In respect of the volume of imports, it has to be examined whether there has been a significant increase either in absolute terms or relative to production or consumption in the importing country. What will be considered "significant" has not been specified.

Price

In respect of the price, it has to be examined whether there has been significant price undercutting, significant price depression, or significant price suppression, i.e., prevention of price increases which would have occurred in the absence of the subsidised imports.

Here again, the criteria for considering what is "significant" have not been spelt out.

Impact

While examining the impact on the domestic industry, the following relevant economic factors and indices having a bearing on the state of the industry will be evaluated:

(i) actual and potential decline in output, sales, market share, profits, productivity, return on investments and utilisation of capacity;

(ii) factors affecting domestic prices;

(iii) actual and potential effects on cash flow, inventories, employment, wages, growth and ability to raise capital or investments, and, in the case of agriculture, an increase in the burden on government support programmes.

This list is only illustrative and is not exhaustive.

Threat of Injury

The threat of material injury is not to be determined based merely on allegation, conjecture or remote possibility. The situation in which the subsidy will cause injury must be: (i) clearly foreseen and also (ii) imminent.

Some of the factors given in the Agreement for examination of the threat are:

(i) the nature of the subsidy and the trade effects likely to arise from it;

(ii) whether there has been a significant rate of increase of subsidised imports, indicating the likelihood of substantially increased importation;

(iii) whether there is freely disposable sufficient production with the exporter, or whether a substantial increase in the capacity of the exporter is imminent, indicating the likelihood of substantially increased exports to the market of the particular importing member; (Here, the possibility of absorption of the additional exports by other markets should be taken into account.)

(iv) whether the prices of the imports will have a significant depressing or suppressing effect on domestic prices, indicating the likelihood of an increase in demand for the imported product;

(v) the inventories of the product.

Causal Linkage

While examining the causal relationship between the subsidised imports and the injury, it is obligatory to examine the other factors, if any, which are also causing injury. The injury caused by these other factors must not be attributed to the subsidised imports. Some relevant factors in this respect, contained in an illustrative list given in the Agreement, are:

- the volumes and prices of non-subsidised imports of the product,
- contraction in demand or changes in the patterns of consumption,
- trade-restrictive practices of the foreign and domestic producers,

- competition between the foreign and domestic producers,
- developments in technology, and
- the export performance and productivity of the domestic industry.

Some typical past cases where material injury or the threat of material injury has been examined are given below for illustration.

In the Panel on New Zealand – Imports of Electrical Transformers from Finland (July 1985), New Zealand argued that the determination of material injury was within the jurisdiction of the government, and that it could not be challenged or scrutinised by other governments. The Panel rejected this view and held that the determination could be challenged, and if found wrong, relief could be given. Thus, it cannot be based purely on the subjective decision of the government making the determination.[66]

This Panel also examined whether New Zealand could make a plea of the existence of the threat of material injury. The Panel found that there had been: (i) high import penetration of the transformer market in New Zealand, (ii) significant increase in imports from all sources over one single year, and (iii) only a minimal impact of imports from Finland. Considering these points, the Panel saw no reason to assume that the imports from Finland would change this picture significantly in the future and concluded that the threat of material injury could not be deemed to have existed.

This Panel further examined whether any material injury had been caused by the imports from Finland. The Panel did find that the industry had been in a poor condition because of the lack of new orders, diminishing profitability, a large increase in imports and uncertainty about new orders. But the Panel took into account the fact that the imports from Finland constituted only 2.4 per cent of total sales of the transformer industry in New Zealand. In terms of the capacities of the transformers, the imports from Finland accounted for only 1.5 per cent of domestic production and imports taken together, and only 2.4 per cent of total imports. The Panel also noted the fact that there had been an increase of 250 per cent in total imports in capacity terms in the two years under consideration and that Finland accounted for only 3.4 per cent of this increase. The Panel concluded that even though the transformer industry in New Zealand might have suffered injury from increased imports, the cause of this injury could not be attributed to the imports from Finland.

This Panel also did not accept the point raised by New Zealand that any given amount of profit lost by the firms was an injury to the domestic industry.

The 1992 Panel on Canadian Countervailing Duties on Grain Corn from the US, established under the Agreement on Interpretation and Application of Articles VI, XVI and XXIII of the General Agreement (the Subsidies Code), (report adopted on 26 March 1992), examined the question of the linkage of subsidies with injury. It found that the Canadian authorities had based their determination of injury on factors other than subsidised imports. In particular, they had taken into account the effect of a dramatic decline in world market prices that resulted in large part from a US subsidy under the 1985 Farm Bill. The Panel was of the opinion that if there was a general and dramatic decline in the world market prices for grain corn, this would affect Canadian producers even if Canada did not import any grain corn from the US. The Canadian price would be directly affected in a material way by the world price decline. The Panel concluded that the Canadian authorities had thus not established that the price depression was caused by the subsidised imports from the US and that, as such, the causal link between the subsidy and the injury was not proved.[67]

Clarifications of Some Terms

Two terms need clarification, viz., "domestic industry" and "like product". These have particular meanings in the context of the determination of injury.

Domestic Industry

Definition

The domestic industry in respect of which the injury is to be examined has been defined in the Agreement (Article 16) as: the whole of the domestic producers of the like products, or at least those of them whose collective output of the products constitutes a major proportion of the total domestic production of those products.

Normally, the term "major proportion" should mean more than half. But in actual practice, even somewhat lower proportions have been treated as "major proportion". The actual interpretation will evolve with the further implementation of the Agreement.

In calculating injury, only the related producers (explained below) have to be left out. All other producers have to be taken into account. One cannot leave out any class of production on the grounds that it constitutes a special situation; for example, one cannot say that production for sale will be taken into account, but not captive production.

Related Producers

There is a further qualification. If some of the producers are themselves importers of the like products, or if they are related to the exporters or importers of the like products, their production will be excluded from calculation while determining the injury to the domestic industry.

Firms will be deemed to be related only if:

(i) one of them directly or indirectly controls the other; or

(ii) both of them are directly or indirectly controlled by a third person; or

(iii) together, they directly or indirectly control a third person.

Here, a firm is said to control another firm if it is legally or operationally in a position to exercise restraint or direction over the latter.

Isolated Markets

There is an additional qualification on the definition of the domestic industry. It is in respect of isolated markets within a country. If, in respect of the products in question, the country is divided into a number of mutually isolated markets, the examination of injury can be conducted in relation to only the industry located in a specific isolated region. In this case, the examination will not be done on the basis of the effect on the total or majority of the domestic producers, but on the basis of the effect on the industry located in that region. Here, the following conditions will have to be satisfied:

(i) the producers within such an isolated region sell all or almost all of their production of the products in question in this region;

(ii) there is no substantial supply of the products by producers from other regions of the country to that region;

(iii) there is a concentration of imports of the products in that region; and

(iv) the imports cause injury to the producers of all or almost all the production in that region. (Here, the condition of an effect on a major proportion of the total production is not applicable.)

Customs Union

When two or more countries have formed a customs union (explained in the chapter on MFN treatment) and, in the process, attained such a level of integration that they have the characteristics of a unified market, the industry in the whole area of the customs union must be taken to be the domestic industry for the purpose of determining injury (Article 16.4).

Gradually, as the globalisation of production advances further, the determination of what domestic production is will become more complex. This problem has to be tackled as an exercise in finalising the rules of origin (described in detail in the chapter on the rules of origin).

Like Products

The determination of injury will depend very much on the extent of the domestic industry which is taken into consideration. The provision in the Agreement is to consider the effect on the producers of like products. A like product is one which is identical, i.e., alike in all respects, to the product under consideration. In the absence of such a product, a like product is another product which has characteristics closely resembling those of the product under consideration, even though it is not totally alike in all respects (Footnote 46, Article 16).

Some specific cases have come up in the past where the examination of what constitutes a domestic industry producing like products was critical. Some of these cases are described below in brief to clarify the definition.

Before the Panel on New Zealand – Imports of Electrical Transformers from Finland (July 1985), New Zealand gave the argument that the transformer industry had four distinguishable ranges of transformers and that these should be considered separately for the purpose of determining injury. The Panel did not consider this argument valid, especially in view of the fact that the industry in New Zealand produced a large range of transformers, most of which were not affected by imports. The Panel was of the view that individual lines of production of an industry should not be protected through such means; what is relevant is to examine the overall state of health of the industry producing the product.[68]

The Panel on US – Definition of Industry Concerning Wine and Grape Products, established under the Agreement on Interpretation and Application of Articles VI, XVI and XXIII of the General Agreement (the Subsidies Code), (April 1992), examined whether wines and grapes were like products. It concluded that they were not. The conclusion of the Panel was based on the consideration that these two products had different physical characteristics and also that the production of grapes and the production of wine were two separate groups of industries in the US.[69]

IMPOSITION OF COUNTERVAILING DUTY

When a final determination has been made regarding the subsidy, injury and linkage, whether positive or negative, a public notice will be given setting forth in sufficient detail the findings and conclusions on all issues. The notice must be sent to the interested Members and interested parties.

If there has been a negative finding in relation to the subsidy, injury or linkage, no further action regarding countervailing duty will be taken. If there has been a positive finding, countervailing duty may be imposed. For this purpose, certain procedures and limitations have been prescribed as detailed below.

Interests of Consumers and Industrial Users

The Agreement suggests that procedures should be established so that domestic interested parties (including, in this case, the consumers and the industrial users of the subsidised imported product) whose interests will be adversely affected by the imposition of countervailing duty are able to make representations and the authorities are able to take due account of such representations (Article 19.2). Thus, these interest groups get two opportunities to put forth their case, first during the investigation when they may present facts on the subsidy, injury and causal linkage, and then again before the imposition of the duty when they may demonstrate the possible adverse effects of such duty on them. After considering the representations of these parties, the Member will decide whether to impose the countervailing duty. If it decides in the affirmative, it may proceed with imposition; but the imposition has to follow certain prescribed limitations as given below.

Limitations

Maximum Limit of the Duty

There is one definitive limitation that the duty cannot be in excess of the subsidy found to exist, i.e., the duty cannot be higher than the subsidy margin. It may, however, be less, at the discretion of the Member.

The Agreement provides a guideline that the duty should be less if such a smaller duty will be adequate to remove the injury to the domestic industry, meaning thereby that the duty should be just enough to compensate for the injury margin. In actual practice, however, the extent of this smaller amount of duty to offset the injury margin may be difficult to work out.

Non-Discriminatory Application

When a decision has been taken to impose the duty, it has to be applied on a non-discriminatory basis to the products of all countries satisfying the conditions of subsidy, injury and causal linkage. The amount of subsidy, of course, will differ among the countries, depending on the extent of subsidy. If either the subsidy has been withdrawn or undertakings have been given on the amount of the subsidy or the price of the product, countervailing duty will not be imposed in the case of that country.

Procedure for Imposition and Collection of Duty

The Agreement does not provide a uniform system of imposition or collection of countervailing duty. Countries may have their own methods for this purpose.

Review and Duration

Review

A review of the need for the continued imposition of the duty or of the adverse consequences of removal of the duty is to be undertaken by the authorities in the following circumstances:

(I) The review may be undertaken by the authorities on their own initiative.

(II) An interested party may request an examination as to whether:

- (i) the continuance of the duty is necessary to offset subsidisation, or
- (ii) it is likely that injury will continue or recur if the duty is removed, or
- (iii) both of the situations mentioned above may materialise.

The conditions for such a request are the following:

(i) a reasonable period has elapsed since the imposition of the duty, and

(ii) positive information substantiating the need for a review is given.

(III) Well before the expiry of the duty, the authorities may start an examination on their own initiative or the domestic industry may ask for an examination as to whether it is likely that the removal of duty will lead to the continuation or recurrence of subsidisation and injury.

Public notices of the initiation and completion of a review have to be given, setting forth all the relevant matters considered in the review and the basis of its conclusions.

Duration

A countervailing duty can be continued only as long as is necessary to counteract injury-causing subsidisation and only to the extent necessary to achieve this objective.

If the countervailing duty is found to be no longer necessary, it will be immediately terminated.

Normally, the duty will be terminated:

(i) before the expiry of five years from its imposition, or

(ii) if, in the reviews, it is determined that the duty is no longer necessary, or

(iii) before the expiry of five years from the date of the most recent review covered by situation (III) or situations (I) and(II), if both subsidisation and injury were the subjects of examination.

If successive reviews indicate the need for the duty to offset subsidisation and injury, the duty, in this manner, can continue without limit.

If a review has been initiated before the expiry of the duty by the authorities on their own initiative or at the request of the domestic industry as mentioned in situation (III) above, the duty may remain in force during the pendency of the review, even beyond the five-year period.

Retroactive Application

Normally, the countervailing duty will be applied to products which enter the importing country only after the decision to impose such a duty comes into force. A similar provision also applies to the provisional measure. However, under certain circumstances, the duty or measure may be applicable even from an earlier date, as explained below.

- If the investigation has shown the existence of actual injury (and not the threat of injury or material retardation of the industry), the countervailing duty may be levied with retroactive effect for the period for which provisional measures have been applied.

- If the investigation has shown only the existence of (i) a threat of material injury or (ii) material retardation of the industry, the countervailing duty can be imposed only with effect from the date of such determination.

- If the investigation has shown the existence of the threat of material injury and if it is determined that the subsidised imports would have led to the determination of the existence of material injury in the absence of the provisional measures, the countervailing duty may be levied retroactively for the period for which the provisional measures have been applied.

INTERMEDIATE STEPS

Some intermediate steps were briefly mentioned towards the end of the section on investigation. These need some elaboration.

Provisional Measures

After the expiry of 60 days from the initiation of the investigation and before the final determination of subsidy, injury and linkage, provisional measures can be applied by the Member. The necessary conditions for taking provisional measures are the following:

(i) an investigation has been formally initiated, public notice of the initiation of the investigation has been given, and interested Members and interested parties have been given adequate opportunity to submit information and make comments;

(ii) a preliminary determination of the existence of subsidy, injury and causal linkage has been made;

(iii) the authorities consider such measures necessary to prevent injury being caused during the investigation.

The disciplines on the provisional measures are the following:

(i) these measures may be in the form of a countervailing duty guaranteed by cash deposits or bonds equal to the provisionally calculated amount of the subsidy;

(ii) the period of application must not exceed four months;

(iii) the measures must not be applied sooner than 60 days from the date of initiation of the investigation;

(iv) the disciplines in respect of the final countervailing duty will also be valid in this case.

A public notice of the preliminary determination must be given along similar lines as those for the final determination. Similarly, a public notice of the imposition of provisional measures must be given, setting forth:

the names of the suppliers, the description of the product, the amount of the subsidy and the basis on which it has been determined, the considerations relevant to the determination of injury and the main reasons leading to the determination.

Undertakings

There is a provision in the Agreement for undertakings from the subsidising Member or from the exporters. If such satisfactory undertakings have been received and accepted, the investigation will be suspended or terminated and no provisional measure or countervailing duty will be imposed.

The undertakings are of the following nature:

(i) the agreement of the exporting Member to eliminate or limit the subsidy or to take other measures concerning its effects; or

(ii) the agreement of the exporter to revise its prices to the extent that the investigating authorities are satisfied that the injury is eliminated.

(iii) There is no provision for an undertaking in respect of a quantitative limit on the subsidised export.

The prior conditions for seeking or accepting the undertakings are:

(i) there has been a preliminary determination of the existence of subsidy, injury and causal linkage; and

(ii) in the case of an undertaking from an exporter, the consent of the exporting Member has been obtained.

The undertakings are to be voluntary and acceptance is to be at the discretion of the investigating Member. Some reasons for non-acceptance could be: the impractical nature of the undertakings because of the number of exporters being too large, or reasons of general policy. The Member should provide the exporters with the reasons for non-acceptance so that they have an opportunity to comment on them.

Even when an undertaking has been given and accepted, the investigation may continue till the end if the exporting Member so requests or if the investigating Member so decides. If a negative determination is made, the undertaking will lapse. If, however, a positive determination is made, the undertaking will normally continue for five years. The provision regarding reviews will be applicable to undertakings as well.

A public notice of acceptance of the undertaking will have to be given, setting forth all the relevant information as well as the non-confidential part of the undertaking.

SOME OTHER PROVISIONS

Judicial Review

A Member must provide for a prompt review of the administrative actions relating to the final determination and the reviews. The judicial or administrative authorities entrusted with such a review must be independent of the authorities that are responsible for the final determination or the reviews.

Notifications

Annual notifications on subsidies will be submitted by Members by 30 June each year.

All specific subsidies must be notified.

The notifications must be clear, detailed and specific, and, in particular, must include:

> the form of the subsidy (e.g., grant, loan, tax concession, etc.); subsidy per unit, or, if it is not possible, the total amount of the subsidy; the average subsidy per unit in the previous year (if possible); the purpose of the subsidy and the policy objective; the duration of the subsidy or time limits relating to it, and statistical data relating to the trade effects of the subsidy.

There is also a provision regarding reverse notification. If a Member considers that any measure of another Member having the effect of a subsidy has not been notified, it may bring it to the notice of that Member. If the latter still fails to notify the measure, the Member may itself notify such a subsidy to the Committee on Subsidies and Countervailing Measures.

Members must notify all actions relating to countervailing duties to the Committee on Subsidies and Countervailing Measures.

Members must inform the Committee about:

(i) the competent authorities for initiating and conducting investigations; and

(ii) the domestic procedures for the initiation and conduct of investigations.

Institutions

The Committee on Subsidies and Countervailing Measures, consisting of the representatives of all Members, has been established to carry out the functions assigned to it in the Agreement.

A Permanent Group of Experts (PGE) will be established by this Committee. The PGE will give advisory opinions on the nature of subsidies.

Dispute Settlement

Beyond the specific provisions on the settlement of disputes explained earlier, the provisions of Articles XXII and XXIII of GATT 1994, as elaborated and applied by the Dispute Settlement Understanding (described in the chapter on the dispute settlement process), will be applicable.

SPECIAL PROVISIONS FOR DEVELOPING COUNTRIES

Some provisions regarding the developing countries have been mentioned earlier. At the risk of repetition, these special provisions are given below in a consolidated manner so as to facilitate ready reference.

Groups of Countries

Developing countries have been divided into two groups, for certain purposes, in this Agreement:

(i) Annex VII developing countries, i.e., (a) the LDCs, and (b) those developing countries which are deemed to have GNP per capita less than US$1,000 per annum (the list of these countries is in Annex VII of the Agreement and includes Bolivia, Cameroon, Congo, Côte d'Ivoire, Dominican Republic, Egypt, Ghana, Guatemala, Guyana, India, Indonesia, Kenya, Morocco, Nicaragua, Nigeria, Pakistan, Philippines, Senegal, Sri Lanka and Zimbabwe)
(As countries reach the critical level of GNP per capita, they will be taken out of this list.);

(ii) All other developing countries.

Export Subsidy

Annex VII Developing Countries

Annex VII developing countries are exempted from the prohibition on subsidies contingent on exports (export subsidies). They can continue with such subsidies and introduce new subsidies of this type.

However, they have to phase out such a subsidy on a product eight years after they reach export competitiveness in respect of that product. Export competitiveness is reached:

(i) when a developing country's export of that product has reached a share of 3.25 per cent in the world trade of that product; and

(ii) if such share continues for two consecutive years.

In determining export competitiveness based on the share of world trade, what is particularly important is the group of products which will be considered together for this calculation. The Agreement prescribes that a product, for this purpose, is defined as a section heading of the Harmonised System nomenclature.

No countervailing duty action can be taken against a product of an Annex VII developing country Member if the overall level of subsidies for the product in question does not exceed 3 per cent of its value calculated on a per-unit basis.

Other Developing Countries

Other developing country Members are exempted from the prohibition of export subsidies for a period of eight years from 1 January 1995. But there are certain disciplines which they will have to follow, viz.:

(i) the level of the export subsidy must not be increased;

(ii) the existing export subsidy should be phased out in eight years, preferably in a progressive manner;

(iii) the subsidy will be phased out even earlier if it is not consistent with the country's development needs.

If a developing country Member considers that some of its export subsidies should continue beyond the eight-year period, it should enter into consultation with the Committee, giving all the relevant facts. If extension is allowed, it will consult with the Committee annually to determine the need for continuing the subsidy. If extension is not allowed, it will phase out the export subsidy within two years of the end of the previous authorised period.

If such a developing country Member attains export competitiveness in a product, it will phase out the export subsidy in two years.

Import-Substitution Subsidy

For this purpose, the developing country Members are divided into two groups, viz.: (i) LDC Members, and (ii) all other developing country Members. Here, there is no grouping based on Annex VII.

LDCs

The prohibition of subsidies contingent on the use of domestic products over imported products (import-substitution subsidies) will not apply to the LDC Members for a period of eight years from 1 January 1995.

Other Developing Countries

For other developing country Members, the prohibition will not apply for five years from 1 January 1995.

Dispute Settlement Process Against Prohibited Subsidy

If a developing country Member maintains an export subsidy or an import-substitution subsidy in accordance with the special dispensations mentioned above, no action through the dispute settlement route can be taken merely for its being maintained.

However, action against these subsidies can be taken in the event of adverse effects to another Member. Thus, remedial action against such measures and practices can be taken if they cause:

(i) injury, or

(ii) nullification or impairment of benefits, or

(iii) serious prejudice

to another Member. The procedure followed for this purpose will be the one applicable as in the case of the dispute settlement route against actionable subsidies, which was explained earlier.

For countervailing duty action, there are separate provisions, which will be mentioned later.

Actionable Subsidy

Absence of Presumption of Serious Prejudice

For developing country Members, there will be no presumption of the existence of serious prejudice as in Article 6.1. This would imply that in the case of (i) *ad valorem* subsidies exceeding 5 per cent, (ii) subsidies to cover the operating losses of an industry, (iii) repetition of subsidies to cover the operating losses of a firm, and (iv) subsidies in the form of direct forgiveness of debt, there is no presumption that serious prejudice exists.

Hence, if a Member wishes to initiate action, it will have to prove the existence of serious prejudice. Thus, there is a shift of the burden of proof. Whereas in the case of a developed country subsidising Member, the burden of proof is on such a Member to establish non-existence of serious prejudice, in the case of a developing country subsidising Member, the burden of proof is on the complaining Member to demonstrate that serious prejudice exists.

Dispute Settlement Process for Article 6.1 Subsidy

If a developing country Member maintains a subsidy as included in Article 6.1, i.e., one of the four mentioned above, remedies may be had against it through countermeasures if such a subsidy causes:

(i) injury, or

(ii) nullification or impairment of benefits, or

(iii) serious prejudice to another Member.

Dispute Settlement Process for Other Actionable Subsidies

For other types of actionable subsidies, there is a limited provision for the dispute settlement process. In such cases, this type of remedy can be had only if a subsidy causes nullification or impairment of benefits under GATT 1994 in such a way:

(i) as to displace or impede imports of a like product of another Member into the market of the developing country Member (here, the importer is the subsidising developing country Member, and the exporter is another Member); or

(ii) as to cause injury to a domestic industry in the market of an importing Member (here, the exporter is the subsidising developing country Member, and the importer is another Member).

The third element of serious prejudice, i.e., the adverse effect in a third country market, is not included here; hence, for such adverse effect caused by the subsidised exports from developing countries, remedial action through this process cannot be taken.

Besides, such a remedy cannot also be had against developing country Members if some specific types of subsidies are linked to and granted within a privatisation programme of the Member. The types of subsidies covered by this special provision are:

(i) direct forgiveness of debt,

(ii) subsidies to cover social costs including relinquishment of government revenue, and

(iii) other transfer liabilities.

The conditions in this special dispensation relating to privatisation are:

(i) the subsidies and the privatisation programme should be for a limited period,

(ii) these should be notified to the Committee, and

(iii) the programme should result in the eventual privatisation of the enterprise.

Countervailing Duty Process

It has to be noted that countervailing duties are not excluded in any of these cases, be it one involving prohibited subsidies or actionable subsidies. Thus, even though countermeasures cannot be taken in some of these cases, countervailing duties can be imposed if the conditions of existence of subsidy, injury and causal linkage are established.

For countervailing duty action, the general *de minimis* provision for developing countries in respect of the margin of subsidy is 2 per cent of the value of the product calculated on a per-unit basis. This limit is 3 per cent for those developing country Members that have eliminated their export subsidies prior to the expiry of the maximum eight-year period allowed for them. The limit is 3 per cent also for Annex VII countries, as explained earlier.

The *de minimis* limit pertaining to the volume of the subsidised import is 4 per cent of the total import of the like product in the importing Member country. If the individual shares are less than 4 per cent each, but the collective share of the subsidised imports from developing countries is more than 9 per cent, action for countervailing duty may be taken. This provision applies equally to all developing countries.

COUNTRIES IN TRANSITION

There are special provisions for Member countries in transition from a centrally planned economy to a market, free-enterprise economy. There is a general provision that these Members may apply the programmes and measures necessary for such transformation.

In particular, the following flexibilities have been laid down in the Agreement:

(i) such Members have seven years to phase out the prohibited subsidies, i.e., export subsidies and import-substitution subsidies;

(ii) remedies through the dispute settlement process cannot be taken against direct forgiveness of debt for seven years, and

(iii) regarding remedies through the dispute settlement process against other actionable subsidies, such Members have the same seven-year flexibility as the developing country Members in general.

Chapter IV.2

ANTI-DUMPING

INTRODUCTION

SOMETIMES, enterprises export products at very low prices in order to capture markets abroad and to eliminate competition. Such a practice, called "dumping", has been considered to be an unfair practice in international trade. Both subsidies and dumping are considered to be unfair practices; the difference is that the former is adopted by Member governments, whereas the latter, by firms and enterprises. Correspondingly, the remedial action in respect of subsidies is targeted at the subsidising Member and is taken against the subsidised product exported by the various enterprises of the subsidising country, whereas the action in respect of dumping is taken against the enterprises that resort to the practice. Those enterprises which do not dump the product are not covered by the anti dumping action.

EFFECTS OF DUMPING, VARYING INTERESTS AND PRESSURES

Like subsidies, dumping has two differing effects in the importing country. The low prices of the imported products may harm the domestic industry which is producing like products. At the same time, the consumers and industrial users of the product in the importing country may benefit from such low prices. However, the latter are not well organised and their voice is not as strong as that of the producer industries which are also usually supported by their labour unions. Hence, the pressure for action against dumping is usually much stronger than that for opposite action.

The Agreement on Anti-dumping authorises counteraction if there is injury to the domestic producer industry. Even though the user industries and consumers have the opportunity to present their own case, the actual point for determination prior to taking any anti-dumping action is, in fact, the injury not to them but to the producer industry. Of course, the government of the importing country has the discretion not to take anti-dumping action even after injury has been established, and one of the important points guiding this option may be the interests of the consumers and user industries. But in actual practice, governments have seldom based their discretion on these interests; they have been influenced more by the interests of the producer industries.

Disciplines

Detailed provisions regarding the identification of dumping and remedial measures against dumping have been made in the Uruguay Round Agreement on Anti-dumping, formally called the Agreement on Implementation of Article VI of the General Agreement on Tariffs and Trade 1994. The original provisions of the discipline regarding anti-dumping are contained in Article VI of GATT 1994. Normally, the Agreement on Anti-dumping is comprehensive and complete in itself; however, the provisions of Article VI of GATT 1994 continue to remain relevant and valid in so far as they are not inconsistent with the Agreement.

The Agreement on Anti-dumping is very complex. It uses terms and concepts which have evolved over the course of a long usage of anti-dumping measures and which have specific connotations. Hence, one has to be very careful in interpreting them.[70] The annexes and footnotes of the Agreement should be read with care as a large number of them contain important definitions, procedures and obligations.

Any action against dumping can be taken by Members only in accordance with this Agreement. If an enterprise is found to be dumping its products and if such dumping is causing injury to the domestic industry in the importing country, the importing Member can impose a countervailing duty on the imports up to the maximum extent of the margin of dumping, i.e., the quantum of dumping. Hence, the remedial process requires the determination of three elements, viz.: (i) existence of dumping, (ii) margin of dumping, and (iii) existence of injury.[71]

DUMPING

Broadly speaking, an enterprise is said to dump a product if it exports the product at a price lower than the price of the like product in the exporting country. Formally, "dumping" is defined as the introduction of a product in the commerce of another country (exporting it to another country) at a price which is less than the normal value. Generally, the normal value is the comparable price of the like product in the exporting country in the ordinary course of trade.

In determining the existence of dumping, therefore, there are three steps of examination, viz.:

(i) determination of the "export price",

(ii) determination of the "normal value", and

(iii) comparison of the export price and the normal value.

The major importing countries have enacted very complex procedures in this regard. The complexity mainly lies in adjusting the available data for the export price and normal value so as to make them reasonably comparable.

EXPORT PRICE

Generally, the export price as shown in the books of the exporter is taken for the consideration of dumping. But in some situations, it is likely that this price may not be available or reliable. Some reasons could be the following:

(i) the exporter and the importer may be associated, or

(ii) the exporter and the importer may have some mutual compensatory arrangement between them.

For such situations, there is a provision for calculating a constructed export price.

Constructed Export Price

The basis for calculating the constructed export price is the price at which the imported product is first sold to an independent buyer. An independent buyer is one who neither controls nor is controlled by the seller, nor, together with the seller, is controlled by a third person.

Difficulties in this process may arise if the product is not resold to an independent buyer or is not resold in its original imported condition. In such situations, the authorities in the importing country may determine the constructed export price on some reasonable alternative basis.

Export from an Intermediate Country

If a product is not directly exported from the country of origin to the importing country, but is exported from an intermediate country, the export price is the one at which the intermediate country exports it to the importing country.

NORMAL VALUE

Main Elements

Generally, the normal value is the comparable sale price for the like product in the exporting country in the ordinary course of trade. (These terms will be explained while discussing comparison.)

Sometimes, it may not be possible to consider the sale price in the exporting country because:

(i) there may not be any sale of the like product in the exporting country in the ordinary course of trade; or

(ii) the sales do not permit proper comparison because of:

(a) a particular market situation, or

(b) low sales volume in the domestic market of the exporting country.

The sale in the exporting country will normally be considered as being of adequate quantity if it constitutes at least 5 per cent of the sale of the product to the importing country.

Clarification of Some Terms

Particular Market Situation

Some examples of a particular market situation which may render the reported sale price unsuitable for comparison are the following:

(i) There may be strict government control on prices and prices may not be determined based on market conditions, but on several other social and political considerations.

(ii) A single sale for some special reason may be at an abnormal price but may, at the same time, be of adequate volume to satisfy the criterion of 5 per cent.

(iii) There may be different patterns of demand for the product in the exporting and importing countries.

Ordinary Course of Trade

This concept has been clarified by citing negative situations. Some examples of transactions not made in the ordinary course of trade are:

(i) the exporters and importers are related,

(ii) the sale price is consistently below the cost price,

(iii) the product is made for a single and specific purpose according to exclusive specifications.

Alternative Methods for Calculating Normal Value

If the recorded sale price for the product in the exporting country cannot be taken for the purpose of calculating the normal value, the normal value will be determined as:

(i) a comparable price of the like product when exported to an appropriate third country, provided this price is representative; or

(ii) a constructed normal value based on the cost of production in the country of origin plus reasonable amounts for:

  (a) administrative, selling and general costs, and

  (b) profits.

Which of these two alternatives should be adopted will depend on the discretion of the importing country. No sequence has been prescribed in this regard. Of course, either of these methods can be employed only if it is not possible to take the normal comparable price of the like product in the exporting country as the normal value.

Sales Below Cost

Main Issues

In calculating the normal value, one has to find out the sale prices of the like product in individual sale transactions in the domestic market of the exporting country. If a large number of transactions have taken place, the technique of sampling is applied. In these calculations, such transactions which have been made in the ordinary course of trade have to be taken into account. An issue which has been controversial for a long time is whether sales at prices below the cost of production should be considered as having been made in the ordinary course of trade.

This issue has particular significance as it has a bearing on the calculation of the dumping margin. If prices below cost in the exporting countries are left out while calculating the normal value, there will naturally be a bias towards arriving at a higher normal value and therefore a higher dumping margin. The argument in favour of considering prices below cost is that it is not uncommon among enterprises to sell goods sometimes at comparatively lower prices, considering overall trade interests. The fear, on the other hand, is that an enterprise might be resorting to persistent predatory practice (by deliberately selling at prices below cost as a strategy) even in its home country; in this case, it would be right to ignore such transactions, as they would clearly not have been conducted in the ordinary course of trade.

The Agreement implies that prices below cost (i.e., fixed costs plus variable costs plus the amounts for administrative, selling and general costs and amounts for profits) will generally be included in calculating the normal value.

Exclusion of Such Sales from Calculation

The Agreement permits the exclusion of sales below cost from the calculation of normal value when there is evidence of persistent sales at lower prices and when large quantities are involved. It specifically prescribes that these prices may be disregarded only if the authorities at an appropriate senior level determine that the following conditions exist:

(i) Such sales are made within an extended period of time, i.e., normally one year, but in no case less than six months;

ii) The sales have been made in substantial quantities. The elements which will satisfy this condition are the following:

(a) the volume of sales below per-unit cost is 20 per cent or more of the volume covered in the transactions under consideration in the determination of normal value;

(b) the weighted average selling price of the transactions under consideration is below the weighted average per-unit cost; and

(iii) The sales are at prices which do not provide for the recovery of all costs within a reasonable period of time.

What a reasonable period of time is has not been specified. However, if the prices are below per-unit cost at the time of sale, but are above the weighted average per-unit cost for the period of investigation, such prices will be deemed to provide for the recovery of costs within a reasonable period of time. Thus, the decline in costs occurring during the period of investigation has to be taken into account.

Cost of Production

Main Elements

Normally, the cost will be calculated based on the records kept by the exporter or producer under investigation if:

(i) such records have been kept in accordance with the generally accepted accounting principles of the exporting country; and

(ii) the records reflect reasonably the costs associated with the production and sale of the product.

Adjustments

Some adjustments in the cost will be required as there may be some items of cost which are spread over products beyond those which have been exported, e.g., development costs, non-recurring costs, costs in connection with new capacity-building, etc. For adjustments regarding these costs, the following principles will be followed:

(i) All evidence on the allocation of costs will be considered if such allocations have been historically utilised by the exporter or the producer, in particular, for (a) amortisation and depreciation periods, (b) allowances for capital expenditures and (c) other development costs.

(ii) Appropriate adjustment will be made for such non-recurring items of cost which benefit future and current production.

(iii) Appropriate adjustment will be made for the costs relating to start-up operations.

The term "start-up operation" needs some clarification. This situation arises when a new line of production is started. It naturally involves substantial additional investment. Capacity utilisation may be low in the beginning. It is likely that the cost of production in the new line will be rather high to start with, but will gradually decline.

The Agreement provides that in the case of start-up operations, the cost at the end of the start-up period will be taken into account, which generally would be the time when the cost of production in the new line would have stabilised. However, if the start-up period extends beyond the investigation period, the most recent cost will be taken into account.

Additions to Cost of Production

Additions to the cost of production for (i) administrative, selling and general costs and (ii) profits, will be based on the actual data of the exporter or producer under investigation. These data should be for like products and relate to production and sale in the ordinary course of trade.

If the calculation of these amounts on this basis is not possible, any of the following bases will be adopted:

(i) The actual amounts incurred or realised by these very producers or exporters in respect of the same general category of products. This basis may be utilised if the data for the product under investigation are not available, but data for other products which are in the same general category are available.

(ii) The weighted average of the actual amounts incurred and realised by other exporters or producers (also subject to investigation) in respect of the like products. This basis may be utilised if some other exporters or producers of the like products have reasonable data on this subject.

(iii) Any other reasonable method, with the stipulation that the profit taken into account must not exceed the level normally realised by other exporters or producers on the sale of the products of the same general category in the country of origin.

By providing that these additions to the cost of production will be based on actual data, the Agreement excludes the practice of using some fixed minimum percentage of the cost of production as the addition for administrative, general and selling costs and profits.

COMPARISON OF EXPORT PRICE AND NORMAL VALUE

Level and Time of Sales

The general guideline is that the comparison of the export price and the normal value has to be done in a fair manner. The authorities determining the margin of dumping by such a comparison must specify to the parties the information which they should supply in order to make a fair comparison possible. The Agreement prescribes that an unreasonable burden of proof will not be imposed on the parties.

To ensure a proper comparison, two precautions have to be taken, viz.:

(i) the comparison must be made at the same level of trade, which normally will be the ex-factory level;

(ii) the comparison must be of sales made, as nearly as possible, at the same time.

By the "level of trade", what is meant is the stage of transaction, e.g., whether the sale is to retailers, to local distributors, or to regional distributors, etc. The Agreement specifies that the level to be considered should normally be the ex-factory level. Thus, if other levels have entered into the calculations, they will have to be reduced to ex-factory level by making suitable adjustments.

Due adjustments should be made for differences which affect price comparability, for example, differences in conditions and terms of sale, taxation, levels of trade, quantities, physical characteristics, etc.

The Agreement does not specify how the adjustments will be made.

In cases where the export price is constructed on the basis of the sale to the first independent buyer, adjustments should be made for costs incurred between importation and resale, e.g., duties and taxes, and also for profits.

Conversion of Currencies

In most cases, the comparison of the export price and the normal value will involve conversion of currencies. In this respect, the following procedure has been prescribed in the Agreement:

(i) the rate of exchange on the date of sale will be considered (the date of sale is the date of the instrument which establishes the material terms of sale);

(ii) if the sale of foreign currency on the forward market is directly linked to the export sale, the rate of exchange in the forward sale will be used;

(iii) fluctuations in the exchange rates will be ignored; and

(iv) exporters will be allowed at least 60 days for the adjustment of export prices to reflect sustained movements in the exchange rates during investigation.

Comparison of Prices

Normal Method

After having made all the relevant calculations, the actual comparison will normally be made according to the following methods:

(i) a weighted average normal value will be compared with a weighted average of the prices of all export transactions; or

(ii) the normal value will be compared with the export price on a transaction-to-transaction basis.

This parity in comparison is important as it ensures a degree of fairness. If the average normal value were to be compared with the export prices in individual transactions, it will generally result in a higher dumping margin. The export prices above the average normal value will be left out in this method, since there is no dumping in these cases and, as such, the dumping margin is zero. In averaging the export prices of various transactions, the higher export prices get balanced with the lower prices and, to that extent, the margin becomes smaller.

Exceptions

Though normally the methods mentioned above will be used, the Agreement does provide for situations when a weighted average normal value may be compared with the export prices of individual transactions. This method can be used when:

(i) there is a pattern of export prices differing significantly among purchasers, regions or time periods, and

(ii) an explanation is provided on why such differences cannot be appropriately accommodated by the use of either of the two normal methods.

To use this method, it must be shown that there is a "pattern" of difference in export prices. The occurrence of sporadic differences will not suffice. To prove a pattern in respect of regions, it will be necessary to show that the prices of products exported to a particular region in the importing country are usually different from the prices for other regions. Alternatively, similar patterns for time periods (for example, significantly differing prices in winter and summer) or for individual purchasers will have to be demonstrated.

INVESTIGATION FOR DUMPING AND INJURY

The investigation for dumping and injury is carried out almost exactly as it is done for subsidies, and the procedure for levying anti-dumping duty is almost exactly similar to that for levying countervailing duty. The descriptions given in respect of these subjects in the chapter on subsidies are also applicable to dumping and should be consulted.

The sections which are almost totally applicable relate to: determination of injury, definition of domestic industry, initiation and conduct of investigation, procedure for evidence, provisional measures, price undertakings, imposition of anti-dumping duty, retroactive imposition of anti-dumping duty, duration and review of anti-dumping duty, public notice and judicial review.

Departures from the descriptions given in the chapter on subsidies on these subjects are mentioned below. It will be advisable to first read these sections in the chapter on subsidies and then go over the points of difference as detailed below.

Consultation

The Agreement on Subsidies and Countervailing Measures provides for a consultation between the importing Member and the Member alleged to be subsidising its product. This consultation is to take place, in the case of subsidies, after the acceptance of the application requesting action against the subsidy and before the initiation of the investigation. The Agreement on Anti-dumping does not stipulate such a consultation. It only makes it obligatory to inform the Member alleged to be resorting to dumping after the application for anti-dumping action has been received and before the investigation is initiated. However, the Members may consult at their discretion.

Determination of Injury

In the examination of the impact of the dumped import on the domestic industry, one additional factor mentioned here is the margin of dumping. (The magnitude of the subsidy is not included as a factor for consideration in the case of the impact of subsidised imports on the domestic industry.)

Investigation, Evidence

The application requesting action against dumping has to contain evidence of the existence of dumping and the margin of dumping. For this purpose, information on the normal value and on the export price will have to be given.

If a request has been made, the investigating authorities must provide an opportunity for all interested parties to meet, so that the presentation of opposing views and the opportunity for rebuttals are facilitated.

It is not obligatory for a party to attend a meeting, and absence must not prejudice its case.

The authorities have an obligation to determine the individual margin of dumping in the case of each known exporter or producer of the product under investigation. If the numbers are so large as to make such individual determination impractical, the authorities may limit their examination to:

(i) a reasonable number of parties or products by using statistically valid samples; or

(ii) the largest percentage of the volume of the exports from the country under consideration which can be reasonably investigated.

In the process of such a limited examination, the following conditions have to be followed:

(i) the selection of exporters, importers, producers or products should preferably be done in consultation with and with the consent of the exporters, importers or producers concerned;

(ii) if an exporter or a producer who has not been selected provides necessary information in time, the authorities must determine the individual margin in that case, except if there is undue burden in this process because of a large number of such requests preventing the timely completion of the investigation.

In the case of such a limited examination, the anti-dumping duty applied to the product of the exporters or producers not covered by the examination will be subject to the following conditions:

(i) it must not exceed the weighted average margin of dumping determined in the limited examination; or

(ii) if calculation of the anti-dumping duty has been made on the basis of a prospective normal value, the duty shall not exceed the difference between the weighted average normal value determined in the limited examination and the export prices of the exporters or producers not covered by the examination.

De Minimis

The margin of dumping is considered *de minimis* if it is less than 2 per cent, expressed as a percentage of the export price.

The volume of the dumped import from a country is considered negligible if it is less than 3 per cent of the imports of the like product in the importing country. However, if enterprises from a number of countries are under investigation and if imports from them individually are less than the *de minimis* limit, anti-dumping action can still be taken if imports from them collectively account for more than 7 per cent of the imports of the like product in the importing country.

Undertaking

An undertaking, in the case of subsidies, comes either from the government regarding the removal of the subsidy, or from the exporter regarding an increase in the product's price to offset the effects of the subsidy. In the case of dumping, naturally the government does not come into the picture; the undertaking comes only from the exporter. The undertaking may take two forms, viz.:

(i) revision of prices so as to remove the effects of dumping; or

(ii) ceasing of exports at dumped prices to the area in question.

Provisional Measure

In the case of subsidies, the provisional measure is in the form of a countervailing duty guaranteed by cash deposits or bonds. In the case of dumping, however, the provisional measure may be in the form of either an anti-dumping duty or, preferably, a security through cash deposit or bond. Though the Agreement prefers a security, the levying of an anti-dumping duty is nevertheless permissible as a provisional measure against dumping.

The maximum duration of a provisional measure, in the case of subsidies, is four months, whereas in the case of anti-dumping, it can be longer. If a request is made by exporters representing a significant portion of the trade involved, the authorities may decide to have the measure for a maximum period of six months.

Further, if the authorities are examining the propriety of applying a duty lower than the dumping margin, these periods may be six and nine months respectively.

Refunds

Time limits have been prescribed for the refund of the cash deposit or anti-dumping duty, whereas in the case of subsidies, the stipulation is merely of prompt refund.

Retroactive Duty

Apart from similar provisions for the retroactive imposition of anti-dumping duty as in the case of subsidies, there is a provision for the imposition of a definitive anti-dumping duty on products imported up to 90 days prior to the date of application of provisional measures, if the authorities determine that:

(i) there is a history of dumping causing injury; or

(ii) the importer was, or should have been, aware that the exporter practises dumping which would cause injury; and

(iii) the injury is caused by a massive volume of dumped imports in a relatively short time, which is likely to seriously undermine the remedial effect of the prospective definitive anti-dumping duty in the light of the timing of the dumped import, its volume and other circumstances like a rapid buildup of the imported product.

In such a case, the importer must be given an opportunity to comment on the proposed action.

NEWCOMERS

During the application of an anti-dumping duty on a product in an importing country, there is a special provision for new exporters and producers from the exporting country whose product is covered by the duty. On the principle that an anti-dumping duty is not applicable in general to all the exporters of a country, but only to those whose products were found to have been dumped, the newcomers who did not export during the period of investigation will not be automatically covered by the anti-dumping duty. In their case, a review will be carried out and individual margins of dumping will be calculated. The anti-dumping duty will be levied on that basis. No anti-dumping duty will be charged on them during the review period, though the duty may be retroactively charged from the date of the initiation of the review, if a dumping margin is found.

For this provision to apply to the newcomers, they will have to show that they are not related to any of the exporters or producers in the exporting country who are subject to the anti-dumping duty on that product.

DISPUTE SETTLEMENT PROCESS

Generally, it is stipulated in the Agreement that the Dispute Settlement Understanding (explained in detail in the chapter on the dispute settlement process) will be applicable to disputes under this Agreement. There are, however, some special provisions, as discussed below, which drastically limit the role of the Dispute Settlement Body (DSB) in cases of anti-dumping.

A dispute is generally anticipated when a Member is not satisfied with the process followed by another Member in respect of the imposition of anti-dumping duty.

A Member may request a consultation with another Member if it considers that:

(i) any benefit accruing to it, directly or indirectly, under the Agreement is being nullified or impaired, or

(ii) any objective is being impeded,

by the other Member.

The Member requesting the consultation may refer the matter to the DSB if:

(i) the Member considers that the consultation has failed to achieve a mutually agreed solution, and

(ii) final action has been taken by the other Member to levy a definitive anti-dumping duty or to accept price undertakings, or

(iii) in the case of a provisional measure which has a significant impact, the Member considers that it was taken contrary to the provisions of the Agreement for such a measure as contained in Article 7.1.

The DSB will establish a panel in accordance with the prescribed procedure. The panel will examine the issue based on (i) a written statement of the complaining Member, and (ii) the facts which would have been made available to the authorities of the respondent importing Member in accordance with its domestic procedure.

The role of the panel is very much restricted. It will only determine:

(i) whether the authorities of the importing Member established the facts properly, and

(ii) whether they evaluated the facts in an unbiased and objective manner.

If the panel makes such a determination, the evaluation of the authorities will not be overturned, even if the panel itself might have reached a different conclusion had it conducted the evaluation.

Further, if more than one interpretation is permissible and if the authorities have acted in accordance with one of these, their conclusion will be deemed to be right.

It is apparent from the description given above that the role of the dispute settlement panel is severely curtailed in the field of anti-dumping. In all other subjects in the WTO agreements, the panel is authorised, and in fact expected, to "make an objective assessment of the matter before it, including an objective assessment of the facts of the case and the applicability of and conformity with the relevant covered agreements" (Article 11 of the Dispute Settlement Understanding).

Further, "where a panel... concludes that a measure is inconsistent with a covered agreement, it shall recommend that the Member concerned bring the measure into conformity with that agreement" (Article 19.1 of the DSU).

It is only in the field of anti-dumping that the panel is excluded from this basic role. The process of dispute settlement appears to have been very much weakened in this area.

The possibility of extending this weak dispute settlement process to other areas has been envisaged. One of the Ministerial Decisions adopted in the Final Act of the Uruguay Round negotiations, viz., the Decision on Review of Article 17.6 of the Agreement on Implementation of Article VI of the General Agreement on Tariffs and Trade 1994, says as follows:

"The standard of review in paragraph 6 of Article 17 of the Agreement on Implementation of Article VI of GATT 1994 shall be reviewed after a period of three years with a view to considering the question of whether it is capable of general application."

Here, the reference is to the Article which applies constraints on the role of the panels. It is significant to note that the objective of the review is limited to the examination of the appropriateness of extending this provision to other areas; it does not extend to examining the propriety of continuing with the constraint.

OTHER PROVISIONS

Developing Countries

There is practically no special dispensation for developing countries in this Agreement.

Third Country Action

A situation is envisaged in the Agreement when the domestic industry of a third country (also an exporting country) suffers injury because of the dumping practices of the enterprises of a Member in an importing Member country. In this situation, the third country Member has to request the importing country Member to conduct an investigation and to take further action for anti-dumping measures.

It is expressly provided here that the injury to the industry of the third country will be assessed as a whole and not only with respect to its exports.

The decision whether to initiate and proceed with an investigation rests with the importing country.

Committee

A Committee on Anti-Dumping Practices has been established. It is composed of the representatives of all Members. It will carry out the functions assigned to it in the Agreement and also those assigned to it by Members from time to time.

Impact on Trade

Generally, it is seen that the very initiation of an investigation on dumping gives rise to uncertainty in the exports from the country under investigation to the investigating importing country. Importers may start shifting their sources of supply. Usually, the investigation takes a long time, and even if finally there is a negative determination of injury or dumping, some damage would already have been done, with some loss of market for the exporting country.

Generally, the developing countries have been facing a large number of anti-dumping investigations, and to that extent, they are exposed to a considerable degree of uncertainty about their export prospects.

PART V

SOME SPECIFIC SECTORS

Some sectors have been covered by specific multilateral agreements, viz., agriculture and textiles. There are also plurilateral agreements in some sectors which will be mentioned later in the relevant Part. The sectors of agriculture and textiles are discussed in this Part.

Chapter V.1

AGRICULTURE

INTRODUCTION

Background

DISCIPLINES in the field of agriculture have been much softer compared to the general disciplines in GATT 1947. Problems arising out of it in international trade have been appreciated for a long time and efforts have been made in the past to work out modalities for introducing stricter disciplines in this sector. This subject found an important place in the Uruguay Round of Multilateral Trade Negotiations, and the final outcome was the Agreement on Agriculture.

The disciplines in this sector are still not on levels similar to those for industrial goods in many ways, yet they are an important landmark on the way to a freer trade regime in this sector. The importance does not lie so much in the actual quantitative commitments as in the initiation of a process and in providing a frame for further commitments on liberalisation. It should be noted, at the same time, that in some ways, the disciplines in this sector are now more stringent than in the sector of industrial products. For example, all tariffs in this sector have been bound by all Members and there are quantitative commitments on the reduction of subsidies.

Differing Interests

Some industrialised countries which are big producers and exporters of agricultural products have been maintaining high levels of protection and support for their domestic producers, and also high levels of export subsidies. This has naturally hurt other major exporters of agricultural products. Hence, the interest of these other major exporting countries, including some developing countries, lies in making the disciplines more stringent, for example, by eliminating import restrictions, domestic support to producers and export subsidies. However, those major industrialised countries which have been maintaining high protective barriers and subsidies find it difficult to increase the pace of liberalisation in these areas because of strong agricultural lobbies in these countries. And those developing countries that are traditional importers fear that this process may result in an increase in the price of agricultural products which will raise their import bill.

Several developing countries have a more deep-seated concern. Agriculture in these countries is not so much a matter of commerce; it is intimately interwoven with the pattern of rural life. Many farmers cultivate their land not as a commercial venture, but more as a family tradition. The land has been with their families for generations and they have been cultivating it as they have no other source of income to support their families. Besides, in the process of the division of holdings, a large number of farmers possess only small parcels of land which are not commercially viable. Such developing countries fear that their small and marginal household farmers will be in great difficulty when they are called upon to face the challenge of world competition.

Then, there is also the interest of the countries, particularly the developing countries with a chronic shortage of foreign exchange, in the indigenous production of their staple food. It is not practical for them to depend on imported staple food, even though it may be cheaper to import, because they may not have adequate foreign exchange to import the food products. Considering the uncertain nature of their foreign exchange availability and also, perhaps, the uncertainty in the supply of food grain even if the necessary foreign exchange were available, several countries would like to develop their own production base for their staple food, rather than depend on imports.

These are some of the main interests in the area of agriculture, and clearly, some of them conflict with one another.

Disciplines

Amidst all these concerns, agriculture has naturally been a very complex subject of negotiation. The resulting Agreement is one of the most complicated ones among the WTO agreements. Various terms used in the Agreement originate in some of the practices of important agriculture producers and exporters and, in spite of explanations in the annexes, remain unclear to varying extents. The annexes are important parts of the Agreement as most of the disciplines are elaborated there. While trying to understand the Agreement, it often becomes necessary to make cross-references among various articles and also between some articles and the relevant annexes.

The main Agreement and the annexes provide the frame of the disciplines, but the actual commitments of Members in quantitative terms are contained in their respective schedules which are not found in the Agreement; these are in the bound volumes containing the Members' schedules on tariffs and commitments in the agriculture sector. Each Member has a serial number for its schedule which contains a table of its bound tariffs, including those on agricultural products, and additional tables of its commitments on domestic support, export subsidies, minimum market access, etc. (to be explained and illustrated later).

Overriding Feature of the Agreement

In respect of the agriculture sector, the provisions of this Agreement override the provisions of GATT 1994 and those of other WTO agreements applicable to trade in goods (Article 21). Hence, if a conflict arises between any provision of this Agreement and any provision of GATT 1994 or a WTO agreement applicable to trade in goods, the former will be applicable.

AREAS OF COMMITMENTS

There are three main areas of commitments in the Agreement, viz.:

(i) market access, i.e., the disciplines on import restraints and import limitations;

(ii) domestic support, i.e., support by governments to domestic producers, and

(iii) export subsidies, i.e., support by governments to exports.

The formulae which formed the basis for the quantitative commitments of Members are not contained in the Agreement; these were decided as agreed modalities in December 1993. These modalities prescribed the base reference levels for the three fields of disciplines mentioned above and the extent of the reduction in tariffs, domestic support and export subsidies which Members were expected to achieve. Though these agreed modalities themselves do not form part of the Agreement and, therefore, are not enforceable, they formed the basis for the quantitative commitments made by various Members which, after scrutiny, were included in the schedules of Members and became enforceable.

One need not go back to these modalities now, as it is perhaps no longer relevant to examine whether the Members have adhered to them in their specific commitments. Whatever is contained in their schedules of commitments is the sole obligation to which they are bound, irrespective of whether or not these commitments conform to the agreed modalities. Nevertheless, the modalities have perhaps some importance for the future. When the next review of the Agreement takes place by the end of 1999, the quantitative parameters of the modalities may provide the basic reference for working out an appropriate framework for the quantitative parameters suitable at that time.

MARKET ACCESS

Scheme of Commitments

The general scheme of the commitments is that non-tariff measures have to be eliminated. They may be converted into equivalent tariffs. The normal tariff and the tariff equivalent of non-tariff measures after conversion, are added together to form the base tariff level. This tariff total has to be reduced over the period of implementation. In this manner, there is a bound tariff level for any particular product which gets reduced from year to year during the implementation period.

All tariffs on agricultural products have to be bound in this manner by all Members, even the least developed country Members.

If a Member does not convert its non-tariff measures for a product into an equivalent tariff, it has the option of allowing a certain minimum level of import of that product each year at a low level of tariff. As will be explained later, only very few countries took recourse to this approach.

A Member that has converted its non-tariff measures and taken the commitment to tariff reduction, has the option of imposing a special safeguard measure (explained later) which is easier to take than the general safeguard measure of GATT 1994.

Tariffication

As is the case with all products, including those in the area of agriculture, constraints on market access, i.e., those on the exports to a country, depend on two factors, viz., tariff and non-tariff measures. In agriculture, non-tariff measures have been particularly significant, mainly because of their complexity, lack of transparency and severity of effect.

The Agreement stipulates the immediate dismantling of non-tariff measures in the agricultural sector. There are, however, three exceptions, viz.:

(i) measures taken under balance-of-payments provisions (explained in the chapter on BOP provisions; these apply particularly to developing country Members);

(ii) other measures taken under the general provisions of GATT 1994 (i.e., those not specifically related to the agriculture sector) or other WTO agreements, e.g., safeguard measures (explained in the chapter on safeguards), measures under the general exceptions (Article XX of GATT 1994), etc.;

(iii) special alternative option adopted by a few countries in respect of one or two products for which tariffication was not adopted but, in lieu of that, a special minimum access opportunity was provided.

All non-tariff measures, excluding these three types, are to be eliminated. They have to be converted into equivalent tariffs which are to be added to the normal customs duties on the respective products. The resulting tariffs are inscribed in the schedule of the Member.

The tariff equivalent of non-tariff measures is to be calculated with the data for 1986-8.

A Member has to reduce its tariff total every year over a prescribed span of time, which, for developed countries, is 1995-2000, and, for developing countries, 1995-2004. The tariff levels on various agricultural products during each of these years are included in the schedule of the Member and are binding on the Member. The guidelines on modalities prescribed an average total reduction of 36 per cent (24 per cent for developing countries) over the implementation period, with the condition that there be a minimum reduction of 15 per cent (10 per cent for developing countries) in each tariff line.

In the case of products subject only to ordinary customs duties (i.e., not subject to non-tariff measures), the reduction is to be made on the bound duty level. In such cases, if the duty had not been bound, the reduction is to be made with reference to the level on 1 September 1986.

In actual practice, major importers of agricultural products have bound the tariffs at very high levels, assuming very high tariff equivalents for non-tariff measures, thus making the entry of imports almost impossible.[72] A United Nations Conference on Trade and Development (UNCTAD) calculation shows some of these typically high tariffs as:

Canada	:	butter (360%), cheese (289%), eggs (236.3%);
EU	:	beef (213%), wheat (167.7%), sheepmeat (144%);
Japan	:	wheat products (388.1%), wheat (352.7%), barley products (361%);
US	:	sugar (244.4%), peanuts (173.8%), milk (82.6%).[73]

These are the initial-year tariffs, and yearly reductions have been made in relation to this base; therefore, the tariffs on these products, even in the final year of the implementation period, would still be very high.

Tariff Quota

As the tariffs existing after the tariffication of non-tariff barriers are very high in several cases, there would be no meaningful market access opportunities. Hence, particular provisions were made in the document on modalities for market access opportunities. There are three types of such provisions.

Current Access Opportunity

Firstly, current access opportunity has to be provided. It means that opportunity has to be provided for a level of import equal to the average annual import level during the base period 1986-8. A practical way to do this is by having very low tariffs for imports up to this extent.

Besides, imports stipulated in bilateral and plurilateral agreements also have to be facilitated by stipulating conditions not inferior to those which are in those agreements.

Minimum Access Opportunity

Secondly, minimum access opportunity has to be provided in 1995 at a level not less than 3 per cent of the annual consumption in the period 1986-8. This level would be raised to 5 per cent by the end of 2000 by developed countries and by the end of 2004 by developing countries. As in the case of current access opportunity, this minimum access opportunity would also be provided by having very low tariffs for imports up to these levels.

Special Minimum Access Opportunity

Thirdly, special minimum access opportunity has to be provided by those countries that have opted for this alternative instead of tariffication. This alternative has been undertaken by only a few countries, and that also for only one or two products: Japan, the Philippines and the Republic of Korea for rice, and Israel for sheepmeat and some dairy products. For developed countries, this special minimum access opportunity means import opportunity in 1995 to the extent of 4 per cent of the annual average consumption in the base period 1986-8, and, thereafter, an increase of 0.8 per cent of the base period consumption every year up to the end of 2000. For a developing country, it means import opportunity in 1995 to the extent of 1 per cent of the annual average consumption in the base period, rising uniformly to 2 per cent in 1999 and then to 4 per cent in 2004.

Allocation of Tariff Quota

These access opportunities are to be provided by tariff quotas, i.e., by having very low tariffs up to the stipulated extent of imports, and above that level, having the normal tariffs which, in the case of agricultural products, are generally very high. Article XIII of GATT 1994 prescribes the discipline that, for such purposes, there should be a global tariff quota which has to be applied on a non-discriminatory basis. However, the importing countries are also expected to prescribe country-specific quotas, in case these are to be provided in pursuance of bilateral and plurilateral agreements. Generally, the country-specific quotas should be given separately from the global quota. However, some countries have mixed and merged the two, which has put constraints on the countries not mentioned in the schedules. But once these entries have been made in the schedules, it is presumed that these were agreed to among the interested Members before being included.

Obligations in the Schedule

The agreed modalities were the guidelines according to which the current access, general minimum access and special minimum access opportunities were to be provided in the schedules of the Members. But, since the guidelines have not been made a part of the Agreement, they are no more binding. What is binding is the access levels and conditions actually mentioned in the schedules, whether or not they are strictly in accordance with the guidelines.

The EEC – Banana Panel has, however, held (and the Appellate Body has confirmed) that the language of Article 4 of the Agreement does not indicate that the schedules of market access are enforceable, if these are in conflict with the obligations in GATT 1994. The general provision of the pre-eminence of this Agreement over GATT 1994 or other WTO agreements (Article 21 of the Agreement), does not apply to the provisions on market access because the language of Article 4, according to the Panel, is not in the nature of an obligation.

Special Safeguard Provision

For imposing restraints on market access as a safeguard for domestic production against problems caused by imports, the general safeguard provisions, covered by Article XIX of GATT 1994 and the Agreement on Safeguards, are of course applicable to agricultural products as well. But, in addition, some special safeguard provisions (SSP) are also applicable under some conditions (Article 5 of the Agreement on Agriculture).

The difference between these two alternative steps is that the general safeguard action can be taken only if there is existence of serious injury or the threat of serious injury to domestic production (explained in the chapter on safeguards), whereas the special safeguard action can be taken without the demonstration of any adverse effect on domestic production. The latter type of action can be taken if the import price falls below a particular level or if the import quantity rises above a particular level, as will be explained later.

A Member can take recourse to either the general safeguard provisions contained in Article XIX of GATT 1994 and the Agreement on Safeguards or the SSP, but not both (Article 5.8).

The actual provisions of the SSP as contained in Article 5 are somewhat unclear and complex. The following description tries to capture the essential elements of the SSP.

Conditions for SSP

The initial conditions for a Member to be able to take SSP measures against a product are:

(i) tariffication has been done in respect of the product, i.e., non-tariff measures have been converted into equivalent tariffs;

(ii) a symbol "SSG" has been marked by the Member against the particular product in its schedule.

Triggers for SSP

There are two alternative triggers for the SSP, i.e., SSP measures can be applied only if either of these two types of situation has arisen. These are:

(i) price trigger, i.e., the price of the import has fallen below a prescribed level; and

(ii) quantity trigger, i.e., the quantity of the import has reached a prescribed level.

Price Trigger

The trigger price is normally to be determined as the average cost, insurance and freight (c.i.f.) import price of the product during the 1986-8 period. If the trigger price is high, the import price may fall below this level more often, and, consequently, it will be easier to take the special safeguard action.

The Agreement provides that the trigger price will be publicly specified so that exporters are cautioned well in time. Though the obligation is to announce the trigger price only after its initial use, some Members have announced it in their notifications to the Committee on Agriculture.

The trigger price, once notified, has to be continued for the rest of the implementation period.

Quantity Trigger

The actual quantity trigger level, i.e., the import quantity level above which SSP action can be taken, is the sum of two components, viz., the increase in the import quantity, and the change (either positive, i.e., increase; or negative, i.e., decrease) in domestic consumption.

The component relating to the increase in the import quantity (called base trigger level in Article 5) is calculated on the basis of a formula explained below:

(i) if the import is 10 per cent of domestic consumption or less, 125 per cent of the average quantity of imports in the three preceding years for which data are available;

(ii) if the import is above 10 per cent, but not more than 30 per cent, of domestic consumption, 110 per cent of the average quantity of imports in the three preceding years for which data are available;

(iii) if the import is above 30 per cent of domestic consumption, 105 per cent of the average quantity of imports in the three preceding years for which data are available.

It is apparent that higher import penetration enables a Member to take SSP action at a lower level of increase in imports.

The change in domestic consumption is measured as the difference between the consumption in the current year (most recent year for which data are available) and that in the preceding year. If consumption has fallen, this change will be negative.

The sum of the increase in import quantity and the change in domestic consumption is the actual trigger import quantity level. The condition mentioned in Article 5.4, however, is that the actual trigger level must not be less than 105 per cent of the average quantity of imports in the three preceding years for which data are available.

SSP Measure

Under the SSP, the measure which a Member can take is an increase in duty. There is no provision for imposing a quantitative restriction on imports.

Ceilings and Limits for Quantity Trigger

In case the SSP measure is taken on the basis of the trigger import quantity level, additional duty can be imposed if the import exceeds the trigger level. There are two conditions in imposing additional duty. These are:

(i) the additional duty must not exceed one-third of the ordinary customs duty (which is the duty recorded in the schedule);

(ii) the additional duty will be maintained only till the end of the year in which it is imposed.

Let us take an example where domestic consumption is 1,000 units and the import quantity is 280 units. Here, the import is 28 per cent of domestic consumption; hence, the base trigger import quantity level will be 110 per cent of 280 units, i.e., 308 units. Let us presume that consumption had grown to 1,000 units from 900 units, which means a change in consumption of +100 units. In this case, an additional duty can be imposed if the import quantity exceeds 308 + 100, i.e., 408 units. The actual trigger import quantity level in this case is 408 units. Suppose the ordinary customs duty on this item is 30 per cent. The maximum additional duty that can be imposed in this case is one-third of 30 per cent, i.e., 10 per cent. The rate of duty is independent of the quantity of imports, except that additional duty cannot be imposed till the import quantity exceeds 408 units.

Ceilings and Limits for Price Trigger

In case the SSP measure is taken on the basis of the trigger price, there is a ceiling on the additional duty which can be imposed. The calculation of the ceiling is as follows:

(i) if the difference between the trigger price and the import price is 10 per cent of the trigger price or less, no additional duty can be imposed;

(ii) if the difference is more than 10 per cent, but not more than 40 per cent, the additional duty will be 30 per cent of the amount by which the difference exceeds 10 per cent;

(iii) if the difference is more than 40 per cent, but not more than 60 per cent, the additional duty will be 50 per cent of the amount by which the difference exceeds 40 per cent, plus the duty in (ii);

(iv) if the difference is more than 60 per cent, but not more than 75 per cent, the additional duty will be 70 per cent of the amount by which the difference exceeds 60 per cent, plus the duty in (iii);

(v) if the difference is more than 75 per cent, the additional duty will be 90 per cent of the amount by which the difference exceeds 75 per cent, plus the duty in (iv).

It is apparent that there is a graduated increasing scale of the additional duty as the import price declines.

An example may clarify this formula. Let us assume that the trigger price is $200 per unit, and the current price falls to $80 per unit. The difference is $120. According to (i) above, there is no additional duty if the difference is only up to 10 per cent of the trigger price. Thus, up to a difference of $20, there is no additional duty. According to (ii) above, the duty is 30 per cent of the amount by which the difference exceeds 10 per cent, up to a difference of 40 per cent of the trigger price. Hence, up to $80, the duty is 30 per cent of $60 (i.e., $80-$20), i.e., $18. Thereafter, up to a difference of 60 per cent (i.e., $120), the duty is 50 per cent of the difference exceeding 40 per cent, i.e., 50 per cent of $40 (i.e., $120-$80), which is $20. Hence, the additional duty may be to the extent of $18 + $20, i.e., $38 on each unit.

Other Provisions

There are further obligations regarding SSP measures, which are as follows:

(i) For taking action based on the import quantity trigger, notice has to be given to the Committee on Agriculture in advance, if possible; otherwise, in any case, within 10 days of taking the action.

(ii) For taking action based on the price trigger, notice has to be given to the Committee within 10 days of taking action.

(iii) As far as practicable, the price trigger will not be used if the volume of imports is declining.

(iv) A Member must afford opportunity to interested Members for consultation regarding the conditions of applying the SSP measures.

(v) Additional duty will not be imposed on imports covered by the current market access opportunity or the minimum market access opportunity, though these imports will be taken into account while calculating the quantity of imports for the volume-based trigger.

Schedules of Market Access

The schedules of market access are contained in part I of the schedule of a Member. A typical schedule of a Member containing the tariff reduction commitment will have the following headings:

Tariff no.	Description of product	Base rate of duty	Bound rate of duty	Implementation period from/to	Special safeguard	Initial negotiating right	Other duties and charges
1	2	3	4	5	6	7	8

The base rate of duty in column 3 is the duty with reference to which the reduction is to take place. The bound rate of duty mentioned in column 4 is the final bound level at the end of the implementation period. The duty will be reduced from the base rate to the final bound rate every year, in equal instalments, over the implementation period. In the first year, i.e., 1995, the level will be the base level reduced by one step.

In column 6, "SSG" will be recorded by the Member if tariffication has been done, and the Member wishes to use the SSP during the implementation period. Column 7 gives the names of Members having initial negotiating rights. This term was explained in detail in the chapter on tariffs. It means a Member with whom initial negotiations were conducted to reduce the tariff on the particular item. It has a relevance in case it is proposed in future to raise the tariff. At that time, negotiations will have to be conducted with that Member and compensation may have to be settled for increasing the tariff above the bound level. Column 8 gives the other duties and charges on imports, which now have to be recorded in the schedule, as explained in the chapter on tariffs.

A typical schedule of the tariff quota containing the commitment regarding the current market access and minimum market access opportunities will have the following headings:

Description of product	Tariff item number(s)	Initial quota quantity and in-quota tariff rate	Final quota quantity and in-quota tariff rate	Implementation period from/to	Initial negotiating right	Other terms and conditions
1	2	3	4	5	6	7

Column 3 contains the quantity to be covered by the tariff quota, i.e., covered by the current market access opportunity or the minimum market access opportunity. It further gives the tariff rate for the import within this quantity limit. Column 4 gives the corresponding figures for the final year of the implementation period. Here, the quantities will be higher and the tariff rates may be lower than those in column 3. There will be a uniform rate of decrease of tariffs every year over the implementation period. The quantity will increase at the stipulated rates mentioned earlier.

DOMESTIC SUPPORT

Scheme of Commitments

The general scheme of commitments is that a Member limits its domestic support, i.e., subsidies, to agriculture in the first year of implementation, i.e., 1995, to a particular level, and, thereafter, progressively reduces the levels in subsequent years during the period of implementation (up to 2000 for developed countries and 2004 for developing countries). The maximum level for each year is mentioned by the Member in its schedule. Domestic support is quantified through what has been called the Aggregate Measurement of Support (AMS).

A clear understanding of the various terms used to denote the measurement of domestic support helps to better comprehend the commitments. The initial level which forms the basis for the committed levels in the implementation period is called the Base Total Aggregate Measurement of Support (Base Total AMS). It is recorded in the schedule, followed by the Annual and Final Bound Commitment Levels. (The method of calculation of the AMS is explained later.) The Final Bound Commitment Level is the maximum Total AMS level permissible in the last year of the implementation period. In between, there are Annual Bound Commitment Levels, which give the maximum permissible Total AMS levels in the respective years during the implementation period. As mentioned earlier, all these are recorded in the schedule of the Member.

The actual level in each year during the implementation period is compared against these maximum committed levels. For this purpose, the Member calculates the Current Total AMS for a particular year. It is compared with the Annual Bound Commitment Level for that year. In the final year of the implementation period, the comparison will be made between the Final Bound Commitment Level and the Current Total AMS for that year.

The commitment is, thus, on the Total AMS. The AMS has two components, as will be explained later, viz., the rate and the quantity covered by the particular support measure. Thus, within this type of commitment, there is a flexibility in choosing the products covered, the quantity of the products covered and the extent of the support measure. A mix of these parameters may be varied within the ultimate obligation that the Total AMS resulting from this mix must not exceed the committed level in a particular year. Clearly, the trade impact of the commitment will depend a good deal on the type of the mix which a Member adopts in a particular year.

Reduction of Domestic Support

Articles 3.1 and 3.2 bind a Member against giving domestic support above what is mentioned by it in its schedule. The disciplines on domestic support are further reiterated and elaborated in Articles 6 and 7.

The schedule on the reduction in domestic support is to be prepared on the basis of the guidelines on modalities which prescribed that the Base Total AMS must be reduced by 20 per cent (for developing countries: 13.3 per cent) over the period of implementation. Thus, for a developed country, the Final Bound Commitment Level, which is the committed ceiling in the final year of the implementation period, should be the Base Total AMS reduced by 20 per cent. The reduction should be done over this period in equal instalments every year so as to reach this targeted reduced level in the final year. It should be recalled that the implementation period for a developed country is 1995-2000 (both inclusive), and for a developing country, it is 1995-2004 (both inclusive).

As mentioned earlier, the implementation of the reduction commitment is to be verified by a comparison of the Annual Bound Commitment Level of a particular year with the Current Total AMS of that year. Annex 3 of the Agreement provides the methodology for calculating the Current Total AMS [definition in Article 1 (a)(ii)]. This is similar to the method provided in the modalities for calculating the Base Total AMS.

Calculation of AMS

If a particular product gets domestic support, the AMS for this product is calculated, taking into account the factors mentioned below. In this manner, the product-specific AMS on all the products are calculated and added together to get the total product-specific AMS. There may be some types of support which are not product-specific. These are added together to get the non-product-specific AMS. The sum of all product-specific and non-product-specific support is called the Total AMS. If a support measure exists but the method of calculation of the AMS cannot be applied to it, the calculation of an equivalent measurement of support will be made [definition given in Article 1(d)], and it will also be included in the Total AMS.

The guidelines on modalities give the manner in which this calculation is made. Some important elements of the calculation are given below.

The AMS for a product has four main elements, viz.:

(i) Market price support: First, the gap between the fixed external reference price and the applied administered price is calculated, and then, it is multiplied by the quantity of the product receiving the price support.

The fixed external reference price is the average unit price during the period 1986-8. It is the free on board (f.o.b) price for the net exporting country and the c.i.f price for the net importing country.

(ii) Direct payments dependent on price gap: It may be calculated either by multiplying the gap by the quantity, or by actual budgetary outlays.

(iii) Direct payments not dependent on price gap: It is measured by using budgetary outlays.

(iv) Other measures: It is measured by budgetary outlays, or, where such outlays do not reflect the full subsidy, by calculating the gap between the price of the subsidised item and a representative market price, and then multiplying it by the quantity of the subsidised item.

In making these calculations, budgetary outlays as well as revenue foregone (for example, remission of some dues) will be taken into account. Further, payments at the national level and lower levels will all be taken into account. Specific levies or fees paid by the agricultural producers will be deducted in the calculations.

Exemption from AMS

Certain domestic support measures are exempted from the commitment of reduction. These are mentioned at two places in the Agreement, viz., in Article 6 and in Annex 2. These measures will, therefore, not be included in the calculation of the Current Total AMS in any year.

Article 6 Exemptions

The exemptions contained in Article 6 are the following:

(i) in the case of developing countries, investment subsidies generally available to agriculture;

(ii) in the case of developing countries, agricultural input subsidies (for example, supply of fertilisers or irrigation at subsidised prices) generally available to low-income or resource-poor producers;

(iii) in the case of developing countries, support to producers to encourage diversification from growing illicit narcotic crops;

(iv) product-specific support which does not exceed 5 per cent of the value of production of that product;

For developing countries, this *de minimis* percentage is 10 per cent.

(v) non-product-specific support which does not exceed 5 per cent of the value of total agricultural production;

For developing countries, this *de minimis* percentage is also 10 per cent.

(vi) direct payments under production-limiting programmes, if such payments are based on fixed area and yields, or if such payments are made on 85 per cent or less of the base level of production, or if such payments are made on a fixed number of heads in the case of livestock payments.

Annex 2 Exemptions

General Requirement and Criteria

Annex 2 to the Agreement lists a large number of policies and measures which are exempted from the reduction commitment under certain conditions that have been mentioned in detail.

The basic requirement is that the domestic support measures for which exemption is claimed must not have more than minimal (i) trade-distorting effects, or (ii) effects on production. This appears to be a very stringent condition. But, immediately after putting this condition, the Annex goes on to say that "[a]ccordingly, all measures ...shall conform to the following basic criteria...", and then, it lists two criteria, as follows:

(i) the support must be provided through a publicly-funded government programme, not involving transfers from consumers; and

(ii) the support must not have the effect of providing price support to producers.

The linkage through the term "accordingly" would seem to mean that the fulfilment of the criteria would imply satisfying the two basic requirements. Hence, all that is needed is the fulfilment of the two criteria mentioned above.

Exempted Policies and Measures

The policies and measures eligible for exemption that are contained in Annex 2 are given below. Qualifying conditions have also been mentioned for different types of policies and measures.

(i) general services, including research, pest and disease control, training, extension and advisory work, inspection, marketing and market promotion including market information, and infrastructure;
The support for marketing and market promotion excludes expenditure for unspecified purposes which could be used by sellers to reduce the selling price or to confer a direct economic benefit to the consumers.
The support for infrastructure is limited to capital works only and excludes subsidies for inputs or operating costs, or preferential user charges.

(ii) stockholding for food security;
The stock must be an integral part of a food security programme identified in the national legislation. There should be predetermined targets, purchases must be made at current market prices, and sales must be made at prices not lower than the current domestic market price.

For developing countries, the purchase and sale may be at administered prices, but the difference between the purchase price and the external reference price must be included in the AMS. It means that this element of the subsidy will get clubbed together with the others which are subject to reduction. Hence, if a country wishes to retain this subsidy, it will have to reduce some other subsidy. This option is available to a country anyway; hence, this provision does not give any particular benefit to the developing countries in so far as the subsidy given for the purchase is concerned. Of course, developing countries will have the benefit of this dispensation in respect of the subsidy for the sales from the stock.

(iii) domestic food aid;
Food purchases must be made at current market prices.
For developing countries, the provision of food to the urban and rural poor on a regular basis at subsidised and reasonable prices will qualify for exemption.

(iv) decoupled income support;
The amount of payment must not be related to the type or volume of production, prices, and factors of production employed.

(v) income insurance and income safety-net;
The income loss should have exceeded 30 per cent of gross agricultural income, and less than 70 per cent of the loss should be covered by compensation. The payment must not be related to the type or volume of production, prices, or factors of production employed.

(vi) payment for relief from natural disasters;
The income loss should have exceeded 30 per cent of production, and payment must not be more than what is needed to compensate for the total cost of replacing the losses.

(vii) structural adjustment assistance through programmes for (a) producer retirement, (b) resource retirement or (c) investment aid;

The subsidy for producer retirement must be conditional on total and permanent retirement of the recipients from marketable agricultural production.
The subsidy for resource retirement must be conditional on retiring land from marketable agricultural production for at least three years, and, in the case of livestock, on its slaughter or permanent disposal. The subsidy for investment should be to assist financial or physical restructuring to overcome structural disadvantages.

(viii) assistance under environmental programmes;

(ix) regional assistance programmes;
Eligibility must be limited to the producers in disadvantaged regions, amounts must not be related to the type or volume of production or price, payments must be generally available to all producers within the disadvantaged region, and payments must be limited to the extra costs or loss of income involved in undertaking agricultural production in the area.

(x) other direct payments;
Paragraph 2.5 of the Annex provides exemption for other types of payments with the condition that these should be decoupled support, i.e., these should not be dependent on volume of production, domestic price, international price, or the factors of production employed.

Some Other Important Implications

Members have to ensure that these subsidies which are claimed to be exempt from the reduction commitment are maintained in accordance with the criteria attached to them.

The burden of proof regarding the fulfilment of conditions for a measure to qualify for being exempted is on the subsidising Member.

There is no specific provision as to how inflation will be taken into account while comparing the Annual Bound Commitment Level with the Current Total AMS. The former is a fixed amount based on a price prevalent in a previous year, and the latter is an amount based on the current price. Article 18.4 provides for the consideration of this matter in the review process. If problems arise, the matter may have to be considered by the Committee on Agriculture.

Subsidies which have not been covered by the reduction commitment and are not exempt, cannot be applied by a Member above the *de minimis* level.

Schedules

The schedule containing the commitments of a Member on the reduction of domestic support is contained in part IV of the schedule of the Member. A typical schedule has the following headings:

Base Total AMS	Annual and Final Bound Commitment Levels 1995-2000	Relevant supporting tables and document reference
1	2	3

Columns 1 and 2 are clear. Column 3 refers to the tables and documents which form the basis of the calculation of the Base Total AMS. A Member is expected to give the tables of the supporting materials to the WTO Secretariat. These have been registered and assigned an official document number. These tables and documents have to be mentioned in column 3.

All developed country Members and 12 developing country Members have made reduction commitments in their schedules. Least developed country Members are not required to make any reduction commitment. Thus, other developing country Members, excluding the 12 that have made commitments, cannot apply domestic subsidies beyond what is exempted or is *de minimis*.

EXPORT SUBSIDY

Reduction Commitments

The general discipline on export subsidies is prescribed in Article 3 and is further reiterated in Article 8. Actual commitments on export subsidies are contained in the schedule of the Member.

According to the guidelines on modalities, a Member is required to reduce its export subsidies from year to year in the implementation period. Such a reduction is to take place in respect of two factors:

(i) the total budgetary outlays on export subsidies in the agricultural sector; and

(ii) the total quantity of exports covered by export subsidies.

The guidelines on modalities prescribed a reduction of (i) budgetary outlays by 36 per cent (24 per cent for developing countries) and (ii) export quantity by 21 per cent (14 per cent for developing countries) over the implementation period. The base period was supposed to be 1986-90. But several countries had increased their export subsidies in the meantime; hence, it was agreed that in specified cases, the reduction commitment could be implemented with respect to the higher levels of 1991-2. But it did not affect the final level at the end of the implementation period which continued to be based on the base period of 1986-90.

Members have included both these types of commitments in their respective schedules. A schedule of a Member on this subject contains the total outlay on subsidies in each year during the implementation period and the total quantity of agricultural exports covered by export subsidies in each year.

Flexibility

A Member has the obligation not to exceed the prescribed levels in any year. However, there is some marginal flexibility, as follows:

In any year from the second year to the fifth year, the prescribed level may be exceeded, provided:

(i) the cumulative budgetary outlay from the beginning of the implementation period up to that year does not exceed 3 per cent of the base period level;

(ii) the cumulative quantity from the beginning up to that year does not exceed 1.75 per cent of the base year quantity;

(iii) the total budgetary outlay and quantity over the whole implementation period does not exceed what is included in the schedule;

(iv) the budgetary outlay and the quantity at the end of the implementation period are not more than 64 per cent and 79 per cent respectively of the levels in the base period.
(For developing countries, these levels are 76 per cent and 86 per cent respectively.)

Coverage of Measures

The export subsidies subject to the reduction commitment are the following:

(i) direct payment contingent on export;

(ii) payment on an agricultural product contingent on its incorporation in the exported product;

(iii) government sale of stock for export at prices lower than the comparable domestic price;

(iv) payment for export on account of some governmental action;

(v) payment to reduce the cost of marketing, including handling, upgrading, processing, and international transport and freight; This is not applicable to developing countries.

(vi) government provision for internal transport and freight in respect of export shipments on terms more favourable than those for domestic shipments.
This is not applicable to developing countries.

Further work will continue towards the development of internationally agreed disciplines relating to export credits, export credit guarantees and insurance programmes. Hence, these programmes and measures are not covered at present by the discipline.

Schedule

The schedule containing the commitments of a Member on export subsidies is contained in part IV of the schedule of the Member. The schedule containing the budgetary outlay and quantity reduction commitments has the following headings:

Description of product and tariff item number at HS six-digit level	Base outlay level	Calendar/ other year applied	Annual and final outlay commit-ment levels 1995-2000	Base quantity	Calendar/ other year applied	Annual and final quantity commit-ment levels	Relevant supporting tables and document reference
1	2	3	4	5	6	7	8

Only 23 Members have schedules of export subsidy reduction commitments. The schedule contains descriptions of the products covered by the subsidy, unlike the schedule on domestic support, which contains only the total amount and not the subsidies on individual products. Hence, the products not included in the schedule on export subsidies cannot get any export subsidy except those export subsidies which, in the case of developing country Members, are exempted from reduction, as mentioned above, or those which are not covered by the reduction commitment. Further, Members that have not given their schedule at all cannot give export subsidies on any agricultural product, except those which are exempted.

EXPORT RESTRICTION

While taking action regarding export prohibitions or export restrictions on foodstuffs, a Member is required:

(i) to give due consideration to the effects of such action on importing Members' food security; and

(ii) to give notice to the Committee on Agriculture before taking the action and provide opportunities for consultation to Members having substantial import interests.

Developing country Members which are not net exporters of the specific foodstuff are exempted from this discipline.

LIMITATIONS ON ACTION AGAINST SUBSIDY

There are special provisions in Article 13 regarding action against subsidies in the case of agricultural products. These provisions are valid for the "implementation period", which, for this Article, is nine years starting from 1995 [definition in Article 1(f)].

As was explained in the chapter on subsidies, two types of remedies are available against subsidies, viz.:

(i) imposition of countervailing duties, if there is material injury or the threat of material injury to domestic production as a result of subsidies given by another Member; or

(ii) taking recourse to the dispute settlement process against the subsidising Member, if, as a result of the subsidy, there is:

  (a) serious prejudice to the domestic industry;

  (b) nullification or impairment of benefits arising due to tariff bindings or other obligations of another Member in GATT 1994;

  (c) material injury or the threat of material injury to the domestic industry.

The domestic support measures exempted from the reduction commitment are found at two places in the Agreement, as mentioned earlier, viz., in Annex 2 and in Article 6. These two sets of measures are subjected to different disciplines in respect of the action to be taken against them.

The measures which are listed in Annex 2, and which satisfy the conditions mentioned there, are exempted from countervailing duty action and the dispute settlement process, including action based on non-violation cases of nullification or impairment of benefits of tariff concessions. (The last situation arises when such effects take place due to some action of a Member, even though such action may not be violating any provision of GATT 1994 or other WTO agreements on goods. This will be explained in the chapter on dispute settlement.) Thus, such measures are fully protected against any action.

The measures which are in Article 6, and which fulfil the conditions mentioned there, have the following protection:

(i) due restraint should be shown in initiating countervailing duty investigations, and countervailing duties will be imposed only after the determination of injury or its threat has been made; This does not provide any additional protection, since countervailing duty action can be taken, in any case, only when the existence or threat of injury has been determined.

(ii) action through the dispute settlement process cannot be taken, provided the measures do not grant support to a specific commodity in excess of the level during the 1992 marketing year;

(iii) these measures are exempt from action based on non-violation nullification or impairment of the benefits of tariff concessions, provided the measures do not grant support to a specific commodity in excess of the level during the 1992 marketing year.

Export subsidies which conform to the disciplines of the Agreement have the following protection:

(i) due restraint should be shown in initiating countervailing duty investigations, and countervailing duty can be imposed only after the determination of injury or its threat;

(ii) action through the dispute settlement process cannot be taken.

OTHER PROVISIONS

Incorporated Products

If a primary agricultural product is incorporated in a processed agricultural product, the per-unit subsidy on the incorporated primary product cannot be higher than what would be payable on this primary product itself.

Developing Country Members

Least developed country Members do not have to adopt any commitment on the reduction of tariffs, domestic support or export subsidies. But they must also bind all tariffs on agricultural items.

As mentioned in the relevant sections, other developing country Members have commitments on lower levels of reduction, and the period in which the reduction is to be made is also longer.

There is a Ministerial Decision accompanying the Marrakesh Declaration which relates to food aid and financing the import of food by net food-importing developing countries and least developed countries. The Decision is to work towards more effective food aid for such countries during the period of implementation of the Agreement on Agriculture. Further, the special difficulties of these countries in importing foodstuff during the implementation period have been recognised.

Committee on Agriculture

A Committee on Agriculture has been established. It will oversee the implementation of the Agreement.

Consultation and Dispute Settlement

The provisions of Articles XXII and XXIII of GATT 1994, as elaborated and applied by the Dispute Settlement Understanding, are applicable to this Agreement.

Chapter V.2

TEXTILES AND CLOTHING

INTRODUCTION

Special Regime

SPECIAL arrangements for restrictions on trade in the area of textiles and clothing, outside the general discipline of the GATT, have been applicable since 1973. This has been a significant case of derogation from the general GATT obligation of free entry of imports. The special regime in this area will finally come to an end on 1 January 2005.

In the beginning of the 1960s, the textile industry in some developed countries found it difficult to face competition from imports. Normally, in such a situation, these countries should have taken safeguard action under the provisions of Article XIX of GATT 1994 to restrain the imports. But such action would have to be taken against the imports from all countries, including the developed countries, something which the importing developed countries wanted to avoid. It was in this background that a special arrangement in the textiles sector was introduced as an instrument for restraining the imports from specific countries; in actual practice, it was used to restrain developed countries' imports from developing countries. The rationale for such a move, as given by the importing developed countries, was that the developing countries were exporting cheap textile products, causing harm to their domestic industry. These developed countries persuaded the main exporting developing countries to restrain the export of their cotton textile products on the grounds that the former's textile industry would need time for adjustment in the light of cheap imports. It was expected that the textile industry in these developed countries would phase out and would need some time for this purpose. However, the textile and clothing industries in the developed countries got used to these special dispensations and went on asking for the continuation and intensification of the restrictions on the exports from developing countries, with the result that this derogation from the GATT, which was supposed to be temporary, continued for nearly a quarter of a century, and is still continuing in another form.

Earlier, there had been a Short-Term Agreement and a Long-Term Agreement covering cotton textiles and clothing. In 1973, a comprehensive agreement in this sector was worked out. Formally, it was called the Arrangement Regarding International Trade in Textiles. Its coverage was expanded to include fibres other than cotton, viz., wool and synthetic fibres. Hence, it was popularly called the Multi-Fibre Arrangement (MFA). This arrangement was extended almost every four years thereafter, and there was further expansion of its coverage to include silk-blends, vegetable fibres, etc.

With the coming into force of the WTO Agreement on 1 January 1995, the MFA has expired. But the special arrangement in this sector will still continue till the end of 2004.

Multi-Fibre Arrangement (MFA)

The MFA provided a special framework for restraints on imports. Within this frame, restraints were worked out in bilateral agreements between an exporting country and an importing country. And under certain situations, even unilateral restraints on imports could be imposed.

The essential features of the MFA were the following:

(i) annual levels of exports were established by an exporting developing country and an importing developed country through bilateral agreements in respect of specific textiles and clothing products;

(ii) growth rates and certain flexibilities regarding the use of the individual export levels were also established by mutual agreement. (These flexibilities were: *swing*, i.e., the use of the export quota of one product partly for the export of another product;

carry over, i.e., the use of this year's quota partly during the next year; and carry forward, i.e., the use of the next year's quota partly for this year.);

(iii) a dispute between members of the MFA could be considered in a body called the Textiles Surveillance Body (TSB).

There were contingency provisions for unilateral restraints in case there was no mutual agreement and the domestic industry in the importing country was suffering from serious damage and market disruption. In case of a dispute on such action, the TSB was to give its opinion and recommendation.

Position at the End of 1994

Within the framework of the MFA, bilateral agreements for export restraints had been worked out which were continuing at the end of 1994. Hence, there were annual quotas for exports from specific exporting countries to specific importing countries for individual product lines. Certain growth rates in the annual quotas were also operative. If market disruption was caused by a new product in an importing country, there was a possibility of seeking a bilateral agreement for an export restraint on that product; in case of failure to reach an agreement, the importing country had the possibility of applying a unilateral restraint.

The New Framework

Now, technically, the MFA is no more operative, as it expired with the coming into force of the WTO agreements on 1 January 1995. But even now, the textiles and clothing sector is subjected to a special discipline. The provisions of the discipline are contained in the Agreement on Textiles and Clothing which forms a part of the WTO agreements. This Agreement starts with the situation as existing on 1 January 1995 and essentially provides for the progressive integration of this sector into the normal WTO disciplines finally by 1 January 2005. Importing countries have got the flexibility to have new export restraints under certain situations through bilateral agreements, and, failing that, to have unilateral restraints. The aggrieved exporting country has the possibility of challenging it in the Textiles Monitoring Body (TMB) (as will be explained later) and also through the normal dispute settlement process of the WTO.

PROGRESSIVE LIBERALISATION

Integration into GATT 1994

The Agreement provides that the quantitative restraints under the MFA which were still in force on 31 December 1994 will all be totally eliminated by 1 January 2005 and that the entire textile sector will be fully integrated into GATT 1994 by that date. This final position will be achieved after three intermediate stages of progressive liberalisation. In each of these stages, some products will be fully integrated into GATT 1994.

Full integration implies that the normal rules of GATT 1994 will apply to products which have been so integrated. For example, it would mean that any importing country intending to restrain the import of any integrated product will have to follow the process of Article XIX of GATT 1994 and the Agreement on Safeguards. Further, once a Member integrates a product into GATT 1994, it cannot withdraw it and bring it back into the folds of the special restraint arrangements covered by this Agreement.

In the four stages of liberalisation (i.e., the three intermediate stages plus the final stage), the Agreement prescribes the effective dates for the stipulated steps and the proportions of past imports which should be covered by the liberalisation process. But the actual choice of the products to be covered by integration at particular stages has been left to the importing country. Its implications will be explained later.

The basis for calculating the proportion for integration at various stages is formed by the list of products contained in the Annex to the Agreement. It is a long list containing nearly 800 tariff lines at the six-digit level of the Harmonised System of nomenclature (HS has been described in the chapter on tariffs). The categories of products under restraint in the bilateral agreements covered by the MFA are defined in terms of these tariff lines, but the categories often get formed by taking some parts from different tariff lines.

A significant point to note is that the Annex contains a large number of products which are not actually under restraint in the importing developed countries. In fact, the Annex contains some such items which were not even included in the coverage of the MFA, e.g., pure silk items and certain jute items, like carpetbacking, etc. This has an important implication for the integration process, as will be explained later.

A Member has first to calculate the volume of its total imports in 1990 of the products included in this list. This volume is the actual base for calculating the percentages for integration at different stages. On the prescribed dates, certain prescribed percentages of this base volume for the Member will have to be integrated into GATT 1994.

The four stages are the following:

(i) on 1 January 1995: at least 16 per cent;

(ii) on the completion of three years, i.e., on 1 January 1998: at least 17 per cent;

(iii) on the completion of seven years, i.e., on 1 January 2002: at least 18 per cent;

(iv) on the completion of ten years, i.e., on 1 January 2005: the entire textiles and clothing sector will get integrated into GATT 1994.

In the first stage of integration, all major importing developed countries mostly included those products which are actually not under restraint. Hence, the prescribed minimum percentage had been achieved without even actually integrating any of the restricted items, except for one solitary case of work-gloves covered by one country.

The long list of products in the Annex, as mentioned above, may perhaps result in this anomaly, between fulfilling the obligations technically and yet not carrying out effective integration, continuing in the later stages as well. One calculation indicates that the list in the Annex contains unrestrained items which account for a high percentage in terms of the volume of imports in 1990. The percentages are 37 per cent for the US, 34 per cent for the EU and 47 per cent for Canada.[74] Thus, if these countries so wish, they need not include any restrained item in the integration process up to the second step of liberalisation. In fact, the coverage of the restrained items by the importing developed countries has been only marginal for the stage of liberalisation which fell on 1 January 1998.

There is a special provision for Members which did not maintain restrictions under the MFA. They will have to notify the TMB as to whether or not they wish to retain the right to use transitional safeguards (to be explained later). If they do not wish to retain that right, they need not make any programme of liberalisation, as they will be deemed to have integrated their textiles and clothing products into GATT 1994.

Growth Rate

Another aspect of liberalisation is the increase in the growth rate of the permissible import level. For this purpose, three stages have been established:

- 1st stage: from 1 January 1995 to 31 December 1997;
- 2nd stage: from 1 January 1998 to 31 December 2001;
- 3rd stage: from 1 January 2002 to 31 December 2004.

In the first stage, the permissible import level for each product for 1994 must be increased annually by an enhanced growth rate, which will be calculated by increasing the growth rate of 1994 by 16 per cent.

For the restrictions continuing in the second stage, the enhanced growth rates for the second stage will be calculated by increasing the respective growth rates of the first stage by 25 per cent. Similarly, for the third stage, the enhanced growth rates will be the respective rates of the second stage increased by 27 per cent.

An example will clarify these provisions further. Let us take a restricted product of a particular exporting country entering a particular importing country, and assume that the bilateral agreement between these two countries under the MFA had put the import level of this product at 100 units in 1994 and the growth rate applied to this product in 1994 was 3 per cent. During 1995, 1996 and 1997, the growth rate for this product will be: 3 + 16% of 3, i.e., 3.48 per cent.

The permissible levels of import during 1995, 1996 and 1997 will be respectively 103.48, 107.08 and 110.81 units.

During 1998, 1999, 2000 and 2001, the growth rate will be: 3.48 + 25% of 3.48, i.e., 4.35 per cent. The permissible levels of import during these years respectively will be 115.63, 120.66, 125.91 and 131.38 units.

During 2002, 2003 and 2004, the growth rate will be: 4.35 + 27% of 4.35, i.e., 5.52 per cent. The permissible levels of import during these years respectively will be 138.64, 146.29 and 154.36 units.[75] For a small supplier country, i.e., one accounting for 1.2 per cent or less of the total volume of the permissible imports of the restricted products in the particular importing country (as on 31 December 1991), the increment in the growth rates will be 25 per cent in the first stage and 27 per cent in the second and third stages.

Flexibility Provisions

Flexibility provisions, i.e., swing, carry over and carry forward, as applicable in 1994 will be continued till the end of the integration period. There can be no quantitative limit to the combined use of flexibility provisions.

CONTINUING RESTRICTIONS

Bilateral Restrictions under the MFA

Restrictions under Article 4 of the MFA, i.e., those which have been taken in accordance with bilateral agreements between the importing and exporting Members, continuing up to 1 January 1995 will continue till:

(i) these get eliminated by virtue of the relevant product being integrated into GATT 1994; or

(ii) the end of the Agreement period, i.e., till 31 December 2004.

The provisions regarding the growth rate and flexibility, as explained earlier, will be applicable.

Unilateral Restrictions under the MFA

The restrictions under Article 3 of the MFA, i.e., those which have been taken unilaterally, which continued up to 1 January 1995 will continue for the duration mentioned in the decision on the restrictions, but, in any case, will not continue beyond a maximum period of 12 months from 1 January 1995. The condition stipulated is that these restrictions should have been reviewed by the Textiles Surveillance Body (TSB) of the MFA. If the TSB has not reviewed them, the Textiles Monitoring Body (TMB) will review such measures.

Restrictive Measures Outside the MFA

With regard to restrictions on textiles and clothing outside the MFA, the following provisions have been made in the Agreement:

(i) If these measures are justified under GATT 1994, they will continue in accordance with the relevant provisions.

(ii) If these measures are not so justified, the Member applying them must:

   (a) bring them into conformity with GATT 1994 within one year of 1 January 1995; or

   (b) phase them out within a period not exceeding the duration of the Agreement, i.e., at the latest, by the end of 2004. A programme for such a progressive phasing-out was to be given to the TMB within six months of 1 January 1995.

SAFEGUARDS

Article XIX Action

After a product has been integrated into GATT 1994, any import-restricting action in the nature of safeguards can naturally be taken only under Article XIX of GATT 1994 and the Agreement on Safeguards.

Special Limitations for Quantitative Restrictions

There are some special provisions for safeguard measures of the non-tariff type, e.g., quantitative restrictions on imports, taken within one year of the integration of the product into GATT 1994. These are:

(i) The level of quota applicable to a Member must not be less than the average level of export from the Member in the last three years for which data are available. If any of these years has had any abnormal condition, the data for that year will not be taken for consideration. Lower levels are permissible, in the Agreement on Safeguards, through quota modulation, as explained in the chapter on safeguards, but are not permissible in these special provisions for textiles and clothing.

(ii) The administration of the quota will be done by the exporting country.

(iii) There will be regular liberalisation of the quota if the measure is applied for more than a year.

(iv) The exporting Member does not have the right to take counter-measures by suspending equivalent concessions or other obligations.

(v) If the exporting Member whose exports had been subject to restrictions under the Agreement at any time during the one-year period preceding the application of the safeguard measure so requests, the importing Member must apply the quota in accordance with Article XIII.2(d) of GATT 1994.
This provision requires the importing Member to seek agreement on the shares of the quota with the Members having substantial interest in the product (explained in the chapter on safeguards), and if there is no agreement, the importing Member may allocate the quota based on the last three normal years of exports. In doing so, due account has to be taken of any special factor which may have affected the trade. Since the export of the Member in this case was restrained earlier, the exports in the previous three years

may not give a fair basis for allocation. Hence, special consideration may have to be made for such Members in allocating the quota.

Transitional Safeguard

Product Coverage

For products which have not yet been integrated into GATT 1994, the provisions relating to transitional safeguards will apply. Under certain prescribed conditions, an importing Member may take a transitional safeguard measure in respect of a product:

(i) which is in the Annex, i.e., to which the Agreement applies;

(ii) which has not been integrated into GATT 1994; and

(iii) which is not already under restraint under the Agreement.

Transitional safeguard measures cannot be taken against the following types of textile products (introduction to the Annex):

(i) developing country Members' handloom fabrics of the cottage industry, or hand-made cottage industry products made of such handloom fabrics, or traditional folklore handicraft textile and clothing products, provided these are covered by proper certification;

(ii) historically traded textile products which were internationally traded prior to 1982, such as bags, sacks, carpetbacking, cordage, luggage, mats, mattings and carpets typically made from fibres such as jute, coir, sisal, abaca, maguey and henequen;

(iii) products made of pure silk.

As was the case with the restrictions under the MFA, a transitional safeguard measure may be taken in respect of a product selectively from one exporting country or more. The difference between transitional safeguard measures and general safeguard measures in this respect is to be noted. The latter have to be taken in respect of the product of all exporting Members.

Conditions

General

Two lines of investigation have to be conducted before taking transitional safeguard measures, viz.:

(i) the impact of imports on the domestic industry, and

(ii) identification of the Member or Members whose exports are causing the impact.

The primary conditions for taking transitional safeguard measures are the following:

(i) the import of the particular product is in increased quantities;

(ii) there is serious damage or a threat of serious damage to the domestic industry producing like or directly competitive products;

(iii) the serious damage or the threat is caused by the increased imports.

Serious Damage

For determining serious damage, the importing Member has to examine the effect of the import on the particular industry as evidenced by changes in some relevant economic factors, like:

> output, productivity, utilisation of capacity, inventories, market share, exports, wages, employment, domestic prices, profits and investment.

What a directly competitive domestic industry is has not been explained in the Agreement. A normal guideline in this respect could be the choice of consumers; for example, whether consumers would treat the products as alternatives. An explanation of the term "directly competitive product" has also been given in the chapter on national treatment, which can also provide some guidelines in this regard.

The causal link is an important point to be determined. If the situation of serious damage is caused by other factors, like changes in consumer preferences, technological changes, etc., it cannot be attributable to the increased imports.

In considering the threat of serious damage, the imminent increase in imports should also be taken into consideration. But such imminence should not be based merely on suspicion; it has to be based on concrete and measurable factors. For example, the mere existence of production capacity in the exporting country will not be considered to be adequate to determine the threat.

The validity of the determination of serious damage is for 90 days with effect from the notification for consultation. Hence, if restraints are not imposed within this period but are still considered necessary, a fresh exercise for determining serious damage will have to be conducted.

Identification of Exporting Countries

Identification of the source of the imports causing serious damage is important. It is to be done based on:

(i) whether there has been a sharp and substantial increase in imports from the Member concerned;

(ii) the level of imports from the Member as compared to the imports from other sources;

(iii) the market share of the Member concerned, and

(iv) import and domestic prices at a comparable level of trade.

Implications of the Criteria

From the angle of the exporting developing countries, there is a significant improvement in the preconditions for transitional safeguard measures as compared to those for unilateral restraints under the MFA. Some points of improvement are given below.

(i) A general guideline in the Agreement is that such a measure should be applied "as sparingly as possible"

(ii) In the MFA, serious damage to the domestic industry in the importing country was linked to the feature of market disruption which, in turn, could be attributed to low prices of the imports from developing countries. The "low-price" criterion does not find a place in the preconditions for transitional safeguard measures.

(iii) While identifying the country(ies) whose exports are causing serious damage, a comparison of exports from various sources will have to be made and market shares will have to be taken into account. In the process of such a comparison, the imports from developed countries cannot be left out, particularly when the criterion of "low-price" imports is no longer present.

Consultation

The importing Member normally has to give notice to the exporting Member for consultation before any decision is made to impose a transitional safeguard measure. Such notice should contain the facts relating to the alleged serious damage or threat of such damage and the identification of the Member as the source of the export to which the serious damage or the threat is attributed. The information should be product-specific and should preferably be related to the 12-month period ending two months before the month in which the notice for consultation is given. The importing Member should mention in the notice, the proposed level at which it intends to restrain the import of the product.

Imposition of the Measure

If the consultation results in mutual agreement on the restraint, the transitional safeguard measure will accordingly be taken. The condition on the measure is that the level of the restrained import must not be lower than the actual level in the 12-month period ending two month before the month in which the notice for consultation was given. For example, if the notice was given on 10 December 1996, the reference minimum level would be the level of the import of the product from the Member during October 1995 – September 1996.

In the event of measures continuing beyond one year, there are provisions for the growth rate and flexibility. The growth rate will generally not be less than 6 per cent per annum. A lower growth rate will need justification before the TMB. In fact, a minimum lower growth rate of 2 per cent has been agreed in the negotiations only for wool products in the US.[76] The carry over and carry forward together will be 10 per cent, of which the carry forward cannot be more than 5 per cent. If more than one product is restrained, there will be a provision of swing up to 7 per cent from one product to the other, i.e., the level of one product can be increased up to 7 per cent, provided the total import of both the products does not exceed the total of the two limits. There will be no quantitative limit on the combined use of swing, carry over and carry forward.

The TMB will be informed of the result of the consultation. It has to determine whether the mutual agreement is justified in accordance with the Agreement. It may make appropriate recommendations to the Members concerned. Thus, the examination by the TMB is mandatory even when the exporting and importing Members have together agreed on the restraints.

If no agreement is reached within 60 days of the receipt of the notice for consultation, the importing Member may apply the restraint within another 30 days and inform the TMB.

The TMB has to conduct an examination of the matter and make appropriate recommendations to the Members concerned within 30 days.

Emergency Action

There is a provision for emergency action which can be taken even before consultation in highly unusual and critical circumstances, when delay would cause damage which would be difficult to repair. Under such situations, an importing Member may impose restrictions on the import of a product of another Member.

Within five working days of taking such action, the importing Member has to:

(i) give a notice for consultation to the other Member; and

(ii) send information to the TMB about the action taken.

The TMB has to be informed of the result of the consultation. It will consider the matter and make appropriate recommendations to the Members concerned.

In the case of failure of the consultation, the examination by the TMB and its recommendations are mandatory, whereas in the case of agreement in the consultation, the recommendation is discretionary.

Duration of Transitional Safeguard Measure

The transitional safeguard measure can be maintained only for three years, and no extension is permitted. The measure will, of course, not continue if the product is integrated into GATT 1994 in the meantime.

Special Considerations

Special considerations have been suggested in four types of cases without being made specific in terms of quantities or proportions.

(i) Least developed country Members must get more favourable treatment than the other Members in overall terms and, preferably, in each element.

(ii) Small exporters (smallness has not been specifically defined here) must be accorded more favourable treatment in terms of quota levels, growth rates and flexibilities.

(iii) Wool-producing developing countries exporting wool products, that are dependent on such exports and that are small exporters, must also receive favourable treatment in terms of quota levels, growth rates and flexibilities.

(iv) Member countries which process textiles and clothing and then re-export them to the source countries must be provided more favourable treatment, if these re-exports are a significant proportion of their total exports of textiles and clothing.

Since the mode of giving special considerations has not been specified, it is doubtful how far these will be implemented in reality. It will depend a lot on the mutual goodwill of the exporting and importing countries.

CIRCUMVENTION

Circumstances

Elaborate provisions have been made to check circumvention of the restraints under the Agreement. Major importing Members have sometimes suspected that the exporters of some exporting countries deliberately try to circumvent the quota restrictions by sending their products through another country and showing as if these are being exported by the latter country. This motivation may arise when the quota of the original country of manufacture and export may be near exhaustion and there is still enough demand for such products in the importing country. Circumvention should, no doubt, be discouraged, but care should be exercised so that the mere suspicion of circumvention does not act as a real barrier to the entry of goods within the quota limits.

Methods of Circumvention

The means of circumvention, as described in the Agreement, are: transshipment, re-routing, false declarations concerning the country of origin and falsification of official documents. Through any of these methods, an exporter or a Member may try to circumvent the provisions of the Agreement, in particular, the restrictions on imports.

For example, circumvention may take place by showing the product as having been exported by another country which does not face a restraint in respect of the product in question, or by giving a wrong description of the product so that it is put in a category which is not subject to restraint.

Obligation of Members

In the Agreement, Members have the following obligations for preventing circumvention:

(i) they should have laws and procedures to take action against circumvention;

(ii) they should cooperate fully in dealing with circumvention.

In particular, cooperation should be extended during the investigation of circumvention cases, relevant information should be provided and visits to plants should be facilitated. All these are required in so far as they are consistent with the domestic laws and procedures.

Consultation and Remedy

General

If a Member believes that circumvention is taking place and adequate steps are not being taken by another Member against it, the former may seek consultation with the latter with a view to arriving at a mutually satisfactory solution. If a solution is not reached, the Member may take certain action in some situations and may refer the matter to the TMB for its recommendations in other situations, as mentioned below.

Indication of False Origin

In the case of circumvention regarding the true origin of the product, if a Member has investigated the case and has established that there is sufficient evidence in this regard, it will hold consultations with the other Member(s) concerned. After the consultation, it may take action, including the following:

(i) It may deny the entry of the goods involved.

(ii) It may charge the goods to the quota of the true country of origin, if the goods have already entered and due consideration has been given to the actual circumstances and the involvement of the true country of origin.

(iii) It may introduce restraints on exports from the intermediate country of transshipment, if there is evidence of the involvement of that country in the circumvention.

The Agreement is not quite clear on the sequence of actions, but it is reasonable to conclude that the importing Member may take action of the type mentioned above if the consultations have not resulted in a mutually satisfactory solution.

If there has been a satisfactory solution of the matter in the consultation, action may accordingly be taken and information sent to the TMB. If no solution has been found and the importing Member takes action, the matter has to be reported to the TMB. The TMB will review the case promptly and make appropriate recommendations.

Other Means of Circumvention

In cases of circumvention relating to false declarations of categories, classification and quantities of the product, consultation should take place. If no solution is found in the consultation, the matter may be referred to the TMB.

SECTORAL BALANCE OF RIGHTS AND OBLIGATIONS

There is a specific provision in the Agreement (Article 7) for a general improvement in market access and general liberalisation in the textiles and clothing sector which appears to be addressed to developing countries. According to this provision, all Members must take actions to achieve access to markets for textiles and clothing through tariff reductions, tariff binding, elimination of non-tariff barriers and facilitation of customs, administrative and licensing formalities.

All Members must also ensure fair and equitable trading conditions in respect of matters like subsidies, dumping and intellectual property rights, and avoid discrimination against textiles and clothing imports while taking measures for general trade policy reasons.

Article 7.3 introduces the concept of balance of rights and obligations in this particular sector. If a Member considers that the balance of rights and obligations under the Agreement has been upset, it may bring the matter before the relevant WTO body for findings or conclusions. The Council for Trade in Goods has to ensure that this balance is not impaired. Further, the Dispute Settlement Body may authorise a reduction of the mandatory growth rates in respect of a Member found not to be complying with its obligations (Article 8.12). Here, the target will naturally be an exporting developing country. There is no similar provision for specified action against an importing developed country if it has not complied with its obligations.

GATT 1994 and the WTO Agreement have been based on an overall balance of rights and obligations; it was particularly in this background that the WTO Agreement was declared open for acceptance "as a whole". [77] But this particular provision of the Agreement on Textiles and Clothing seeks to establish a sectoral balance which has generally not been the practice in the multilateral trade negotiations.

TEXTILES MONITORING BODY

The implementation of the Agreement is to be supervised by the Textiles Monitoring Body (TMB) which is a standing body composed of a Chairman and 10 members.

As explained earlier, the TMB has to examine even measures for which agreements have been reached between exporting and importing Members, and it has to decide whether the measures are in conformity with the Agreement. When agreements have not been reached in the consultation and a Member has taken unilateral measures, the TMB will, of course, have to examine the measures and decide on their conformity with the Agreement.

The Agreement prescribes that Members must endeavour to accept the recommendations of the TMB. The term "endeavour" makes it less than a mandatory obligation.

The Agreement provides for a matter to be considered twice by the TMB, before it is brought to the Dispute Settlement Body (to be explained in the chapter on the Dispute Settlement Understanding). When the TMB has made its recommendations and a Member considers itself unable to accept these recommendations, it must provide the TMB with the reasons. The TMB will again consider the matter and, if it considers it appropriate, will issue further recommendations. If even then a Member is not satisfied, it may refer the matter to the Dispute Settlement Body.

In the case of a dispute between Members, if the TMB is called upon to make recommendations or findings, the Agreement makes it obligatory on the TMB to make such findings or recommendations within a stipulated time.

TERMINATION OF THE AGREEMENT

The Agreement will stand terminated on 1 January 2005, and thereby, all restrictions covered by it will also automatically stand terminated. The entire textiles and clothing sector will then be deemed to be covered by the general rules of GATT 1994 and the WTO agreements. There is a specific provision at the end that this Agreement shall not be extended.

PART VI

PROCEDURAL AND OTHER MATTERS RELATING TO GOODS

There are some important procedural and other matters relating to goods which have a significant bearing on international trade. This Part covers these subjects. In particular, the following topics have been taken for detailed consideration:

1. Customs valuation,
2. Import licensing,
3. Rules of origin,
4. Preshipment inspection,
5. State trading enterprises,
6. Part IV of GATT 1994, and
7. Plurilateral agreements.

Chapter VI.1

Customs Valuation

INTRODUCTION

IN most cases, a tariff (customs duty) is fixed on an *ad valorem* basis, i.e., as a percentage of the price of the product. Hence, the customs duty payable on a product depends a good deal on the base on which the percentage is calculated. This base is called the customs value. Article VII of GATT 1994 originally laid down the principles on which the customs value should be calculated. But a number of problems kept cropping up. The Tokyo Round evolved a Code for this purpose with the aim of introducing a certain objectivity and uniformity in this process. Finally, there is now the WTO Agreement on Implementation of Article VII of the General Agreement on Tariffs and Trade 1994 (commonly called the Agreement on Customs Valuation), which forms a part of the WTO agreements. This Agreement provides a comprehensive set of rules on this subject.

The need for discipline in this area arises as sometimes, it is apprehended that the exporter and the importer may collude to show a lower value for the imported product with the objective of having a lower liability for customs duty on the importer. To prevent such a practice, the customs authorities in the importing country should be able to probe deeper into the value of the good. However, if they are given too much discretion, it may result in uncertainty about the expected customs duty on an imported product, and there may even be cases of harassment. Keeping all this in view, there is a need for balancing these two opposing apprehensions.

DISCIPLINE

The Agreement starts with a general introductory commentary which helps one to understand the sequence of steps to be taken in determining the customs value as included in the articles of the Agreement. Some of the basic terms have been defined in Article 15 and elaborate interpretative notes have been given in Annex I to the Agreement. These definitions and notes have to be read along with the relevant articles of the Agreement. The interpretative notes clarify various problems which may emerge in the course of the operation of various articles. Several useful and simple illustrations have been included in the notes to facilitate the understanding of various phrases and concepts.

The main points to be understood in this Agreement are: the various alternative methods for determining the customs value of an imported product, the sequence of priority of these methods, the various adjustments which have to be made to the basic reported amounts and the conditions guiding such adjustments.

The customs value is normally based on the transaction value, i.e., the invoice price with some prescribed adjustments. When this price cannot be taken as a basis, there are five other methods which have to be adopted as preferred alternatives in sequence, as will be explained later.

Ministerial Decision of Marrakesh

What the situation is in which the transaction value will not be taken to be the customs value has been clarified in a Ministerial Decision taken in Marrakesh at the time of approving the WTO agreements. This Decision prescribes a two-step process. When a declaration about the transaction value has been given, the customs authorities will examine it. If they have reason to doubt the truth or the accuracy of the documents or the particulars, they may ask the importer to provide further explanations, evidence or documents. If, on examining all the materials, or if the importer has not responded, the customs authorities still have reasonable doubts about the truth or accuracy of the documents or the particulars, it will be deemed that the customs value cannot be determined on the basis of the transaction value.

Hence, after such a two-stage examination by the customs authorities, there will be a presumption about the transaction value being not appropriate for the purpose of calculating the customs duty, and then, other methods will be applied.

TRANSACTION VALUE

As mentioned earlier, the customs value is to be based primarily on the transaction value, i.e.: (i) the price actually paid, or (ii) if no actual payment has been made, the price which is payable. It is normally shown in the invoice for the import of the product. All forms of payment have to be taken into account. The payment may be direct, e.g., through an actual transfer of money or through a letter of credit or a negotiable instrument. The payment may also be indirect, e.g., through a settlement of some past debt of the exporter. All this has to be considered as the price.

Limitations on Transaction Value

There are certain conditions of eligibility for the transaction value to be the basis for calculating the customs value. It will qualify for this purpose only if the following conditions are satisfied:

(i) There are no restrictions regarding the use of the product, except:

  (a) those which are imposed under the laws and regulations of the importing country; or

  (b) those which limit the regions in which the product may be resold; or

  (c) those which do not substantially affect the value of the product.

  As an example of the last exception, the interpretative notes cite the restriction when a buyer of automobiles is prohibited from reselling them before a fixed date which represents the beginning of a model year.

(ii) The transaction or the price is not conditional on factors which cannot be translated into a specific value in respect of the product. Some examples of such conditions, as given in the interpretative notes, are:

(a) a commitment of the buyer to buy specific quantities of other goods as well;

(b) a commitment of the buyer to sell some other products at specified prices to the seller;

(c) in the case of the import of a semi-finished product, a condition that the buyer will sell a specified quantity of the finished product to the seller and the price of the semi-finished product is fixed on this basis.

(iii) When the product is resold by the buyer, no part of the proceeds accrues to the seller, except where an adjustment for this purpose is made, as will be explained later.

(iv) The buyer and the seller are not related. In the event of their being related, there are procedures for still accepting the transaction value, as will be explained later.

Related Buyer and Seller

Definition

Specific conditions have been given to determine when the buyer and the seller will be considered to be related (Article 15). Any one of the following conditions, when fulfilled, will make the buyer and the seller related:

(i) they are officers or directors of one another's business;

(ii) they are legally recognised partners in business;

(iii) they are employer and employee;

(iv) any person owns, controls or holds at least 5 per cent of the outstanding voting stock or shares of both of them;

(v) any of them directly or indirectly controls the other;

(vi) both of them are directly or indirectly controlled by a third person;

(vii) together, they directly or indirectly control a third person;

(viii) they are members of the same family.

The interpretative notes mention that one is deemed to control the other when one is legally or operationally in a position to exercise restraint or direction over the other.

Acceptability of Transaction Value

Price not influenced

Even if the buyer and the seller are related, the transaction value has to be accepted, provided the relationship did not influence the price. Thus, the customs authorities may satisfy themselves about it. The onus is on them to indicate that the relationship has influenced the price. If they are satisfied that it has, they have to communicate the grounds to the importer.

Price close to an acceptable value

Another situation in which the transaction value has to be accepted is when the importer demonstrates that it is close to an acceptable value. Three such alternative "test" values which may be used for this purpose have been prescribed in Article 1.2(b). These are:

(i) the transaction value in the sale of identical or similar goods, if the sale is to unrelated buyers for export to the same importing country (the terms "identical" and "similar" goods will be explained later);

(ii) the customs value of identical or similar goods "deduced" on the basis of the resale price in the importing country (to be explained later); and

(iii) the customs value of identical or similar goods "computed" on the basis of the cost of production, profits, etc. (to be explained later).

The interpretative notes mention that in case the test criterion is satisfied, it is not necessary to examine whether the price has been influenced by the buyer and the seller being related.

The test values should be used only for the purpose of comparison, and not for establishing a substitute value on this basis.

Adjustments to Transaction Value

The adjustments to the transaction value to convert it into the customs value have been laid down in Article 8. The adjustment is by the addition of amounts related to certain prescribed factors. These are:

(i) commissions and brokerage (except buying commissions, i.e., except the fees paid by an importer to its agent for representing the importer abroad in the purchase of the goods under valuation), the cost of containers and the cost of packing;

(ii) the value of materials, components, parts and similar items incorporated in the goods, supplied by the importer free of charge or at reduced rates, to the extent such values have not been included in the price;

(iii) the value of the materials which, though not actually incorporated in the goods, are consumed in the production of the good, under the conditions mentioned in item (ii) above;

(iv) the value of engineering, development, artwork, design work, and plans and sketches undertaken outside the importing country, if these were necessary for the production of the goods and if the conditions in item (ii) are satisfied;

(v) the value of tools, dies, moulds and similar items used in the production of the goods, if the conditions in item (ii) are satisfied;

(vi) royalties and licence fees related to the goods which the buyer is obliged to pay as a condition of sale, to the extent these are not included in the price;

(vii) any portion of the subsequent resale, disposal or use of the goods which accrues to the seller.

The Agreement stipulates that items (ii) to (vii) have to be added, whether they occur directly or indirectly in relation to the goods being valued. Item (i) is, of course, a direct expenditure.

The items (i), (ii), (iii), (vi) and (vii) are all related to the particular goods under consideration, whereas the items (iv) and (v) may be covering amounts spread over other goods. In that case, the amounts have to be appropriately apportioned to the goods under consideration. The method of apportionment has been given in detail in the interpretative notes.

OTHER METHODS OF DETERMINATION OF CUSTOMS VALUE

If the method for determining the customs value based on the transaction value cannot be adopted, the following values will form the basis for this purpose:

(i) the transaction value of identical goods;

(ii) the transaction value of similar goods;

(iii) the deduced value based on the sale of the goods in the importing country;

(iv) the computed value based on the cost of production, profits, etc.;

(v) any other reasonable means.

These can be used only in this sequence, i.e., the later method can be adopted only if adoption of the previous one is not possible. There is, however, a stipulation that the importer may have a choice to reverse the order of sequence in the case of methods (iii) and (iv). Thus, normally, method (iii) will have priority over method (iv), but (iv) will have priority over (iii) if the importer indicates such a preference.

Basis of Identical Goods

Definition

The phrase "identical goods" means goods which:

(i) are the same in all respects, including physical characteristics, quality and reputation;

(ii) have been produced in the same country;

(iii) have been produced by the same entity.
The goods produced by another entity will be considered identical only if there are no identical goods produced by the same entity.

If some goods incorporate or reflect engineering, development, artwork, design work, and plans and sketches, and adjustments had not been made for them because of their being undertaken in the country of importation, such goods will not be considered as identical goods.

Application

As mentioned earlier, if the normal method of determining the customs value based on the transaction value of the imported goods under valuation cannot be applied, the customs value has to be determined on the basis of the transaction value of identical goods, with the following conditions:

(i) the goods should have been sold for export to the same importing country;

(ii) the goods should have been exported at the same time or nearly the same time as the goods under valuation;

(iii) the sale should have been made at the same commercial level; (Here, the commercial level refers to the stage of sale, e.g., retail sale, sale to regional distributor, ex-factory sale, etc.)

(iv) the sale should have been made in substantially the same quantity;

(v) if the sale had been made at a different commercial level or in a different volume, the transaction value has to be adjusted to take account of these differences;
(Special care has to be exercised in this adjustment. It should be done only if it can be demonstrated that it is possible to make a reasonable and accurate adjustment on account of these factors. The interpretative notes in Annex I give some examples to explain it.)

(vi) an adjustment has to be made for the cost of transport, insurance, loading, unloading and handling, taking into account any significant difference in such costs between the imported goods and the identical goods under consideration;

(vii) if more than one such transaction value for identical goods is found, the lowest value should be used to determine the customs value of the imported goods.

Basis of Similar Goods

Definition

The phrase "similar goods" means goods which:

(i) have like characteristics and like components, perform the same functions and are commercially interchangeable;
(The quality, reputation and trademark are among the factors to be considered.)

(ii) have been produced in the same country;

(iii) have been produced by the same entity.
The goods produced by another entity will be considered similar only if there are no similar goods produced by the same entity.

If some goods incorporate or reflect engineering, development, artwork, design work, and plans and sketches, and adjustments had not been made for them because of their being undertaken in the country of importation, such goods will not be considered as similar goods.

Application

The conditions of application are the same as in the case of identical goods.

Basis of Deduced Value

Main Elements

In this method, the customs value is deduced on the basis of the unit price at which the imported identical or similar goods are sold in the country of importation after the import has taken place. There are two basic conditions:

(i) if several sales have taken place, the unit price involving the greatest aggregate quantity should be considered;
(The interpretative notes in Annex I give examples to clarify this criterion.)

(ii) only such sales which are made to unrelated persons have to be taken into account.

Deductions

The following deductions have to be made from the unit sale price:

(i) commissions, profits and general expenses in connection with the sales of goods of the same class or kind in the importing country;
(The interpretative notes in Annex I clarify that the same "class or kind" should be determined on a case-by-case basis by referring to the circumstances involved.)

(ii) costs of transportation and insurance and other associated costs incurred in the importing country;

(iii) customs duties and domestic taxes payable in the importing country;

(iv) costs and charges relating to transport, insurance, loading, unloading and handling in the course of importation.

Additional Conditions

There are additional conditions regarding the timing of the sale in the importing country and the form in which the goods are sold after importation. These are:

(i) the sale should have taken place close to the time of importation of the goods being valued;

(ii) if such a sale has not taken place close to the time of importation, the sale at the earliest date after the importation will be taken into account, but the time gap must not be 90 days or more;

(iii) the goods should have been sold in the condition as imported, i.e., there should have been no processing;

(iv) if no such sale has taken place in the condition as imported, the unit price at which the imported goods, after further processing, are sold, will form the basis of calculation with due deduction for the value addition during processing.

Basis of Computed Value

In this method, the customs value is determined as the computed value, which is calculated by adding the following:

(i) the cost of production, including the costs and values of materials, fabrication and other processing employed in the production;

(ii) profit and general expenses usually applicable to goods of the same class or kind produced in the exporting country for export to the importing country;

(iii) necessary amounts for transport, insurance, loading, unloading and handling, depending on the practices employed in the importing country.

The interpretative notes point out the difficulties in using this method and indicate that it will be generally limited to those cases where the buyer and seller are related, and the producer is prepared to supply information on costing and also to provide facilities for verification.

Other Bases

In this method, any reasonable means may be applied. These means must be consistent with the principles and general provisions of Article VII of GATT 1994 and this Agreement.

In this method, the following bases must not be applied:

(i) the price at which the goods produced in the importing country are sold in that country or the price of goods in the domestic market of the exporting country or the price of goods for export to another country;

(ii) minimum customs values, or arbitrary or fictitious values;

(iii) any system which provides for the acceptance of the higher of two alternative values; or

(iv) the cost of production other than what is employed in the method of computed value.

The interpretative notes clarify that the methods of valuation in this case should also be similar to those for the other alternatives described previously, but a reasonable flexibility may be applied.

OTHER PROVISIONS

Domestic Legal Provisions and Judicial Review

The domestic legislation, rules, procedures, etc. have to be published so that interested parties have an opportunity to know about them and to consult them.

There must be a right of appeal against the decisions of the authorities determining the customs value. The first appeal may be to an authority in the customs administration or to an outside independent body. There must be a provision for an appeal to a judicial authority, at least at a subsequent stage.

Institutions

The Committee on Customs Valuation has been established, with representatives from each of the Members. There will be a Technical Committee under the auspices of the Customs Cooperation Council. Its functions and method of operation have been laid down in Annex II to the Agreement.

Consultation and Dispute Settlement

The provisions of the Dispute Settlement Understanding are applicable to this Agreement.

A panel established to examine a dispute regarding the provisions of this Agreement may refer any matter requiring technical consideration to the Technical Committee. The panel must take into consideration the report of the Technical Committee, but is not bound to accept its opinions.

Developing Countries

Some developing country Members had earlier joined the Tokyo Round Code on Customs Valuation. They will have no problems in implementing the provisions of this Agreement. There are some relaxations of time for those developing country Members who had not joined that Code. They may delay the implementation of the Agreement for a maximum period of five years from 1 January 1995. They may also delay the adoption of the computed value method for a maximum period of three years beyond the start of their implementation of the other provisions of the Agreement.

A Ministerial Decision in Marrakesh says that a developing country may seek to retain officially established minimum values for customs valuation, which is generally not allowed under the Agreement. If it gives good reasons for this option, the Committee on Customs Valuation must give sympathetic consideration to such a request.

This Decision also refers to the concern of developing countries about problems of valuation in the case of imports by sole agents, sole distributors and sole concessionaires. But it gives no relief, except that these countries may conduct appropriate studies and take other necessary actions in this regard during the five-year period in which they are not required to undertake the obligations.

Chapter VI.2

IMPORT LICENSING

INTRODUCTION

SOMETIMES, governments introduce a system of licensing for the import of some products. The need arises when the import of a product has to be controlled or monitored. The introduction and implementation of import licensing can sometimes act as impediments to trade; hence, it has been considered necessary to lay down disciplines on import licensing. The Agreement on Import Licensing Procedures contains these disciplines. It mentions two types of import licences, viz., automatic licences and non-automatic licences, for which different disciplines have been prescribed. In addition, there are some disciplines which are applicable to both.

GENERAL DISCIPLINES

Import licensing is defined as the administrative procedures requiring the submission of an application or other documentation as a precondition for imports.

The following general disciplines have been prescribed in the Agreement:

(i) All information regarding the licensing procedure must be published so that governments and traders are able to become acquainted with them. Generally, the publication should be done 21 days prior to the effective date of requirement.

(ii) If there is a closing date, the period available to the applicant to file an application should be at least 21 days.

(iii) Generally, the applicant should not be required to approach more than one administrative body; in any case, the applicant must not be required tc approach more than three bodies.

(iv) An application should not be refused for minor errors which do not alter the basic information.

(v) If the actual import has a minor variation in value or quantity from what is designated in the licence, it should not be refused, provided the variation occurs during shipment, is incidental to bulk loading or is otherwise of a small magnitude consistent with normal commercial practice.

(vi) If a mistake lies in documentation or procedure and was committed without any fraudulent intent or gross negligence, and if a penalty is to be imposed, the penalty should be just enough to serve as a warning.

AUTOMATIC LICENSING

Automatic import licensing is one where approval is granted in the case of all valid applications. It is employed mainly for the purpose of monitoring imports in specific sectors.

The process of automatic licensing has to be applied in such a manner that it does not have trade-restrictive effects. The Agreement prescribes some conditions which must be followed; otherwise, the automatic licensing will be deemed to have trade-restrictive effects. These conditions are the following:

(i) If an applicant fulfils the legal requirements to obtain a licence, the applicant must be eligible to submit the application and obtain the licence. There should be no discrimination between eligible persons in respect of filing applications or obtaining licences.

(ii) The applicant should be able to submit the application on any working day prior to the customs clearance of the goods.

Developing country Members that did not join the Tokyo Round Code on Import Licensing, may delay the implementation of this provision for a maximum period of two years from 1 January 1995.

(iii) The applications should be processed and approval granted quickly; in any case, approval must be given in eligible cases within 10 days of the filing of the application.
In this case also, the developing country Members mentioned above have the discretion to delay its implementation by two years.

NON-AUTOMATIC LICENSING

This licensing practice is normally used when there is a quantitative restriction on the import of a product and the import is permitted only through licences. This process can be used, for example, to allocate the permissible quantity of imports among different importers in the country or among different supplying countries.

The process is to be applied as an administrative procedure for implementing an import restriction. It cannot be applied as an import restriction by itself.

The Agreement prescribes some conditions on the procedure, as described below:

(i) No discrimination can be made between applicants fulfilling the legal and administrative requirements.

(ii) If an application has been rejected, the applicant should have the right to know the reasons and to file an appeal against the decision.

(iii) If the applications are to be considered on the basis of first come first served, the time of processing should not be more than 30 days. In case the applications are to be considered simultaneously, i.e., where choices have to be made among those who have filed the applications, the time of processing should not be more than 60 days.

(iv) If the process of licensing is applied for the administration of an import quota, i.e., for the distribution of an import quota, the following additional conditions are applicable:

(a) The quantity/value of the quota, and the opening and closing dates should be published so that the interested Members and traders are able to become acquainted with them.

(b) If the quota is to be distributed among various supplying countries, the allocated shares of different countries have to be notified to all Members having an interest in supplying the product.

(c) While allocating the quota, the past import performance of the applicant should be considered. Consideration should be given to a reasonable distribution of licences to newcomers. Besides, special consideration is to be given to the importers importing products from developing countries.

(d) There are some other conditions; for example, the validity period of the licence should be reasonable; consideration should be given to issuing licences for economic quantities; if quotas are not meant for specific countries, the importers should be free to import from any source; imports in accordance with the licence must not be prevented; if the interested Members so desire, they must be provided information on the administrative procedure, the licences granted recently and import statistics, if practicable; etc.

OTHER PROVISIONS

Notification

Members introducing a licensing practice must notify the Committee on Import Licensing about it. The notification requirement also applies to the introduction of changes in existing practices. The notification should contain the following information:

a list of products covered, whether the procedure is for automatic or non-automatic licences, the administrative purpose of the licensing and the trade measures being implemented through it, the details of the publications containing the procedures, the contact point for information, the administrative body to which applications are to be sent, and the probable duration of the practice.

There is also a provision for counter-notification. Thus, if a Member considers that another Member has not notified its licensing process, it may bring it to the notice of that Member; if the notification is still not made promptly, the Member may itself send the notification to the Committee based on its information.

Consultation and Dispute Settlement

The normal process of consultation and dispute settlement, as explained in the chapter on the Dispute Settlement Understanding, applies to this Agreement.

Institutions

A Committee on Import Licensing has been established to assist Members in the implementation of the Agreement.

Chapter VI.3

Rules of Origin

INTRODUCTION

RULES of origin are a set of rules which determine the country in which a product will be deemed to have originated. When a product has been produced entirely in one country, a problem does not arise. For example, if a country C produces a clothing product out of its own fabric, which in turn has been manufactured with its own cotton, using only domestically produced processing chemicals and other inputs, the country of origin for this product is clearly country C. A problem, however, arises when the fabric or other major inputs have been imported from other countries, or when some minor operations, like sewing the buttons or folding and pressing, have been done in the country from which the product is finally exported.

The determination of the country of origin becomes relevant, and sometimes extremely important, when some of the rules of GATT 1994 and the WTO agreements are applicable to products from a particular country. For example, if an anti-dumping duty is to be applied by an importing country to the passenger cars of a country C, it is necessary to determine whether a particular import of passenger cars coming from country C should be considered to be the product of country C. Complexities may arise if country C has used the components and parts of several other countries to assemble the passenger cars for sale to this importing country.

Countries have formulated their own criteria to determine which country will be considered the country of origin of a particular product. These are called the rules of origin. A country may have general rules of origin applicable to all countries and all subjects in GATT 1994. It may also have some special rules of origin for preferential trade, for example, for the Generalised System of Preferences (GSP), and for regional arrangements, like free-trade areas and customs unions in which it is a member.

DISCIPLINE

In order to make the rules of origin simpler, uniform and stable, it has been considered desirable to prepare a harmonised set of rules of origin to be adopted by all countries. The WTO Agreement on Rules of Origin aimed at initiating, in 1995, work on having a harmonised set of rules and completing it within three years. The Agreement lays down guidelines for broad approaches in formulating the harmonised rules. It also prescribes some disciplines which have to be observed during the transition period, i.e., from 1 January 1995 till the new harmonised rules are adopted.

The disciplines are for general rules of origin, i.e., those not applicable to the rules of origin for preferential trade, e.g., GSP or regional arrangements. A Declaration is made in Annex II to the Agreement which contains the agreements of Members on certain general disciplines on the rules of origin for preferential trade. It will be explained later.

MAIN CRITERIA APPLIED IN THE RULES OF ORIGIN

There are three types of criteria to determine the country of origin of a product:

(i) change in the classification of the product;

(ii) percentage of value addition, commonly called the *ad valorem* criterion;

(iii) manufacturing or processing criterion.

Change in Classification

Now, countries generally follow the Harmonised System of tariff nomenclature (described in detail in the chapter on tariffs) for the classification of products. The criterion of change of classification for determining the origin of a product involves finding out whether the manufacturing or processing done in the particular country changed the tariff classification of the product. For example, if iron ore has been converted into steel slabs, or if the steel slab has been converted into a coil or rod, changes in the classification of the products have taken place, and the countries where these operations took place will be the countries of origin for these respective products.

Ad Valorem Percentage

In this criterion, the determining factor is whether a certain minimum percentage of value addition was done in a particular country. When the iron ore is converted into steel slabs or when the steel slab is further converted into a steel coil or steel rod, at each stage of such manufacture or processing, there is a value addition which is generally calculated on the basis of the difference between the price of the new product and the price of the earlier product which was converted into the new product. Thus, the difference between the prices of the steel coil and the steel slab will be the value addition in converting the steel slab into the steel coil. In this criterion, it is prescribed that for a country to be the country of origin, a certain minimum value addition must have been done in that country.

In this criterion, sometimes a minimum domestic content is prescribed, while sometimes a maximum import content is prescribed.

This criterion may result in different conclusions in different situations. For example, the same process may involve different value additions, depending on whether the process is carried out in a high-cost country, like an industrialised country, or in a low-cost country, like a developing country.

Specific Operation

The chain of activities in manufacturing and processing has several important operations. In this criterion, the particular operation in the chain which will determine the origin is prescribed. For example, in the case of the steel coil, it may be laid down that the operation of pressing the slab into the coil will be the criterion, and not merely cutting the coil into particular sizes, or putting a particular coating over it.

DISCIPLINES IN THE TRANSITION PERIOD

In the transition period, different Members will have their own rules of origin. But in the formulation and implementation of their rules, they must follow the following disciplines:

(i) the prescribed requirements must be clearly defined, in particular:

 (a) while using the change of classification criterion, the rules must specify the headings or subheadings which will determine the origin;

 (b) while using the *ad valorem* percentage criterion, the required percentage will naturally be mentioned, but the method of calculating the percentage must also be indicated;

 (c) while using the specific operation criterion, the particular manufacturing or processing operation which will determine the origin must be precisely specified.

(ii) the rules must not be used as instruments to achieve trade objectives; for example, these must not be used to restrict the import of a product in general or from particular sources;

(iii) the rules must not themselves create restrictive, distorting or disruptive effects on trade, and there must not be any condition unrelated to manufacturing or processing;

(iv) the rules must not be more stringent than those applied by the Member to determine whether a product is of domestic origin, and these must not be discriminatory as between Members;

(v) the rules must be implemented in a consistent, uniform, impartial and reasonable manner;

(vi) the rules must be based on positive standards, i.e., these should include criteria of eligibility for being treated as the country of origin, and not criteria of ineligibility, except:

(a) as a clarification of a positive standard; or

(b) where a positive determination of origin is not necessary;

(vii) laws, rules, etc. relating to the rules of origin must be published promptly in such a manner as to enable other governments and traders to become acquainted with them;

(viii) when a request is made to indicate what origin will be accorded to a particular product, the response must be issued within 150 days of the request;

(ix) the rules and modifications in the rules must not be applied retroactively;

(x) there must be a provision for prompt judicial, arbitral or administrative review of the administrative actions relating to the determination of origin; the reviewing authority must be independent of the authority making the determination;

(xi) information which is of a confidential nature or which is provided on a confidential basis must be treated confidentially.

HARMONISATION OF RULES OF ORIGIN

Institutional Arrangement

The final objective is to have a harmonised set of rules of origin. The harmonised rules, when ready, will be adopted at a Ministerial Conference of the WTO. Detailed guidelines and timetables have been provided in the Agreement for the preparation of the harmonised set of rules.

The work on the harmonised set of rules will be done in the Committee on Rules of Origin (the Committee) and the Technical Committee on Rules of Origin (the Technical Committee). The Agreement has created these two institutions and mentions that the latter is being established under the auspices of the Customs Co-operation Council (CCC). The Committee will place requests with the Technical Committee at different stages, and the latter will take up the work accordingly and complete it according to a prescribed time schedule.

The work will be carried out by the Technical Committee on a product-sector basis, as represented by various chapters or sections of the Harmonised System.

Broad Guidelines

The objectives and principles of the harmonised rules prescribe that the origin of a product should be:

(i) the country where the product has been "wholly obtained", or

(ii) in case more than one country is concerned in the production of the product, it should be the country where the last "substantial transformation" has been carried out.

"Wholly obtained" would imply that the entire manufacture or processing has been done in that country, except, of course, some minor operations, like cutting to size, polishing, packing, etc. The exact definition is to be evolved, as will be explained later.

Work Programme

"Wholly Obtained" Criteria

The Technical Committee will first develop the criteria of:

(i) products considered as being "wholly obtained" in one country; and

(ii) minimal operations or processes which are not, by themselves, determinants of the country of origin (for example, simple operations like cutting into specific dimensions, splitting up, etc.).

This work will be done within three months of the request from the Committee.

Substantial Transformation Criteria

For cases where the manufacturing or processing operations have been done in several countries, the Technical Committee will develop various sets of criteria. First, it will develop the change in classification criterion for substantial transformation to determine the origin of a product. The change in tariff heading or subheading in the Harmonised System of tariff classification will be used for this purpose. This work will be done within one year and three months of the request of the Committee.

Thereafter, the Technical Committee will develop the *ad valorem* percentage, and manufacturing or processing operation criteria for substantial transformation for determining the origin. This will be done within two years and three months of the request of the Committee.

Work in the Committee

The Committee will consider the work of the Technical Committee and may request additional work or suggest alternative approaches to the Technical Committee. Finally, the Committee will make recommendations to the Ministerial Conference.

Objectives and Principles

In the preparation and finalisation of the harmonised rules of origin, the following principles will be followed:

The principles mentioned earlier in (ii), (iii), (v) and (vi) in the section on Disciplines in the Transition Period are applicable here also. Besides, the following additional principles have been laid down:

(i) The rules of origin should be applied equally for all purposes. It will mean that a Member will not have different sets of rules of origin for use in connection with different provisions of GATT 1994, e.g., MFN treatment, national treatment, subsidies, anti-dumping, safeguards, quantitative restrictions, etc.

(ii) The rules should be objective, understandable and predictable.

DISCIPLINES AFTER TRANSITION PERIOD

After the harmonised set of rules has been prepared by the Technical Committee and the Committee, and after its adoption by the Ministerial Conference, the rules will come into operation with effect from a specified date. Till then, the disciplines for the transition period will continue to remain applicable. On the coming into effect of the harmonised rules, the following disciplines will be applicable:

Those mentioned in the section on the objectives and principles related to harmonisation will continue to be applicable even when the harmonised rules come into operation.

Besides, those mentioned in (iv), (v), (vii), (viii), (ix), (x) and (xi) in the section on Disciplines in the Transition Period will also be applicable.

COMMON DECLARATION ON PREFERENTIAL RULES OF ORIGIN

There is a Common Declaration with regard to the rules of origin applied by Members to preferential trade. It is contained in Annex II.

In this Declaration, Members have agreed to the disciplines as mentioned in (i), (vi), (vii), (viii), (ix), (x) and (xi) in the section on Disciplines in the Transition Period.

Besides, Members have agreed to provide to the WTO Secretariat their rules of origin applicable to preferential trade as on 1 January 1995. They have also agreed to provide to the Secretariat any new rules which may be formulated in this regard and modifications to the rules.

OTHER MATTERS

Notification

Members are required to provide to the Secretariat their general rules of origin and related judicial and administrative decisions within 90 days of 1 January 1995.

Modifications in the Rules of Origin

During the transition period, if any rules are introduced by a Member or if modifications are made to existing rules, the Member must publish a notice to this effect at least 60 days before the entry into force of the new rules or the modifications. In exceptional circumstances, however, a Member need not give prior notice, but must publish the new rules or modifications as soon as possible.

Consultation and Dispute Settlement

The provisions of Articles XXII and XXIII of GATT 1994, as elaborated and applied by the Dispute Settlement Understanding, apply to this Agreement. These provisions will be described in detail in the chapter on the Dispute Settlement Understanding.

Chapter VI.4

Preshipment Inspection

INTRODUCTION

A PRESHIPMENT inspection is an arrangement made by an importing country for the verification of an import consignment in the exporting country before the export takes place. Generally, this practice is adopted by countries which want to lighten the burden of their own customs authorities in inspecting the consignment on arrival in the country. In order to ensure that the exporters do not face unnecessary problems in this process and to bring about some degree of uniformity in the process, the WTO Agreement on Preshipment Inspection lays down certain disciplines.

DEFINITIONS AND THE PROCESS

The importing country organising the inspection is called the "user Member" in the Agreement. The inspecting agency which is assigned this task is called the "preshipment inspection entity" in the Agreement.

The inspection may involve the verification of the quality, the quantity, the price and the customs classification of the product being exported. The verification the price may include the currency exchange rate and the financial terms .

DISCIPLINES

The Agreement prescribes the disciplines for the user Member, the inspection entity and the exporting Member. The user Member is responsible for the observance of the disciplines by the entity, as will be explained later.

Obligations of the User Member

The main direct obligations of the user Member are given below.

Non-Discrimination

The preshipment activities have to be carried out in a non-discriminatory manner. The procedures and criteria have to be objective and applied equally to all exporters covered by the inspection. There has to be a uniform performance of inspection by all the inspectors.

National Treatment

In the process of inspection, it has to be ensured that the products being inspected are not accorded treatment less favourable than that accorded to the like products of national origin in respect of laws, regulations and requirements, in so far as it is relevant in the particular case of inspection.

Site of Inspection

The inspection will normally be carried out in the country of export. In special cases, however, it may take place in the country of manufacture, if both the parties agree or if there is particular complexity involved in the inspection.

Standards

Normally, the standards as laid down in the purchase agreement will be the basis of the standards of the products. If there is no stipulation in this regard in the agreement, the relevant international standards will be applicable.

Price Verification

Normally, the price in the contract will be accepted. If this is to be rejected, the rejection has to be based on a verification process in respect of the prices of identical or similar goods. In this respect, there are certain conditions. Such products should be exported from the same country at about the same time and under competitive and comparable conditions of sale in conformity with customary commercial practices. In the comparison process, due adjustments will be made for some relevant factors, like the quantity of the goods, delivery periods, price escalation clause, etc. The Agreement prohibits certain elements being used for price verification. These are: the selling price in the country of importation of goods produced in that country, the price of goods exported from another country, the cost of production and arbitrary or fictitious prices or values.

Redressal of Grievances

There must be an arrangement for the redressal of grievances. An independent entity will be constituted jointly by an organisation representing preshipment inspection entities and an organisation of exporters. This entity will arrange for the independent review of grievances. There is a provision for the formation of panels to look into such cases.

Obligations of Inspection Entities

The inspection entities also have some obligations, but, as indicated earlier, it is the responsibility of the user Member to ensure that they fulfil their obligations. Perhaps this may be done through clear stipulations in their contract of appointment. The entities have to provide full information to the exporters on the requirements for the inspection. They have to protect the confidential information given by the exporters. They are prohibited from seeking information on certain elements, like manufacturing data related to patented processes, unpublished technical data, internal pricing, profit levels, etc. They have to conduct the inspection promptly on request. They must quickly issuc a Clean Report of Findings, and if they are not able to do so, they must give a detailed written explanation specifying the reasons. They must also designate some officials who would promptly receive, consider and decide on the appeals and grievances of the exporters.

Obligations of the Exporting Member

Exporting Members have to ensure that their laws and procedures in respect of the preshipment inspection are applied in a non-discriminatory manner.

OTHER OBLIGATIONS

Notification

All laws and regulations of a Member are to be notified to the WTO Secretariat. No changes must come into effect before they are officially published.

Consultation and Dispute Settlement

The normal process of consultation and dispute settlement as contained in Articles XXII and XXIII of GATT 1994 and elaborated and applied by the Dispute Settlement Understanding (to be explained in the chapter on the Dispute Settlement Understanding), will be applicable in this case.

Review

There was to be a review at the end of the second year from 1 January 1995. In future, there will be a review every three years. The Ministerial Meeting will conduct these reviews with a view to amending the provisions of the Agreement as considered necessary.

Chapter VI.5

State Trading Enterprises

INTRODUCTION

SOMETIMES, governments establish state enterprises and vest them with monopoly functions of importing and exporting. It is often apprehended that such enterprises, which operate within the control of governments, may not follow general commercial practices, and may be used by governments for restricting imports and exports or for diverting imports and exports to preferred sources and destinations. All these may have distorting effects on international trade. Hence, disciplines have been laid down on the establishment of state enterprises and their general functioning. Basically, the disciplines are contained in Article XVII of GATT 1994. These have been further specified and strengthened by the Understanding on the Interpretation of Article XVII of GATT 1994 (the Understanding), which is a part of GATT 1994.

DEFINITION

The Understanding gives a working definition of a state enterprise. It is an enterprise which has been granted exclusive or special rights or privileges, in exercise of which it influences the level or direction of imports or exports. Such an influence comes through its purchasing and selling activities.

The enterprise may be a government or a non-government enterprise, meaning, thereby, that the management or ownership of the enterprise is not relevant for this purpose. What is important is the rights or privileges granted to it by the government, and its manner of operation. The Understanding specifically mentions that marketing boards will be covered by this definition, and also that the rights and privileges include statutory or constitutional powers.

In the Panel on Republic of Korea – Restrictions on Imports of Beef – Complaints by the US (November 1989), the US argued that the very existence of a producer-controlled import monopoly was inconsistent with Article XVII of GATT 1994. The particular enterprise in the Republic of Korea had been granted exclusive privileges as the sole importer of beef. The Panel considered this argument, but noted that Article XVII permitted the establishment of state enterprises and the granting to them of exclusive or special privileges. Hence, the Panel held that mere establishment or granting of such privileges could not violate the GATT.[78]

An explanatory note to Article XVII of GATT 1994 further clarifies that privileges granted for the exploitation of national natural resources but which do not empower the government to exercise control over the trading activities of the enterprise in question, do not constitute exclusive or special privileges.

GENERAL DISCIPLINES

Disciplines on Enterprises

The general disciplines on the enterprise are the following:

(i) In its trading activities, it must act in a manner consistent with the general principles of non-discriminatory treatment prescribed in GATT 1994 for governmental measures affecting imports or exports by private traders. This has been further elaborated to imply that the enterprise must make its purchases and sales solely in accordance with commercial considerations, including factors like price, quality, availability, marketability, transportation, etc. The Panel on Canada – Administration of the Foreign Investment Review Act (February 1984) considered Canada's argument that only the MFN, and not the national treatment, obligations fall within the scope of the general principles referred to here. The Panel "saw great force in Canada's argument", but did not consider it necessary to pronounce on this matter, as it had already found the action inconsistent with Article III of GATT 1994.[79]

(ii) The enterprise must afford the enterprises of other Members an adequate opportunity to compete for participation in its purchases and sales.

Disciplines on Members

The disciplines on Members in relation to the functioning of such enterprises are the following:

(i) A Member must not prevent an enterprise from acting in accordance with commercial considerations and in a non-discriminatory manner.
It is to be particularly noted that this obligation of the Member extends to all enterprises, whether or not they are state trading enterprises.
The Panel mentioned earlier also examined the US argument that Canada's provision obliging investors to export specified quantities is violating Article XVII.1(c) because the export levels of companies subject to such undertakings cannot be assumed to be based on commercial considerations. The Panel found that there is no provision in the GATT which forbids requirements to sell goods in foreign markets in preference to the domestic market; accordingly, it decided that Canada was not violating Article XVII.1(c) by asking for export obligations.

(ii) A Member must inform other interested Members, if so requested, about the import mark-up on the product in a recent representative period, or about the price charged for the product on its resale. The import mark-up is defined in an explanatory note as the margin by which the price charged by the import monopoly exceeds the landed cost.

(iii) A Member must send notification to the WTO Secretariat about its state enterprises, whether or not imports or exports have taken place. The notification should contain the particulars of the enterprises, the products covered by their trading activities, the procedures followed by them, etc. The details of the information which is required are in the questionnaire adopted on 24 May 1960, contained in BISD 9S/184-185.

The disciplines mentioned above do not apply to imports for consumption in governmental use or in the use of the enterprise, if they are not for resale or used for production for sale.

There is a provision for reverse notification. If a Member has reason to believe that another Member has not notified its enterprise properly, it may take it up with the Member concerned. If the matter does not get resolved, the Member may send notification to the Secretariat on its own.

INSTITUTION

A working party has been established on behalf of the Council for Trade in Goods. It will review the notifications and counter-notifications, and work further towards preparing a list showing the relationship between governments and enterprises and also the activities of enterprises which are relevant for Article XVII of GATT 1994.

Chapter VI.6

Part IV of GATT 1994

INTRODUCTION AND BACKGROUND

AFTER about a decade of the functioning of the GATT, it was perceived that developing countries were not in a position to derive benefits from the system which was based on the principle of reciprocity. They were in no position to offer concessions, and therefore, in such a system, they would not be able to get concessions in return. Further, it was difficult for them to fully undertake the obligations of the GATT at their stage of development. Therefore, consideration started being given to changes which would improve the situation. It was in this background that Part IV was formulated and incorporated in the GATT. It contains provisions for the special consideration of developing countries. It was approved on 8 February 1965, and entered into force on 27 June 1966. The time limit for acceptance was extended from time to time until the end of 1979. All contracting parties to the GATT accepted it by that time.

Part IV contains three articles: Article XXXVI, containing the principles and objectives; Article XXXVII, containing the commitments; and Article XXXVIII, containing the provisions for joint action of contracting parties to further the objectives contained in Article XXXVI.

Though these provisions have not been generally accepted by developed countries as contractual obligations which can be subjected to the dispute settlement procedure, the obligations which these Articles impose on the developed countries are very clear. Whether or not these countries act according to these provisions is clearly verifiable. But these have not been taken seriously in the course of implementation.

(The term used for the developing countries in these provisions is "less-developed contracting parties".)

ARTICLE XXXVI

The principles and objectives contained in this provision go to the root of the problem. Some of these are summarised below.

(i) There is a need for a rapid and sustained expansion of the export earnings of the developing countries.

(ii) There is a need to ensure that they secure a share in the growth of international trade commensurate with their economic development needs.

(iii) There is a need for more favourable conditions of market access for the primary products on which many developing countries depend for their export earnings.

(iv) There is a need for increased market access in the largest possible measure for processed and manufactured products of current or potential export interest to developing countries.

(v) The developed countries do not expect reciprocity for commitments made by them in trade negotiations to reduce or remove tariffs and other trade barriers.

ARTICLE XXXVII

In this background, the "commitments" contained in Article XXXVII are particularly important. This Article starts as follows:

"The developed contracting parties shall to the fullest extent possible – that is, except when compelling reasons, which may include legal reasons, make it impossible – give effect to the following provisions..."

This provision may appear to be non-contractual and of the type that is called the "best endeavour" clause, but the language of the commitment is specific, precise and capable of being implemented in terms of actual measures. A developed country is, in fact, liable to be invited to explain what compelling reasons prevented it from taking a particular action.

After this introductory phrase, this Article goes on to specify the actions to be taken. In particular, it provides for the reduction and elimination of trade barriers facing the products of developing countries, including the reduction and elimination of tariffs and tariff escalation in respect of the products of developing countries. Besides, the developed countries are to refrain from introducing or increasing the customs duties on these products and also from imposing new fiscal measures.

The developed countries are also required to give active consideration to the adoption of other measures designed to provide greater scope for the development of imports from developing countries. Such other measures have been further specified in an explanatory note to include steps to promote domestic structural changes, to encourage the consumption of particular products, or to introduce measures of trade promotion.

ARTICLE XXXVIII

This provision stipulates that the contracting parties shall collaborate jointly to further the objectives of Article XXXVI of GATT 1994.

THE COMMITTEE ON TRADE AND DEVELOPMENT

The operation and implementation of these provisions is monitored by the Committee on Trade and Development.

Chapter VI.7

Plurilateral Agreements

THERE were originally four plurilateral agreements in the WTO. These were:

1. Agreement on Trade in Civil Aircraft,

2. Agreement on Government Procurement,

3. International Dairy Agreement, and

4. International Bovine Meat Agreement.

Subsequently the signatories to the last two agreements decided not to continue with them. Hence, now, there are only two plurilateral agreements, viz., (1) and (2) above.

As mentioned earlier, these agreements are not applicable to all Members of the WTO; these are applicable to only those Members that have accepted them. The obligations in these agreements, therefore, are limited to only those Members.

PART VII

AREAS OTHER THAN GOODS

The WTO agreements cover two areas other than goods, viz., services and intellectual property rights. These two areas are discussed in this Part.

The inclusion of these subjects in the framework of GATT/WTO is a significant step. As mentioned in Chapter I.1, the GATT traditionally dealt with only trade in goods. Now, the jurisdiction of the WTO has expanded to cover other areas which are totally unconnected with the trade of goods. Further, the earlier coverage was of measures at the border, whereas now, with the inclusion of services and intellectual property rights, particularly patents, the coverage, in some ways, extends to the production process as well.

Chapter VII.1

SERVICES

INTRODUCTION

THE disciplines in the area of trade in services are prescribed in the General Agreement on Trade in Services (GATS). It is an agreement outside GATT 1994, but is a constituent part of the WTO agreements and is inscribed as Annex 1B of the WTO Agreement. (Annex 1A contains GATT 1994 and other agreements on goods, and Annex 1C contains the Agreement on Trade-Related Aspects of Intellectual Property Rights (TRIPS). GATS has links with the agreements on goods and the Agreement on TRIPS through the dispute settlement process.

FRAME OF COMMITMENTS

This Agreement is in the nature of a framework agreement establishing a framework within which liberalisation commitments in the area of services are to be undertaken and implemented. There are broadly two types of obligations and commitments, viz.:

(i) General obligations, including that of most-favoured-nation (MFN) treatment, i.e., non-discrimination as between Members. These commitments are general in the sense that they are applicable to all sectors, irrespective of the fact whether or not specific commitments have been made in that sector. It is permissible to have initial exemptions from the MFN treatment commitment, and there is a provision for a schedule where all such initial exemptions from MFN treatment should be recorded.

(ii) Specific commitments related to specific sectors. The sectoral commitments are applicable to specific sectors to which they relate. These are included in the respective schedules of the Members which form an integral part of the Agreement.

The Agreement provides a frame for initial commitments, and also for progressively increasing commitments through successive rounds of negotiations.

The general commitments are applicable to all Members and all sectors of services trade. The specific commitments in services sectors are those undertaken by individual Members in particular sectors. The operation of the Agreement started on 1 January 1995 with some specific commitments of Members which had been negotiated by them beforehand with the other Members; further specific commitments will be added through negotiations in the future. The general commitments emerged out of the general negotiations in this area among all the Members. In giving the details of these two types of commitments, the specific commitments will be taken up first, followed by the general commitments. The commitments regarding trade in services, particularly the specific commitments, relate very closely to the mode of supply of the service, i.e., the manner in which the particular service is supplied.

MODES OF SUPPLY

Services can be provided in many ways. Four modes of supply of service have been specified in the Agreement. These are:

(i) supply of service from one country into another country;

(ii) supply of service in a country to the service consumer of another country;

(iii) supply of service by a service supplier of one country through commercial presence in another country;

(iv) supply of service by a service supplier of one country through the presence of natural persons of a country in another country.

The commercial presence mentioned in (iii) above may be had by maintaining an establishment in that country.

A natural person of a country means a person who resides in that country and is a national of that country. In case the country does not have nationals or in case it accords substantially the same treatment to its permanent residents as it does to its nationals, a natural person is one who has the right of permanent residence in that country.

The modes of supply will be further explained in detail later.

SPECIFIC COMMITMENTS

Specific commitments, as mentioned earlier, are those undertaken by individual Members in specific sectors of services. In each of the selected sectors, a Member will have taken commitments in three areas, viz., (i) market access, (ii) national treatment, and (iii) other commitments.

Market Access

In the frame of the Agreement, a Member has to select the sector in which it makes commitments. The sectors left out by the Member are those in which it has not made any commitment on market access. In the sectors selected by the Member for commitments, access has to be freely granted, except if the Member has specified in its commitments some terms, limitations and conditions in the particular service sector. Thus, the schedule of a Member includes the terms, limitations and conditions under which it will allow a particular service to be supplied in its territory by the service suppliers of another country.

A Member has the obligation to allow market access to services in accordance with these commitments.

In sectors where market access commitments have been undertaken, the Agreement specifies some types of measures which the Member "shall not maintain or adopt..., unless otherwise specified in its Schedule..." This seemingly mandatory provision becomes very much discretionary, as exceptions are allowed to be inscribed in the schedule. However, if a Member has not inscribed any limitations regarding these measures in its schedule, it will be bound by the obligation that it will not apply these measures in these sectors. These measures relate to:

(i) limitation on the number of service suppliers, for example, annual quota on the establishment of branches of banks and need for licences for new restaurants based on an economic needs test, i.e., based on the evaluation whether or not a new restaurant is needed in that area;

(ii) limitation on the total value or the total assets of service transactions, for example, limitation of the transactions or assets of branches of banks to a specified percentage of the total domestic transactions or assets of all banks;

(iii) limitation on the total number of service operations or the total quantity of service output, for example, prescribing the maximum weekly duration of the telecast of films;

(iv) limitation on the total number of natural persons that may be employed in supplying a service, for example, the restriction that in computer software services, only a prescribed maximum number of workers can be employed in a year;

(v) restriction or requirement regarding the type of legal entity or joint venture, for example, a restriction that in a particular sector, commercial presence can only be in the form of a company in which the citizens of the country must have a majority shareholding, and

(vi) limitation on the participation of foreign capital, for example, a restriction that a particular form of commercial presence will have a foreign equity ceiling of a specified level.

In successive stages of the liberalisation of service sectors, Members may undertake further market access obligations which will be included in their schedules.

National Treatment

The national treatment obligation of a Member in this context means that the treatment accorded to the services and service suppliers of any other Member must not be less favourable than what the Member accords to its own services and service suppliers.

A Member may, however, prescribe conditions and qualifications to the general obligation of national treatment in any service sector mentioned in its schedule. The treatment could be formally identical or formally different but it will be considered less favourable if it modifies the conditions of competition in favour of domestic services or service suppliers compared to like services or service suppliers of any other Member.

Like in the case of the limitations on measures relating to market access, here, too, a Member will be presumed to be bound by the obligation of unrestricted national treatment in a service sector mentioned in its schedule, except if conditions and qualifications have been inscribed by the Member in its schedule.

Other Commitments

Members may enter into other types of commitments, e.g., those involving competition policy, or qualifications, standards or licensing in respect of trade in services.

Schedules of Specific Commitments

All these specific commitments, as mentioned earlier, are inscribed in the schedule of the particular Member. The obligation of a Member extends to what is in its schedule which includes, along with the commitments and related conditions, the time frame of implementation of the commitments and the date of the entry into force of such commitments.

The schedule of a Member is finalised through negotiations with other Members concerned. Naturally, a Member starts with an offer of low levels of commitments, and when it enters into negotiations with other Members, it has to expand its commitments, keeping in view the interests of other Members and the expectation which it has of other Members regarding their own commitments that may be of interest to it. In this manner, through a series of bilateral and plurilateral (involving a limited number of Members) negotiations, the schedule of a Member is finalised. The general objective is to arrive at an overall balance of costs and benefits and have an overall reciprocity among the Members as a whole. There is no set criterion for establishing this; it evolves through a process of pragmatic approach.

If a sector is not included in the schedule of market access commitments, it would mean that there is no obligation of the Member in that sector in this regard, and it is free to have market access restrictions in that sector, subject, of course, to the general obligations which are applicable to all sectors.

Illustrations of Schedules of Specific Commitments

Some entries of typical schedules are illustrated below.

Mode of supply:
1.cross-border supply 2.consumption abroad 3.commercial presence 4.presence of natural persons

Sector	**Limitation on market access**	**Limitation on national treatment**	**Additional commitment**
Horizontal commitment: All sectors: taxation measures	1.none 2.none 3.none 4.unbound, except as indicated in the horizontal section	1.,2.,3. At federal level with respect to direct taxes: differential tax treatment may be provided between trusts created or organised in the country to provide employment benefits and trusts not created or organised in the country	

Mode of supply:
1.cross-border supply 2.consumption abroad 3.commercial presence
4.presence of natural persons

Sector	Limitation on market access	Limitation on national treatment	Additional commitment
Horizontal commitment: All sectors included in this schedule	3.Services considered as public utilities at a local or national level may be subject to public monopolies or to exclusive rights granted to private operators In the case of collaboration with public sector enterprises as joint venture partners, preference will be given to foreign service suppliers/entities which offer the best terms for transfer of technology 4.unbound, except for measures affecting the entry and temporary stay of natural persons who come on a visit for business negotiations or for preparatory work for establishing a commercial presence in the country	3.Purchase of real estate by foreigners may be subject to authorisation. Eligibility for subsidies may be limited to juridical persons established within the country.Subsidies available to natural persons may be limited to the citizens.	

Mode of supply:
1.cross-border supply 2.consumption abroad 3.commercial presence 4.presence of natural persons

Sector	Limitation on market access	Limitation on national treatment	Additional commitment
Engineering service	1.unbound 2.unbound 3.only through incorporation with a foreign equity ceiling of 51 per cent 4.unbound, except as indicated in the horizontal section	1.unbound 2.unbound 3.none 4.unbound, except as in the horizontal section	
Construction work for civil engineering: Roads and bridges	1.unbound 2.unbound 3.only through incorporation with a foreign equity ceiling of 51 per cent 4.unbound, except as indicated in the horizontal section	1.unbound 2.unbound 3.none 4.unbound, except as indicated in the horizontal section	
Accounting services	1.unbound 2.none 3.Access is restricted to natural persons. Professional associations among natural persons are permitted.Sole proprietorships or ownerships are limited to persons licensed as accountants.	1.unbound 2.none 3.Foreign accountants may enter into partnership with domestic authorised accountants after obtaining permission from Authorised Agency. 4.unbound, except as indicated in the horizontal section.	

Reference to Mode of Supply

The "mode of supply" mentioned above each table refers to the manner in which the service is supplied and is defined in Article I. This was briefly mentioned in the beginning. Now, some more details are explained below.

Cross-border supply:

It is the supply of service from one country into another country. It covers those cases where a service is supplied to a person in a country by a service supplier from outside this country, i.e., by a service supplier that is located in another country. Examples of this mode may be: international transport, supply of service through telecommunication or mail, service embodied in exported goods, like a computer diskette, an engineering drawing, etc.

Consumption abroad:

It is the supply of service by a service supplier in one country to a service consumer of another country. This mode will cover ship repair services when the ship of one country is sent to another country for repair and is repaired there, or it may cover medical services in a hospital of another country.

Commercial presence:

It is the supply of service by a service supplier of one country through commercial presence in another country. In this mode, the service is provided by having an establishment in the country where it is provided. For example, a banking service may be provided by having a subsidiary or a branch of a foreign bank. It may involve the presence of corporations, joint ventures, representative offices, etc.

Presence of natural persons:

> It is the supply of service by a service supplier of one country through the presence of natural persons of that country in another country. This mode of supply of service involves the actual movement of persons across the border. For example, a foreign consultant may travel to the country to supply consultancy services, or some employees of a firm may travel to the country to provide the service which the firm is meant to supply.

In the first two modes of supply of service, the provider of the service is not present in the country which receives the service or where the purchaser of the service is located, whereas in the last two modes, the supplier is present within the country where the service is being supplied and received.

In any mode of supply of service, the obligations and commitments under the Agreement relate to the treatment accorded to the service or the service supplier, and not to the consumer of the service. A Member is able to impose restrictions affecting consumers in its own country, but not those in another country.

Service Needing More Than One Mode of Supply

A special case needs consideration here. There may be cases where a service may need more than one mode of supply. For example, a particular consultancy service may be provided through telecommunication and the presence of natural persons. If, in the schedule of the country relating to this sector, only cross-border supply is allowed, and there is a full limitation on the presence of natural persons, the only way in which this service can be provided is by cross-border supply, e.g., by telecommunication. The consultant or the employees of the consultancy firm will not be able to move to the country to provide this service. Hence, if more than one mode of supply is essential for providing a particular service, such a service can be supplied only if the limitations recorded for this sector permit all these modes of supply.

Horizontal Commitment

The first two illustrative tables given above contain commitments which apply to all sectors covered by the specific commitments. These, of course, do not imply any commitment in respect of sectors which have not been included by a Member in its specific commitments. The third illustrative table relates to the commitments of this country in some specific sectors, namely the engineering services sector, construction services for roads and bridges, and accountancy services.

Details of Different Columns

The first column in the table gives the name of the sector or sub-sector covered by the commitments. It may be based on the Services Sectoral Classification List maintained by the WTO Secretariat, or on the Central Product Classification (CPC) numbers which are contained in the UN Provisional Central Product Classification. One is able to understand the content of the sector or the sub-sector in the schedule by the description given there, and it may not always be necessary to consult these classification systems.

The second column in the table specifies the limitations on market access which the Member wishes to impose. The term "limitations" includes terms, limitations and conditions on the supply of service as envisaged in Article XVI of GATS. The numbers 1, 2, 3 and 4 mentioned in this column as also in the third column relate to the four modes of supply.

The term "unbound" means that the limitations on market access are unbound, i.e., the Member has taken no commitment in respect of that mode in this sector. Hence, the Member is free to impose any restriction on market access in respect of that mode in this sector.

The term "none" means that the Member commits that it will not put any limitation on market access relating to this mode in this sector.

In between these two extremes, there are commitments regarding conditions imposed on market access. A Member will not be permitted to impose more stringent conditions than what are recorded here.

In some places in some schedules, an asterisk is put against "unbound", which would mean that this particular mode of supply may not be technically possible in this sector.

The third column in the table records the limitations on national treatment. The term "limitations" means conditions and qualifications on national treatment. Here, again, the levels of commitments are recorded, as in the second column, by inscribing "unbound" or "none" or by prescribing specific limitations in the form of conditions and qualifications.

If a particular limitation relates to both market access and national treatment, it is given in the second column.

The last column contains additional commitments which do not relate to market access or national treatment. These may, for example, mention commitments regarding qualifications, standards, etc.

The general exceptions (Article XIV of the Agreement) or balance-of-payments measures (Article XII of the Agreement) are not required to be included in the schedule.

Future Rounds of Negotiations

Programme

The initial commitments had been negotiated among the Members before the coming into force of the WTO Agreement and these have been included in their schedules. The Agreement provides for successive rounds of negotiations. The first such round has to start within five years of 1 January 1995 and subsequent rounds will be held later.

Objectives

The objective of the rounds will be to have a progressively higher level of liberalisation. This process has to promote the interests of all participants on a mutually advantageous basis and has to ensure an overall balance of rights and obligations.

Special Treatment of Developing Countries

In respect of the negotiations for specific commitments, there are special provisions for developing countries, as given below.

(i) There will be due respect for national policy objectives and the level of development of individual Members, both as an overall consideration and as a consideration in individual sectors.

(ii) Individual developing countries will have the flexibility of opening up fewer sectors and liberalising fewer types of transactions.

(iii) They will have the flexibility to extend market access progressively in line with their development situation.

(iv) While allowing market access to foreign service suppliers, they may attach conditions aimed at achieving the objectives of strengthening their domestic services capacity, access to technology, improvement of access to information channels and networks, etc.

In this respect, particular priority must be given to the least developed country Members and particular account must be taken of their serious difficulty in undertaking specific commitments in view of their special economic situation and their development, trade and financial needs.

Modification of Schedules

General Limitations and Conditions

A Member may modify its schedule of specific commitments if it is prepared to offer alternative equivalent concessions. A detailed procedure has been laid down for the modification of the schedule by a Member.

The withdrawal or modification of a commitment in the schedule can be done only after three years since the particular commitment became applicable.

Notice

A Member wishing to modify or eliminate any commitment in its schedule (a modifying Member) has first to give a notice of its intention to the Council for Trade in Services at least three months prior to the date when it wants the modification or elimination to take place.

Negotiations

Members will examine this notice and if a Member considers that its benefits under this Agreement may be affected by the action of the modifying Member, it may request for a negotiation. The modifying Member has the obligation to hold a negotiation with such a Member (affected Member). There may be one affected Member or more. The objective of the negotiation will be to arrive at an agreed compensatory adjustment. The general guideline for such a negotiation is that there must be an endeavour to maintain a general level of mutually advantageous commitment which is not less favourable than what was available earlier.

The process of such a negotiation is that the modifying Member makes an offer of new commitments by including either new sectors in the schedule or new commitments in respect of existing sectors. The affected Members examine if it is satisfactory to them. They may accept it or propose some alternative or enhanced commitments from the modifying Member. The negotiation proceeds in this manner, each side weighing the costs and benefits of the offers and requests. A final settlement is arrived at through a practical and pragmatic approach.

Agreement in Negotiation

If an agreement is reached on the new compensatory commitments, they will be included in the schedule of the modifying Member and will be applicable not only to the affected Members but to all Members in accordance with the principle of MFN treatment (to be explained later).

Arbitration in Absence of Agreement

If no agreement is reached within a reasonable time, the affected Members may refer the matter to arbitration. All Members claiming to be affected have to join in the arbitration; otherwise, they lose the benefit of taking countermeasures.

If arbitration has been resorted to, the Members have to abide by its decision. The modifying Member will make compensatory adjustments, i.e., it will introduce new alternative commitments in accordance with the findings of the arbitration, and then carry out the modification or elimination as was proposed.

If the modifying Member has effected the modification or elimination without making compensatory adjustments in accordance with the findings of the arbitration, an affected Member is free to modify or withdraw substantially equivalent benefits from the modifying Member. Such modification or withdrawal will be effected only in respect of the modifying Member, i.e., it will not be operated on an MFN treatment basis.

No Agreement and No Arbitration

If no agreement is reached in the negotiation and yet the request for arbitration is not made, the modifying Member is free to modify or eliminate its commitments as was proposed in its notice.

GENERAL OBLIGATIONS AND DISCIPLINES

As mentioned earlier, there are several obligations and disciplines in the Agreement which are of a general nature, in the sense that they are applicable to all Members in all areas of services. These are explained below.

Most-Favoured-Nation Treatment

Disciplines

The MFN treatment principle, i.e., the principle of non-discrimination as between one Member and another, is applicable in respect of the measures covered by the Agreement. In general, this principle prescribes that the treatment accorded to any country (whether a Member or not) in respect of any measure covered by this Agreement must be accorded to all Members. It is, of course, permissible to accord more favourable treatment to Members than what is provided to a non-Member in respect of the measures covered by this Agreement.

Initial Exemptions

This obligation, however, is not absolutely mandatory. Members are allowed to have measures which are inconsistent with the MFN treatment principle, but such measures should be listed in a schedule which will be an integral part of the Agreement. The conditions for such deviations are mentioned in an Annex to the Agreement.

The Annex provides that the deviations from the MFN treatment principle are in the nature of exemptions from the obligations of the Agreement. Individual Members have listed their exemptions in their schedules. Of course, these would not have been totally unilateral decisions; rather, they would have been finalised only after consultation with interested Members. A Member could take advantage of such exemptions only in the beginning, i.e., only at the time of entry into force of the Agreement, when the exemptions were recorded in the schedule. If one wants to know about the MFN treatment obligations of a Member, this schedule will have to be consulted.

The Council for Trade in Services will review these exemptions within five years of 1 January 1995 and examine if the conditions causing the need for these exemptions are still continuing. The time of any subsequent review will also be fixed.

Generally, these exemptions should not continue for more than 10 years, but there is no binding time limit on their continuance. Of course, during the subsequent rounds of negotiations, these exemptions are likely to come up for consideration.

Later Exemptions

If any Member intends to have an exemption after the coming into force of the WTO Agreement, the process of a waiver under the WTO Agreement will have to be followed. A request for such a waiver will have to be made to the Council for Trade in Services. The Council will consider it and send a report to the Ministerial Conference within 90 days. The Conference will decide on this issue. A waiver can be allowed only by a decision of three-fourths of the Members. The waiver will state the exceptional circumstances in which it has been allowed and the date of its termination.

Illustration of a Schedule of Exemption

An illustrative schedule for MFN exemptions is given below.

Sector or sub-sector	Description of measure indicating its inconsistency with Article II	Countries to which the measure applies	Intended duration	Conditions creating the need for the exemption
Land use: All sectors	Foreigners may not acquire land unless the country of which they are citizens extends a reciprocal right to the citizens of this country	All	Indefinite	Lack of reciprocity
Shipping: Cargo sharing	Special treatment to bilateral treaty partners; equality in freight liftings originating in the ports of partners to the agreement and equality in freight earnings	CI,CII, CIII (countries which are partners to the agreement)	Indefinite	In the context of overall trade relations
Transport: Road transport	Government has discretion to issue trucking licence to persons from contiguous countries on the basis of reciprocity.	CI,CII (countries which are contiguous)	Indefinite	Need to have authority to ensure cross-border operations on the basis of reciprocity

The meaning of the various columns given in this table should be quite clear.

Possibility of Conflict Between General Obligation of MFN and Specific Commitments

Generally, the specific commitments will be applicable on an MFN basis. If a Member has recorded an exemption from MFN treatment, it can grant more favourable treatment to some Members without according it to other Members in terms of the exemption which it has recorded. A problem will arise when a Member records the discriminatory application of a specific commitment in its schedule of specific commitments.

The provision relating to MFN treatment (Article II) and that relating to specific commitments (Articles XVI, XVII, XVIII) appear to have equal validity. There is no provision in the Agreement specifying any precedence of one over the other. Moreover, the language of Article XVI does not clearly rule out non-MFN application of the specific commitments. It says "...each Member shall accord services and service suppliers of any other Member treatment no less favourable than that provided for under the terms, limitations and conditions agreed and specified in its Schedule". The possibility of the terms, limitations and conditions themselves providing for non-MFN treatment is not ruled out. Of course, such a possibility will arise only when a Member is able to carry it through the negotiations for the finalisation of the schedules.

This type of possible conflict will probably get resolved in the course of the operation of the Agreement, based on the actual experience of Members.

Domestic Regulations and Practices to Implement the Agreement

Specific disciplines have been prescribed for domestic regulations which would be adopted to implement the obligations of this Agreement. In particular, disciplines have been prescribed in respect of the review of administrative decisions; the authorisation for supply of service; qualifications, standards and licensing; and the recognition criteria for service suppliers.

Review of Decisions

For implementing the obligations under this Agreement, a Member must establish an administrative or judicial procedure for the review of administrative decisions affecting trade in services. Recourse to such a review should be possible if a service supplier is dissatisfied with an administrative decision. Generally, the review should be carried out by a body which is independent of the administrative agency taking such decisions. In any case, it has to be ensured that the review process provides for an objective and impartial consideration of the issues.

Authorisation for Supply of Service

In case any authorisation is needed for the supply of a service for which specific commitments have been made, the decision of the authorities has to be conveyed within a reasonable period of time. This provision has been made to ensure that unnecessary delays in this regard should not act as a barrier to the supply of services.

Qualification, Standards, Licensing

The Council for Trade in Services will develop, in due course, disciplines for qualification requirements (necessary qualifications of the service supplier), technical standards (of the service) and licensing requirements (for providing the service in a Member country). Pending the formulation and implementation of such disciplines in the Council, a Member must ensure that:

(i) its qualification requirements are based on objective and transparent criteria;

(ii) its technical standards are not more burdensome than necessary to ensure the quality of the service; and

(iii) its licensing procedures are not in themselves a restriction on the supply of service.

Recognition Process

It is expected that Members will adopt criteria or standards for the authorisation, licensing or certification of service suppliers. In order that there be at least some degree of harmonisation among these standards and criteria, the Agreement provides that a Member may recognise:

(i) the education or experience obtained in another country,

(ii) the requirements met in another country, and

(iii) the licences or certifications granted in another country.

Such recognition may be had through harmonisation or through any other process. There may also be a mutual recognition agreement between two Members. Members may strive to have an agreement on harmonisation. They should afford adequate opportunity to other Members to join such harmonisation agreements.

A Member would have had to notify the Council for Trade in Services about its existing recognition measures within 12 months of 1 January 1995. It must inform the Council promptly about any negotiation for harmonisation so that other interested Members may seek the opportunity to join such negotiations. New recognition measures and substantial modifications to existing measures must also be promptly notified to the Council.

Balance-of-Payments Provision

If there is a situation of serious balance-of-payments (BOP) difficulties and external financial difficulties, or if there is a threat of such difficulties, a Member may:

(i) adopt or maintain restrictions on trade in services on which it has undertaken specific commitments, and

(ii) adopt or maintain restrictions on payments or transfers for transactions related to such commitments.

Such measures have to be non-discriminatory as between Members and must not exceed the extent necessary to deal with the BOP problem. These will be temporary measures and must be phased out progressively as the BOP situation improves. A Member, while taking BOP measures, must avoid unnecessary damage to the commercial, economic and financial interests of any other Member.

A Member applying such measures will consult with the Committee on BOP Restrictions in accordance with the procedure established by the Ministerial Conference for this purpose.

A restriction of this type has to be notified by the Member to the General Council.

Exceptions

General Exceptions

There are provisions in the Agreement which allow Members to take measures necessary to protect public morals; to maintain public order; to protect human, animal or plant life; to protect human, animal or plant health; and to secure compliance with laws or regulations relating to: (i) prevention of deceptive and fraudulent practices or dealing with the effects of a default on services contracts, (ii) protection of the privacy of individuals, and (iii) safety.

A Member may take measures inconsistent with the national treatment obligations if the difference in treatment is aimed at ensuring the equitable or effective imposition or collection of direct taxes in respect of the services or service suppliers of other Members.

Measures inconsistent with the MFN treatment obligations may be taken if the difference in treatment is due to an agreement or arrangement on the avoidance of double taxation by which a Member is bound.

Security Exceptions

A Member has the flexibility to take measures which it considers necessary for the protection of its essential security interests and also those which it takes in pursuance of its obligations under the UN Charter for the maintenance of international peace and security.

Government Procurement

The obligations of MFN treatment, specific market access commitments and specific national treatment commitments will not apply to laws, regulations or requirements governing procurement by government agencies for governmental purposes. This exception does not extend to government procurement for commercial resale or for use in the supply of services for commercial sale.

Notification and Transparency

A Member is required to publish promptly all relevant measures of general application which relate to or affect the operation of this Agreement. If publication is not practicable, such information must be made available publicly. A similar requirement concerns the publication of international agreements pertaining to or affecting trade in services to which the Member is a signatory.

A Member has to inform the Council promptly about the introduction of new laws, regulations or administrative guidelines as well as changes in existing ones, if these have significant effects on trade in services covered by its commitments. Such information has to be given at least annually.

A Member may also take recourse to reverse notification, i.e., it may notify the Council about any measure taken by another Member which affects the operation of this Agreement.

A Member has to respond promptly to all requests by any Member for specific information on its measures of general application or on the international agreements mentioned above.

A Member has to establish one or more enquiry points to provide information to other Members, when so requested, on measures of general application, international agreements or measures which the Member is bound to notify to the Council. Such enquiry points must be established within two years of the entry into force of the WTO Agreement. The Council may allow flexibility to developing country Members over this time frame.

Developing Countries

While negotiating specific commitments, special consideration has to be given to certain objectives relating to developing countries which were explained earlier in the section on specific commitments. The inclusion of these objectives in the general obligations makes it obligatory for Members to adhere to them.

Developed country Members, and also developing country Members, to the extent possible, have to establish contact points to facilitate access of developing country service suppliers to information in relation to:

(i) the commercial and technical aspects of the supply of services in their respective countries;

(ii) the registration, recognition and obtaining of professional qualifications in their respective countries; and

(iii) the availability of service technology in their respective countries.

These contact points had to be established within two years of 1 January 1995.

Special priority must be given to the least developed countries in respect of the special provisions made for developing countries as mentioned above.

Economic Integration

A Member may enter into an agreement providing for liberalising trade in services among the parties to the agreement. Though it may not satisfy the condition of MFN treatment, it is permitted in line with the regional arrangements allowed in Article XXIV of GATT 1994.

An important point to note is that such an agreement need not be only among Members. Hence, a Member may even join an agreement of integration where non-Members are also parties.

Such an agreement must have substantial sectoral coverage. It must also provide for the absence or elimination of substantially all discrimination among parties in the sectors covered. This condition does not apply in relation to the provisions regarding restrictions on transfers and payments, BOP measures, security exceptions and general exceptions.

Notification about such agreements or their modification has to be given to the Council.

A Member may also enter into an agreement providing for full integration of labour markets among parties to the agreement. The Agreement clarifies that such integration typically provides the citizens of the parties with a right of free entry into the employment markets of the parties and includes measures concerning conditions of pay and other conditions of employment.

Monopoly Suppliers of Service

There are disciplines regarding the operation of monopoly suppliers of service, somewhat along the lines of those for state trading enterprises in GATT 1994. A monopoly supplier of service in a country could be, for example, a government-owned insurance company which has an exclusive role in the field of insurance in the country, or a railway which may have an exclusive role in this type of transport service, etc. The coverage is, in fact, wider. These disciplines apply even to cases where a government establishes or provides authority to a small number of service suppliers, and substantially prevents competition among those suppliers in the country. In the course of implementation, the connotation of the phrases, "small number of service suppliers" and "substantially prevents competition", will be further clarified.

There are two requirements in respect of monopoly suppliers of service, viz.:

(i) a Member has to ensure that a monopoly supplier of service of its territory does not act in a manner inconsistent with the obligations of the Member regarding MFN treatment and specific commitments;

(ii) when such a supplier competes for the supply of a service outside the scope of the monopoly and yet in a sector covered by the obligations of the Member, the Member has to ensure that the supplier does not abuse its monopoly position to act in a manner inconsistent with the commitments of the Member.

If a new monopoly right is granted in the area of trade in services after 1 January 1995, the Member has to follow the procedure for modification of its commitments which has been explained above.

Competition-Restrictive Practices

There is a provision for consultations between Members on trade-restrictive business practices of service suppliers. If a Member considers that the business practices of a service supplier are restraining competition and are thereby restricting trade in services, it may request consultation with the Member concerned. The other Member has to enter into consultation with a view to eliminating these practices.

In actual practice, how far this provision will be effective is doubtful. The Agreement merely provides for consultation among Members and an obligation to cooperate through supplying publicly available non-confidential information. However, the very entry of this provision is significant as GATT 1994 does not have such a provision in respect of goods. The closest that the GATT came to handling this subject was in 1960, when a decision was taken by the CONTRACTING PARTIES which provided for consultations on a bilateral or multilateral basis on this question. The decision required a government to take such measures as it deemed appropriate to eliminate these measures if, during a bilateral consultation, it was agreed by the responding party that harmful effects of restrictive business practices (RBPs) were present in a particular case. This decision has remained almost totally inoperative.[80]

The provisions on RBPs in the area of services may evolve over a course of time depending upon the perception of Members about the impact of restrictive trade practices on the development of services trade. The seriousness with which Members will view this problem will depend on the intensity of this perception.

Payments and Transfers

Disciplines

The Agreement prohibits the application of restrictions on international transfers and payments for current transactions which are related to the specific commitments of a Member. Besides, it also prohibits the imposition of restrictions on any capital transaction which are inconsistent with the specific commitments of a Member regarding such transactions. The only exception to this discipline in respect of current transactions is action for BOP reasons. The exceptions in respect of capital transactions are: (i) action for BOP reasons and (ii) action at the request of the International Monetary Fund (IMF) in pursuance of the Articles of Agreement of the IMF.

Certain specific disciplines have been prescribed in the footnote to Article XVI of GATS. If a Member has undertaken a commitment of market access through the cross-border mode of supply of service and if cross-border movement of capital is an essential part of the service itself, the Member, in such a case, is committed to allowing such movement of capital. Further, in the case of a commitment of market access through the mode of commercial presence, a Member is committed to allowing related transfers of capital into its territory.

Possibility of Conflict with Specific Commitment

As in the case of MFN treatment, there is a scope for conflict between the operation of the disciplines on transfers and payments on the one hand and the specific commitments on market access on the other. Article XVI on market access prescribes that a Member cannot accord a treatment less favourable than what is contained in its schedule. The schedule can have terms, limitations and conditions. The Article relating to payments and transfers and this Article relating to market access have equal validity and neither is specified as having priority over the other. A conflict will arise when a Member has included in its schedule restrictions on payments and transfers. (Of course, a restriction can be put in the schedule only after the Member is able to persuade other Members about it during the negotiations on this entry in its schedule. Such an eventuality may arise when a Member seeks to balance a larger coverage of sectors in its specific commitments with a possible flexibility regarding payments and transfers. Other Members may sometimes find this attractive and permit it.)

Such conflicts between the general and specific commitments may probably get resolved in the course of the operation of GATS, as mentioned in the case of MFN treatment earlier.

SAFEGUARD MEASURES, SUBSIDIES, GOVERNMENT PROCUREMENT

Disciplines in respect of safeguards and subsidies will be evolved in future negotiations. In the meantime, some interim provisions have been prescribed in the Agreement. Disciplines relating to government procurement will also be evolved in future negotiations.

If a Member considers that it must take safeguard measures in respect of any service sector covered by the Agreement, i.e., if it considers the necessity of withdrawing or modifying any specific commitment within three years of the coming into force of this commitment, it may notify the Council about it. Two following preconditions are laid down for this action:

(i) An emergency safeguard measure cannot be taken in respect of a commitment within one year of the coming into force of that commitment.

(ii) The Member has to show to the Council that the modification or withdrawal of the commitment cannot await the lapse of the three-year period when, in any case, the Member can give notice for modification or withdrawal.

There is no specific provision regarding compensatory adjustments in respect of the emergency safeguard measure, as in the case of the modification or withdrawal of a commitment after three years. But since the emergency safeguard measure is not likely to have a softer passage than the modification of commitments, it can be presumed that compensatory adjustments, at least on the scale relevant for the modification process, will also be applicable for the emergency safeguard process.

There is one clear guideline regarding future negotiations on the question of emergency safeguard measures. It has been stipulated that these will be based on the principle of non-discrimination.

In respect of future negotiations to evolve disciplines in the field of subsidies, there is a provision in the Agreement that these negotiations shall recognise the role of subsidies in relation to the development programmes of developing countries and take into account the needs of Members, particularly developing country Members, for flexibility in this area.

There is no restriction on the application of subsidies in the field of services in the meantime, except what is implied in the provisions of the Agreement. For example, the provision of a subsidy may be construed to violate the national treatment principle contained in Article XVII, if the particular sector has been included in the schedule of specific commitments, but conditions and qualifications regarding subsidies have not been recorded in it. If any Member considers that it is adversely affected by a subsidy applied by any other Member, it may enter into the process of consultation with the other Member.

On government procurement, there is already an exception in respect of the commitments on market access and national treatment. The Agreement provides that there will be multilateral negotiations on government procurement in services within two years of 1 January 1995.

CONSULTATION AND DISPUTE SETTLEMENT

There are special provisions for consultation and dispute settlement, some of which do not exactly follow Articles XXII and XXIII of GATT 1994.

If a Member considers that there is any matter affecting the operation of the Agreement which needs solution, it may request consultation with any other Member concerned with this matter. The other Member so requested has to enter into consultation with the requesting Member and has to accord sympathetic consideration to the representation made by the requesting Member.

The occasion for such a consultation arises when a Member having a grievance against another Member for some of its actions or for its failure to take some action, considers that it is necessary to have the grievance redressed.

The process of the Dispute Settlement Understanding (DSU), explained in the chapter on the dispute settlement process, applies to such consultations.

If a matter is not satisfactorily resolved through the consultations mentioned above, the Council for Trade in Services or the Dispute Settlement Body (DSB) may hold consultations with a Member or Members to resolve the matter.

A Member may take recourse to the DSU if:

(i) it considers that any other Member has failed to carry out its obligations or specific commitments under this Agreement; or

(ii) it considers that any benefit reasonably expected under a specific commitment of another Member is being nullified or impaired as a result of any measure which is not in conflict with the provisions of this Agreement (the so-called "non-violation" case).

Once recourse to the DSU is taken, the process of the DSU will be followed, which is described in detail in the chapter on the dispute settlement process.

In the "non-violation" cases, if the DSB finds that the allegation is true, the affected Member shall be entitled to a satisfactory adjustment of the matter. Such an adjustment may be in the form of the modification or withdrawal of the measure, or compensation. If no adjustment has been possible, the Member may be allowed to take retaliatory action through the suspension of concessions or other obligations in respect of the offending Member. This process will be described in detail in the chapter on the dispute settlement process.

ANNEXES ON SPECIFIC ISSUES AND SECTORS

Annexes have been included in this Agreement on the movement of natural persons and on some specific service sectors, viz., air transport, maritime transport, financial services and telecommunication services. The objective in having these specific sectors in the Annex was to have negotiations on these issues and sectors in order to finalise their coverage, and the related obligations and specific commitments of Members. Negotiations have since been conducted in these areas in the WTO.

The negotiations in the maritime services sector have been postponed. The negotiations in the area of movement of natural persons have been closed. Comprehensive agreements have been reached in the telecommunication services and financial services sectors.

Chapter VII.2

Trade-Related Aspects of Intellectual Property Rights (TRIPS)

INTRODUCTION

The Title

THE title, "trade-related aspects of intellectual property rights", of this WTO agreement owes its origin more to the historical process of the negotiations of the Uruguay Round than to the actual content of the subjects covered. There is actually nothing related to trade in this agreement; it is all about the protection of intellectual property rights (IPRs).

A large number of countries participating in the negotiations had initially objected to the inclusion of IPRs in GATT negotiations on the grounds that the subject was covered by another organisation, viz., the World Intellectual Property Organisation (WIPO) and also because the GATT had jurisdiction only in the field of trade. As a compromise, the subject of the negotiations was termed trade-related intellectual property rights, and it was thought that it would cover only the matters related to trade. For a long time, several countries continued to oppose the inclusion of substantive matters of intellectual property in the negotiations, and kept on insisting that only the trade effects should be discussed. But finally, it was agreed that all issues relating to IPRs, including the standards of protection, would be negotiated. In this process, the link with trade has almost vanished, and yet the original name remains. In this way, the agreement is called the Agreement on Trade-Related Aspects of Intellectual Property Rights (the Agreement on TRIPS). It forms a part of the WTO agreements.

Differing Interests

An intellectual property is a creation of the mind; for example, a technological innovation, a poem or a design of a dress. Those who make these creations deserve adequate returns so that there are enough incentives for creativity. For this reason, their creations should be accorded protection. However, the general public that benefits from such creations should not be expected to pay unreasonably high prices. The balance between the remuneration to the innovator and artist on the one hand, and the genuine interests of the public on the other, has been a subject of debate for a long time. Various countries tried to have their own balance. Multilateral agreements were also reached in the WIPO, laying down the rules for the protection of intellectual property and the limitations on protection.

Importance of Intellectual Property

Many developed countries felt, for some years, that the protection of IPRs needed much more strengthening than what was possible through the WIPO agreements. In the wake of rapid technological development, reaping the full benefits of their technological innovations was important for them. In the emerging world economic and trade scene, their prospects lay mainly in knowledge-intensive, high-technology sectors of industrial production and services. It was vital for them to provide strengthened and assured protection to their innovations. This objective assumed added urgency in view of their perception that their technological innovations, particularly in the sectors of pharmaceuticals and electronics, were liable to be copied easily in several countries, reducing their own rents on novelty.

Relevance of the GATT as a Forum for IPRs

In this background, though the GATT had nothing to do with IPRs, the developed countries' aim was to bring IPRs into its folds, where the obligations on protection could be expanded during the multilateral trade negotiations, and enforced along with the obligations on international trade. Their main objectives were to enhance the protection standards in respect of patents in developing countries and to ensure effective implementation. This would benefit the present and future patent-holders who, in large measure, were and were likely to be in developed countries. With this aim in view, the developed countries got the subject introduced in the Uruguay Round of MTNs, and finally, a comprehensive agreement on the standards of protection and enforcement was concluded.

Area Covered and Disciplines

The Agreement prescribes minimum standards for Members in various areas of intellectual property. There is, however, some flexibility in the manner of application, as will be explained later while discussing various areas covered by the Agreement.

The Agreement includes in its folds, seven types of intellectual property, viz. (i) patents, (ii) copyright, (iii) trademarks, (iv) geographical indications, (v) industrial designs, (vi) layout-designs of integrated circuits and (vii) undisclosed information. These terms will be explained in the respective sections.

The disciplines contained in the Agreement include minimum standards of protection of IPRs, limitations and other conditions, and enforcement of obligations.

Role of Governments

The provisions of the Agreement are addressed to Members, and the disciplines contained in the provisions are applicable to them. They have to discharge these obligations by implementing the Agreement through their respective domestic legislation which are expected to incorporate the rights and obligations of an IPR-holder and the manner in which these will be enforced in a particular Member country. The IPR-holder and the user of intellectual property will take recourse to the domestic administrative or legal means to enforce the rights and obligations. In the multilateral forum of the WTO, a Member is responsible for the establishment of the necessary administrative and legal framework and for ensuring that the machinery works.

BASIC OBJECTIVES, PRINCIPLES AND GENERAL OBLIGATIONS

Objectives and Principles

The broad objectives of the incorporation and enforcement of the disciplines on IPRs, as mentioned in the Agreement, are:

(i) promotion of technological innovation;

(ii) transfer and dissemination of technology;

(iii) contribution to the mutual advantage of producers and users of technological knowledge conducive to social and economic welfare; and

(iv) contribution to the balance of rights and obligations.

While formulating the implementing legislation, Members have some flexibility in adopting measures which are necessary to:

(i) protect public health and nutrition;

(ii) promote the public interest in sectors of vital importance to their socio-economic and technological development;

(iii) prevent the abuse of IPRs by right-holders;

(iv) prevent resorting to practices which unreasonably restrain trade; or

(v) prevent resorting to practices which adversely affect the international transfer of technology.

If a Member uses such flexibility, it has to be done in a manner that is consistent with the provisions of the Agreement.

The inclusion of these basic objectives and principles in the Agreement is very significant. These will be the main guiding factors for the Members in the exercise of their discretion provided for at various places in the Agreement. For example, there are provisions for exceptions, conditions and limitations on IPRs and also ample scope for discretion at various other places. A Member will be well justified in making appropriate provisions in its legislation based on these objectives and principles, which are quite broad and yet very specific. For example, the concern for the public interest and for the prevention of abuses of IPRs by the right-holder may motivate a Member to prescribe appropriate restrictions on the rights.[81]

Most-Favoured-Nation Treatment and National Treatment

The general most-favoured-nation (MFN) treatment is applicable in respect of the protection of intellectual property. Thus, the benefits of the provisions of the Agreement have to be extended to all Members in a non-discriminatory manner. The particular importance of the MFN treatment obligation is that Members cannot exchange special concessions on these subjects in bilateral deals.

The national treatment principle is also applicable, which means that a Member must not accord less favourable treatment to the nationals of other Members than what it accords to its own nationals.

The implication of national treatment, in the areas covered by the Agreement, lies in the restriction that a Member cannot give any special protection to its domestic innovators or innovations which it does not give to foreign ones.

These obligations are subject to some conditions which largely cover the obligations on these subjects taken by a Member in various international agreements outside this Agreement.

Exhaustion

National laws and procedures in the area of exhaustion of IPRs cannot be challenged through the dispute settlement process. The only condition is that the principles of MFN treatment and national treatment have to be respected in this regard. The concept of exhaustion and the significance of its exclusion from the dispute settlement process need some elaboration. Although it appears to have been accorded only a passing reference in the Agreement, it is very important. It has an implication for the limitation on the exclusive rights of the IPR-holder.

According to the principle of exhaustion of IPRs, once the IPR-holder has sold the product covered by the IPR, the IPR-holder cannot thereafter have any control on the later stages of the marketing of the product. The IPR is deemed to have been exhausted after the first sale. Various countries have different provisions regarding the exhaustion of IPRs in their domestic laws and practices.[82]

The implication of the application of the principle of exhaustion of IPRs is significant. For example, when a patent-holder sells the patented product, the buyer is free to use it in any way he/she likes, including selling it and exporting it to another country. Let us presume that a product is patented in a country C and it is sold to a buyer in that country. A person in another country D imports it for sale in country D where this product is also patented. Since the patent right has been exhausted in country C after the first sale in that country, the patent-holder cannot stop the export of the product to country D, which can consider it legal to import this product from C, after it has been put on the market in C. This process has been called "parallel import", to distinguish it from the normal import of the product with the authorisation of the patent-holder. If the patented product normally sells at higher prices in D, the parallel import from C may push the prices down, whereby the consumers will benefit.

As various countries have their own systems on this subject, the effect of exhaustion will depend on the particular system and practice prevalent in the country. A Member is free to have its own provisions in this regard. In fact, it may be an important tool to protect the interest of consumers and to ensure the availability of industrial and agricultural inputs as well as essential drugs at competitive prices.[83]

PATENTS

General, Paris Convention

Patents relate to scientific and technological innovations in various industrial and service sectors. A government registers the patent and, thereby, confers certain exclusive rights on the patent-holder regarding the subject of the patent.

The multilateral agreement on patents has been the Paris Convention for the Protection of Industrial Property (1967), popularly called the Paris Convention (1967).[84] It covers the protection of industrial property, which includes patents, utility models, industrial designs, trademarks, service marks, trade names, and indications of source or appellations of origin. Utility models, which relate to minor functional modifications as distinct from significant innovations covered by patents, are left out of the Agreement on TRIPS. Further, the subject of trade names has also been left out. The rest of the subjects are covered by various parts of the Agreement on TRIPS.

The Agreement incorporates Articles 1 to 12 and Article 19 of the Paris Convention (1967). These articles cover the protection of various industrial property rights, national treatment, right of priority, compulsory licensing, provision for seizure of articles, safeguards against unfair competition, special agreements among countries, etc. The Agreement specifically provides that Members must comply with these provisions of the Paris Convention (1967). Thus, the implementation of these provisions of this agreement administered by the WIPO is ensured through the implementation machinery of the Agreement on TRIPS in the WTO.

Eligibility for Patenting

Patentable Subjects

Basic Eligibility

The Agreement makes it obligatory on Members to make patents available to all inventions. The conditions are that the invention should be:

(i) new, i.e., it should not have been invented by somebody earlier, or, at least, should not have been publicly disclosed;

(ii) involving an inventive step, i.e., it should be non-obvious, meaning, thereby, that it should be the result of a serious exercise of mind; and

(iii) capable of industrial application, i.e., it should be useful, meaning, thereby, that it should not be limited to the thought process, but should be applicable in having a new product or process, or in improving the functioning of an existing product or process.

The obligations on Members are that:

(i) the patent must be available to both products and processes;

(ii) the patent must be available and patent rights enjoyable without discrimination regarding: (a) the place of invention, (b) the field of technology, and (c) whether products are imported or locally produced.

Possibility of Flexibility

The various terms mentioned here have not been defined in the Agreement. In fact, there is considerable flexibility for the Member to define these terms in its domestic legislation so as to reflect its own objectives in this field. For example, if the Member wishes to give protection to the interests of an established innovator, it may define "invention" in a wider way, so that new innovations which approximate the earlier ones are not considered to satisfy the condition of novelty. On the other hand, if it wishes to encourage new innovators, it may define this term narrowly, thus permitting the patenting of innovations which approximate the already patented matter. It can also use the flexibility of definitions to reflect its national objectives in balancing the interests of innovators and consumers.

The subject of a patent should be an invention, and not merely a discovery of something already existing in nature which was not known earlier. For example, it is possible for a Member to refuse patents for biological or genetic materials which have been in existence, though these were not known earlier.

Implication of Product Patent

It is important to note the significance of the patent of a product as against the patent of a process. In a case of the patent being limited to a process, it is possible for another innovator to develop the same final product through an alternative process. On the other hand, in a case of the patent covering a product, another innovator is debarred from producing that product even through any alternative method which this innovator might have developed. Thus, the whole process of further scientific and technological research on obtaining the particular product by various alternative methods is stopped by allowing the patent of the product.

Coverage of All Areas

The significance of the obligation to grant patents and permit the enjoyment of patent rights without discrimination regarding the field of technology lies in the fact that Members do not have the discretion to exclude patents from any specific sector, nor can they abridge patent rights exclusively in any sector. This is important in the context of several countries which have had a somewhat relaxed patents regime in some sectors, particularly pharmaceuticals.

Countrywise Patent

A patent is applicable to each jurisdiction, i.e., the registration for the patent is done in each country and validity is limited to the jurisdiction of that country. Thus, if an innovator wants to have the patent rights in different countries, registrations will have to be obtained in all of them.

Exceptions to Patentability

Certain types of inventions may be excluded from patentability at the discretion of a Member.

If it is necessary to prevent the commercial exploitation of an invention, the Member may leave it out of the scope of patentability. The reasons for this prevention could be any of the following:

(i) to protect *ordre public* or morality,

(ii) to protect human, animal or plant life or health, or

(iii) to avoid serious prejudice to the environment.

The following subjects may also be excluded from patentability:

(i) diagnostic, therapeutic and surgical methods for the treatment of humans or animals.

(ii) plants and animals.

(iii) essentially biological processes for the production of plants or animals.

However, it is clarified in the Agreement that, in spite of the above exclusions, some subjects must be covered by patentability. These are:

(i) micro-organisms, e.g., bacteria, viruses, fungi, algae, protozoa, etc., and

(ii) non-biological and microbiological processes for the production of plants and animals.

The various terms mentioned here have not been defined in the Agreement; there is a considerable scope of flexibility in this regard for a Member to define them in harmony with its national objectives.

It is relevant to note that plants and animals have been excluded from the obligation of patents, irrespective of their mode of production. For example, plants and animals, even though produced by modifications through genetic engineering (transgenic plants or animals) or other methods, need not be covered by patents.

However, the "processes" for the production of plants and animals have to be given patents, if these are non-biological or microbiological.

Plant Varieties, **Sui Generis** *System*

Even though plants themselves are excluded, plant varieties have to be covered by some form of effective protection, either by patents or by an effective *sui generis* system, or by a combination of both. The making of varieties refers to bringing about improvements by breeding techniques to create stable and uniform objects with different characteristics. This obligation does not extend to the protection of animal varieties.

UPOV, Objectives

There is considerable flexibility for a Member to introduce its own *sui generis* system. One example of such a system is UPOV (UPOV stands for Union Internationale pour la Protection des Obtentions Végétales, i.e., the International Convention for the Protection of New Varieties of Plants). UPOV was signed in 1961 and came into force in 1968. Earlier, the applied version of this Convention was UPOV 1978. Then, a revised version, UPOV 1991, was negotiated and it has come into effect.[85]

The objective of UPOV is to grant certain exclusive rights to plant breeders who develop new varieties of plants. Normally, farmers provide the source material to the breeders for the development of new varieties. They are also the users of the new varieties developed by the breeders. There is a need for a balance between the breeder's rights and what has been called the farmer's privilege.

UPOV 1978

UPOV 1978 confers exclusive rights to breeders in respect of the marketing, selling and producing for commercial marketing of the propagating material (e.g., seeds, cuttings, etc.) of the new plant variety. There are some important limitations as given below:

(i) The right does not extend to the harvests from these plants; for example, the fruits from fruit plants are not covered.

(ii) The right is limited to production for commercial marketing, and thus, does not extend to production of seed by a farmer for use in his own farm.

(iii) The use of the protected variety by another breeder for creating further new varieties is allowed (breeder's exemption).

(iv) Not all genera and species need be protected. A minimum of five genera has to be covered at the time of acceding to the agreement, with progressively higher coverage, providing for the coverage of at least 24 genera after eight years.

UPOV 1991

UPOV 1991 is much more heavily weighted in favour of the breeder's rights. Some of the important differences with UPOV 1978 are given below.

(i) The right extends also to the harvested material under certain conditions.

(ii) The coverage of protection is also much more extensive; for example, it covers rights in respect of reproduction, propagation, conditioning, stocking for these purposes, etc.

(iii) It extends the breeder's rights to all production and reproduction of the variety.

(iv) The farmer's privilege is an exception here, which may be incorporated by States in respect of seeds saved and retained on the farm.

(v) A variety essentially derived from a protected variety cannot be exploited without the permission of the breeder of the variety from which the new one has been derived. Thus, the right of the breeder of the source variety has been taken care of, but the right of the farmer, who is the real original source, has not been considered.

It is really not necessary for a Member to adopt either of these models, but they can provide guidelines. Members are quite free to evolve their own effective *sui generis* system of protection.

The provisions of the Biodiversity Convention also provide some guidelines in this respect.

What will be considered "effective" has not been clarified;

perhaps it may be a subject of consideration in the Council for TRIPS; hence, a Member should be prepared to argue that the system it has adopted is effective.

Rights of Patent-Holder and Exceptions

Rights

The rights of a patent-holder have been separately prescribed for a patent in respect of a product and that in respect of a process.

For a patent on a product, the patent-holder has the right to prevent any other person from making, using, selling, offering for sale, or importing the patented product without the consent of the patent-holder.

For a patent on a process, the patent-holder has the right to prevent any other person from:

(i) using the process without the consent of the patent-holder;

(ii) using, selling, offering for sale, or importing the product directly obtained by the process, without the consent of the patent-holder.

The footnote to Article 28 clarifies that the rights relating to use, sale, importation and distribution of goods are subject to the provisions relating to exhaustion. It can be construed that parallel imports, as explained earlier, are permissible.

Exceptions

Limitations to Exceptions

The Agreement allows limited exceptions to the rights of the patent-holder. The conditions are the following:

(i) such exceptions do not unreasonably conflict with a normal exploitation of the patent;

(ii) the exceptions do not unreasonably prejudice the legitimate interests of the patent-holder; and

(iii) the exceptions take into account the legitimate interests of third parties.

Various qualifying terms used here have not been clarified; hence, there may be ample scope for differences of opinion. Clarity will emerge during the course of the operation of the Agreement.

Exception for Experimental Use

Based on prevailing practices, it does appear reasonable to assume that the limited exceptions cover the use of patented products or processes for scientific or technological experiments in pursuit of further scientific development. In fact, for countries which wish to encourage domestic innovation, it may be desirable to provide a limited exception that patented matter may be put to experimental use without the authorisation of the patent-holder. It may enable domestic innovators to experiment with this matter and bring about further improvements, particularly those suited to local conditions. A certain degree of reverse engineering (i.e., proceeding backwards from the patented product to learn how it has been produced) is inevitable in this process, which may be of help to new innovators working on the further development of patented matter.

Obligation While Filing Application

Full Disclosure of Patentable Matter

Members are obliged to prescribe that an application for a patent must disclose fully the invention sought to be patented. In particular, the disclosure has to be clear and complete, so that an expert in the field can carry out the same invention. Further, Members may require the applicant to indicate the best mode for carrying out the invention as known to the inventor.

This obligation of the applicant is meant to ensure that the subject of the patent comes within the public domain of knowledge, and does not remain a secret. The advantages of such a disclosure are that:

(i) all interested persons come to know the source of a particular technology;

(ii) other innovators may be in a position to carry forward further scientific and technological development; and

(iii) at the expiry of the patent period, it may be possible for all interested persons to use the patented subject freely.

This obligation of disclosure is particularly useful for countries that do not have much domestic innovation and wish to encourage it. The information can be of immense help to domestic innovators who can work around a particular innovation and also come up with new processes and products based on the existing patented matter.

Treatment of Application in Other Countries

There is an enabling provision that a Member may require an applicant for a patent to provide information about the treatment of its application in other countries if it has been filed there. This will facilitate the examination of the application. The facts considered by the authorities in other countries while accepting or rejecting the application can be taken into account while considering the application in this country. It may be particularly useful to determine novelty.

Term of Patent

The minimum term of a patent is 20 years counted from the filing date.

Determination of Equivalents

The qualification of a particular innovation to be patented will depend a good deal on the determination of equivalents by the Member. If the patent equivalents are kept narrow, there will be more scope for competition among prospective innovators, as another innovator can come up with an innovation which is close to one patented earlier and yet falls outside the range of equivalents. For countries which do not have, at present, a high base of domestic innovation and want to encourage small innovators, it may be preferable to have a narrow range of equivalents so that, amidst the flow of foreign innovations, domestic innovators also have some chance of evolving patents in ranges outside those covered by the existing patents.

Use Without Authorisation, Compulsory Licensing

There are elaborate provisions for the use of a patent without the authorisation of the patent-holder. A government may sometimes give a licence to a person to use a patent without the authorisation of the patent-holder. This is called compulsory licensing or non-voluntary licensing to distinguish it from the licence given voluntarily by the patent-holder. Further, instead of giving a licence to another person, a government may itself use a patent without the authorisation of the patent-holder.

The grounds on which such use without authorisation, either through compulsory licensing or through direct government use, can be allowed have not been specified in the Agreement. Certain conditions, procedures and limitations have, however, been laid down. Since the grounds have not been specifically prescribed, there is a certain degree of flexibility in this process. A Member may draw on the basic guiding objectives and principles which are contained in Articles 7 and 8, particularly the latter, viz., the need to protect public health and nutrition or to promote the public interest in the context of socio-economic and technological development or to prevent the abuse of IPRs. These have been explained earlier. The Agreement does not require a Member to justify the grounds on which the compulsory licensing process is resorted to.

A point which has been the subject of extensive discussion is whether the non-working of a patent (patented product not being produced or patented process not being applied in the country where the patent has been granted) can be a valid ground for granting a compulsory licence. The argument against it is derived from Article 27.1 of the Agreement which mentions that patent rights will be enjoyable without discrimination whether the products are imported or locally produced. Hence, it is argued that even if a patented product is not locally produced, but is made available through imports, this situation of non-working, by itself, may not be a sufficient ground for granting a compulsory licence.

On the other hand, the arguments for it are the following. The Paris Convention allows it and its related provision has been incorporated in the Agreement on TRIPS. Article 2 of the Agreement says that Members shall comply with these provisions of the Paris Convention.

The Agreement does not specifically prohibit it. Further, in respect of Article 27.1, one should be guided by what has been directly said and not draw conclusions by implication. This Article merely requires that the patent-holder must be allowed to enjoy the patent rights, irrespective of the fact whether a product is locally produced or imported. All it means is that the patent-holder should have similar rights in respect of the product obtained in either of these ways.

On considering all this, some experts have held that having a provision in the national legislation for compulsory licensing for non-working will not be considered to be a violation of the Agreement.

There is, of course, the aspect of the public interest. Imports imply an outgo of foreign exchange, and the public interest may be adversely affected in this process if the country does not have an abundance of foreign exchange. Besides, the price of the product may be high because of sole dependence on imports, and this may also adversely affect the public interest. In such circumstances which flow out of the non-working of patents, it may be reasonable to conclude that compulsory licensing could be a justified course of action.

Conditions and Limitations

As mentioned earlier, specific conditions, limitations and procedures for use without authorisation have been prescribed. The primary conditions are that:

(i) the proposed user of the patent should have made efforts to get authorisation from the patent-holder on reasonable terms and conditions; and

(ii) authorisation could not be obtained within a reasonable period.

What is "reasonable" in these cases has not been clarified; as such, there may be considerable flexibility in laying down these conditions in the domestic legislation.

There are some specific limitations, viz.:

(i) the scope and duration of the authorisation (of uses not authorised by the patent-holder) will be limited to the purpose for which it was given;

(ii) there may be earlier termination of the authorisation if the circumstances leading to it do not exist any more and are not likely to recur;

(iii) the authorisation must be non-exclusive and non-assignable;

(iv) the use of the patent must be predominantly for the supply of resultant products to the domestic market;

(v) the request for authorisation must be considered on a case-by-case basis.

Remuneration

The patent-holder has to be paid adequate remuneration. Guidelines on what would be adequate have not been given; hence, there is considerable discretion in this respect. The remuneration has to be decided in accordance with the circumstances in each case. Further, the economic value of the authorisation will be taken into account. While considering the circumstances, one may, for example, differentiate between the proposed use of the patent for meeting some social need and use for purely industrial or commercial interests. The determinants of the economic value could be: the size of the possible market, the type of technology, the degree of competition from substitute products, the speed of obsolescence, etc.[86]

Judicial Review

There must be provisions for the review of the decisions on authorisation and remuneration by a judicial or other independent authority.

Anti-Competitive Practice

When a judicial or administrative process has determined a practice to be anti-competitive, and if a remedy is to be applied through compulsory licensing, two of the above conditions and limitations will not apply, viz.:

(i) the condition that the proposed user must make prior efforts to get authorisation is not necessary;

(ii) there will be no limitation that the use of the compulsory licence will be predominantly for supply to the domestic market.

While determining the amount of remuneration, the need to correct anti-competitive practices may be taken into account.

Government Use

In the case of use of the patent by governments in cases of national emergency or other circumstances of extreme urgency or in cases of public non-commercial use, the requirement that the proposed user should have made efforts to obtain authorisation may be waived. However, in these cases, the patent-holder has to be informed. The other conditions, limitations and procedures will, of course, be applicable even in such cases.

Dependent Patent

This provision relates to cases where a patent (second patent) cannot be exploited without infringing another patent (first patent). For a compulsory licence in the case of the second patent, the following additional conditions will apply:

(i) the second patent must involve an invention which is an important technical advance of considerable economic significance compared to the invention involved in the first patent;

(ii) the owner of the first patent will be entitled to a cross-licence to use the second patent on reasonable terms;

(iii) the use of the first patent will be non-assignable except with the assignment of the second patent.

Burden of Proof in Process Patent

If there is a process patent for manufacturing a product, and if an identical product is produced without the consent of the patent-holder, the presumption will be that it has been produced by using the patented process. In such a case, the burden of proof is on the defendant to show that the product has, in fact, been produced by using another process. The condition, however, is that:

(i) the product obtained by the patented process should be new; or

(ii) there is a substantial likelihood that the identical product was made by the patented process, and the patent-holder is unable to determine the process actually used even though reasonable efforts have been made to ascertain it.

The definition of "new" could give some flexibility to the Member to define the scope of the burden of proof in this case.

Exclusion of Semi-Conductor

There is a specific provision for the use without authorisation of the patent-holder in the case of semi-conductor technology. It can be permitted only in two situations, viz. (i) government use for non-commercial purposes, and (ii) to remedy any anti-competitive practice which has been determined to be such in a judicial or administrative process.

COPYRIGHT AND RELATED RIGHTS

This part of the Agreement covers copyright and other related rights which are sometimes called the "neighbouring rights" or "rights neighbouring on copyright", covering, generally, the rights of performing artists in their performances, the rights of producers of phonograms (i.e., sound recordings) in their phonograms, and the rights of broadcasting organisations in their radio and television programmes.

Copyright

Coverage

The Agreement incorporates Articles 1 to 21 of the Berne Convention (1971), excluding Article 6*bis*. The Berne Convention (1971)[87] covers the protection of the rights of authors in their literary and artistic works and the protection of cinematographic works as well as works of architecture. The articles of the Berne Convention referred to here define the various types of works getting protection and the works derived from them, e.g., translations, etc., which also get protection. The articles further lay down the specific rights which are protected, the exceptions to the rights, e.g., political speeches, etc., the conditions of protection, the terms of the rights, the provision of national treatment, the seizure of works infringing the rights, the special provisions of developing countries, etc.

Article 6*bis*, which has been excluded, contains what is called the "moral rights" of authors, viz., the rights which still remain with the author even after the transfer of economic rights, e.g., the right of being cited as the author and the safeguard against distortion or other modification of the work which would prejudice the author's honour and reputation.

One basic stipulation is that the copyright protection extends only to expressions and not to the ideas behind those expressions. The literal copying of the work of an author will be an infringement of copyright, but the exposition of similar ideas in different ways will not.

Term of Protection

The term of protection of a literary or artistic work, generally, is the life of the author and 50 years after his/her death.

In the case of cinematographic works, the term is 50 years after the work has been made available to the public with the consent of the author. If this condition is not satisfied, the term will be 50 years from the making of the work.

The term of photographic works and of works of applied art will be at least 25 years from the making of the work.

If the term in a case other than a photographic work or a work of applied art is not fixed on the basis of the life of the author, it must not be less than 50 years from the end of the year of the authorised publication. If publication has not taken place within 50 years of the making of the work, the term must be at least 50 years from the end of the year of making.

Rental Right

In respect of cinematographic works, the right-holders must have the right to authorise or prohibit the commercial rental of their works which enjoy copyright, provided the commercial rental has led to widespread copying of the works, impairing materially the right of the authors regarding reproduction.

Conditions, Limitations, Exceptions

Members may provide for limitations or exceptions to the copyrights in special cases, but while doing so, must ensure that these do not conflict with the normal exploitation of the work and do not unreasonably prejudice the legitimate interests of the copyright-holder.

Various qualifying terms used here, e.g., special, normal and unreasonable prejudice, have not been elaborated. There is, therefore, considerable flexibility in this regard.

Computer Programs and Compilation of Data

Coverage

Computer programs are covered by the copyright discipline.

Similarly, compilations of data which constitute intellectual creations because of the process of selection or arrangement of their contents will also be covered by the copyright discipline.

Implications

The copyright protection to computer programs has some significance. No registration in an individual country is necessary to enjoy the protection, as is the case with patents. It also does not require disclosure, which is necessary in the case of patents; hence, the secret of the programming can be retained with the author. Besides, the conditions to be satisfied for copyright are less stringent than those for patents.[88] But the protection through copyright is weak compared to that through patents. Copyright prohibits the copying of the creative expression, but permits independent creations even though based on the same ideas. Thus, such independent creations can be easily defended against charges of copying.[89] The proponents of the protection of computer programs are not quite satisfied, and it is likely that the appropriate mode of protection of computer programs may continue to remain under serious discussion in the future.

Rental Rights

In respect of computer programs, the authors must have the right to authorise or prohibit the commercial rental of their works which enjoy copyright. Here, the qualifying condition which applies to cinematographic works is absent.

Rights Regarding Performers, Phonograms, Broadcasting

Coverage

Performers must have the possibility of preventing:

(i) the fixation of their unfixed performances (e.g., recording their performances on tapes or records);

(ii) the reproduction of such fixation (e.g., making copies of the tapes or records containing their performance);

(iii) the broadcasting by wireless of their live performances; and

(iv) the communication to the public of their live performances;

if these acts are being done without their authorisation.

Producers of phonograms (i.e., sound recordings) must have the right to authorise or prohibit:

(i) the reproduction of their phonograms;

(ii) the commercial rental of the phonograms or their copies.

Broadcasting organisations must have the right to prohibit:

> the fixation, the reproduction of fixation, the rebroadcasting and the communication to the public of their television broadcasts;

if these acts are being undertaken without their authorisation.

The Agreement envisages a situation when such a right is not granted to the broadcasting organisation; in such cases, the copyright-holders of the subject of broadcast must have the possibility of preventing these acts.

Term of Protection

The term of the protection to performers and producers of phonograms must be at least 50 years from the end of the year of fixation or performance.

The term of the protection to broadcasting organisations must be at least 20 years from the end of the year of broadcast.

Conditions, Limitations, Exceptions

In respect of performers, producers of phonograms and broadcasting organisations, Members may provide for conditions, limitations, exceptions and reservations as permitted by the Rome Convention.[90] The Convention provides for exceptions for private use, short excerpts, teaching and scientific research, etc.

The provisions of Article 18 of the Berne Convention (1971) are also applicable. This Article provides for protection to those works which had not fallen into the public domain through the expiry of the term of protection at the time of the coming into force of the Convention. It prohibits new protection in such cases.

TRADEMARKS

Coverage

The disciplines on trademarks are covered by Articles 6 to 10 ter of the Paris Convention (1967) which are incorporated into this Agreement by Article 2.1 of the Agreement. Additional disciplines are contained in Articles 15 to 21 of the Agreement.

Registration

A trademark is defined as any sign which distinguishes the goods or services of one undertaking from those of other undertakings. The following conditions may be applied by a Member in the registration of trademarks:

(i) if the sign is not inherently capable of distinguishing the goods or services, distinctiveness acquired through use may be considered as a criterion for registration;

(ii) the sign should be visually perceptible;

(iii) registration may be made dependent on the use of the trademark by the applicant, but the filing of the application must not be made conditional on actual use;

(iv) the nature of the goods or services cannot be the sole basis for refusal of registration;

(v) registration will be refused if the trademark is a reproduction, imitation or translation of another well-known mark used for identical or similar goods or services, and is liable to create confusion;

(vi) if the goods or services are not identical or similar, and yet the proposed trademark would indicate a connection of these goods or services with the holder of the earlier trademark, damaging the interests of the holder, registration will be refused;

(vii) registration of state emblems as trademarks will normally be refused.

Rights Conferred

A trademark confers the following rights:

(i) A trademark-holder must have the right to prevent any person from using identical or similar signs for identical or similar goods, if such use will result in the likelihood of confusion.

(ii) A trademark-holder must have the right to assign the trademark, with or without the transfer of the business to which the trademark belongs.

(iii) The compulsory licensing provision cannot be made for a trademark.

Limited exceptions to the rights may be provided, but in this process, the legitimate interests of the trademark-holder and other interested parties must be taken into account.

Term

The initial registration must be for a minimum period of seven years. The renewal will also be for the same minimum period, and there will be no limit to the number of times the trademark is renewed.

Requirement of Use

If there is a condition of continuity of use for maintaining the trademark, the registration will be liable to cancellation only after continuous non-use for at least three years.

Other Conditions

There is an obligation that the use of a trademark must not be unjustifiably encumbered by special requirements. One example given in the Agreement is the requirement of use with another trademark. This would appear to prohibit the condition that a foreign trademark must only be used when linked with a domestic trademark, a requirement stipulated in some countries in some cases. However, the qualifying phrase "unjustifiably encumbered" may give some flexibility in this regard. If such a linkage is prescribed, it must be justifiable.

GEOGRAPHICAL INDICATIONS

Definition

A geographical indication identifies a product as originating in a particular place to which its quality, reputation or other characteristics are essentially attributable. This is particularly relevant in the case of wines and spirits, for example, scotch whisky, champagne, etc.

Protection of Geographical Indication

Members must provide for the prevention of:

(i) the use of means indicating that a product originates in a place other than the true place of origin, and thereby misleading the public as to the true origin of the product;

(ii) any use constituting an act of unfair competition within the meaning of Article 10*bis* of the Paris Convention (1967), which includes:

  (a) indications which are liable to mislead the public as to the nature, manufacturing process, characteristics, suitability or quality of the product;

  (b) acts creating confusion with the establishment, goods, or industrial or commercial activities of a competitor;

(c) false allegations so as to discredit the establishment, goods, or industrial or commercial activities of a competitor.

Members must refuse or invalidate the registration of a trademark if the trademark has a geographical indication which misleads the public regarding the true place of origin of the product.

In the case of wines and spirits, there are some additional disciplines. In these cases, even if the true origin is indicated in translations or if there is a use of expressions such as "kind", "type", "style", "imitation", etc. (for example, "champagne-type wine", "imitation scotch whisky"), a Member has to provide for the prevention of false geographical indications. Negotiations will be undertaken to enhance the protection of individual geographical indications of wines and spirits.

Exceptions

A Member is not required to prevent the use of a geographical indication in the case of wines or spirits, if it has been used: (a) for at least 15 years before 15 April 1994 or (b) in good faith preceding that date.

If a trademark has been applied for or registered or acquired by use in good faith before the application of these provisions of discipline or before the geographical indication is protected in the country of origin, the eligibility for or validity of registration, or the right to use the trademark, shall not be prejudiced on the basis that such a trademark is identical with or similar to a geographical indication.

There is also a flexibility of discipline in cases where a geographical indication of another Member is identical with the customary name for such a product in the Member country considering the case.

INDUSTRIAL DESIGNS

Coverage

Industrial design refers to the features concerning the look of an article, for example, the shape, ornamentation, pattern, configuration, etc. It is different from the designs related to the functional utility of products, for example, an improvement in a machinery. The latter are sometimes protected in some countries as "utility models", which, in fact, are minor innovations.[91]

The Agreement covers only industrial designs, and not utility models.

Members are required to provide for the protection of industrial designs. The necessary conditions are that the designs should be independently created and should be new or original. It has been clarified that novelty or originality may not be present if the design does not significantly differ from known designs.

Probably considering the importance of industrial designs in the textiles sector, there is a special provision that requirements, particularly in respect of costs, examination or publication, should not unreasonably impair the opportunity to get the protection.

Protection

Members must provide that the owner of a protected design will have the right to prevent the making, selling or importing of articles having a copy of that design for commercial purposes, without his/her consent.

Limited exceptions to the right are permissible, provided the exceptions do not unreasonably conflict with the normal exploitation of the design or unreasonably prejudice the interests of the right holder.

LAYOUT-DESIGNS OF INTEGRATED CIRCUITS

Coverage

The Agreement incorporates some provisions of the Washington Treaty, more formally called the Treaty on Intellectual Property in Respect of Integrated Circuits (1989) (IPIC Treaty),[92] and also lays down some additional provisions.

The relevant provisions of the IPIC Treaty contain the definitions of integrated circuit and layout-design (topography), the obligations of protection, the conditions for protection, the elements of protection, and exceptions. The additional provisions given in this Agreement marginally qualify the scope of the protection and specify the term of protection.

Definition

"Integrated circuit" is a product, having an electronic function, in which the elements and at least some interconnections are integrally formed on a piece of material. Here, at least one of the elements must be active.

"Layout-design (topography)" is a three-dimensional arrangement of the elements and at least some interconnections of an integrated circuit. At least one element must be active. It may also include a three-dimensional arrangement prepared for an integrated circuit intended for manufacture.

Conditions for Protection

Subject of Protection

In order to have a right to protection, the layout-design has to be original in the sense that it is the result of the intellectual efforts of the creator and is not a subject of common knowledge among the experts and manufacturers of integrated circuits. In case the elements and interconnections are subjects of common knowledge, the layout-design itself will be entitled to protection if the combination, taken as a whole, is original.

Disclosure

If an application for protection is required, it must be accompanied by an adequate disclosure of what is sought to be protected. If the integrated circuit has been commercially exploited, a sample may be required to be provided. In any case, a copy or a drawing of the layout-design has to be given. Information on the electronic function which it will perform also has to be provided. The material should be sufficient to allow the identification of the layout-design, though the copy or drawing of parts relating to the manner of manufacture of the integrated circuit need not be given.

Time Limit

A Member may prescribe a maximum duration between the first commercial exploitation of the layout-design by the applicant anywhere in the world and the date of filing the application, when required. This duration, however, cannot be less than two years.

Scope of Protection

The following acts, if undertaken without the authorisation of the right-holder, must be considered unlawful:

(i) reproduction of a protected layout-design, whether by incorporation in an integrated circuit or otherwise;

(ii) importing, selling or otherwise distributing for commercial purposes:

   (a) a protected layout-design, or

   (b) an integrated circuit incorporating a protected layout-design, or

   (c) an article incorporating such an integrated circuit. (items (a) and (b) according to the IPIC Treaty, and item (c) according to this Agreement)

Exceptions

The exceptions to the scope of protection are the following:

(i) acts of reproduction done for private purposes;

(ii) acts of reproduction done for the purposes of evaluation, analysis, research or teaching;

(iii) if a person creates a new and original layout-design on the basis of the evaluation or analysis of an earlier layout-design, the use by this person of this new layout-design without the authorisation of the right-holder of the earlier layout-design;

(iv) use of an identical but original layout-design created independently by a person other than the right-holder;

(v) importing, selling or commercially distributing a protected material (either an integrated circuit or an article incorporating an integrated circuit), where the person performing or ordering any of the acts mentioned above did not know, nor had reasonable grounds to know (an innocent infringer), that the material incorporates an unlawfully reproduced layout-design;
(Once it comes to the notice of the person that the material incorporates an unlawfully reproduced layout-design, the person must be liable to pay a reasonable royalty to the right-holder.)

(vi) importing, selling or commercially distributing a protected layout-design or an integrated circuit incorporating such a layout-design, after it is put on the market with the consent of the right-holder (exhaustion of rights).

Use Without Authorisation

The provisions regarding use without the authorisation of the right-holder (i.e., use by governments for non-commercial purposes, or compulsory licensing), as applicable in the case of patents, are also applicable to layout-designs.

Term of Protection

Where registration is required for protection, the term must be at least 10 years from the date of filing the application for registration, or from the first commercial exploitation in the world.

Where registration is not required for protection, the term must be at least 10 years from the date of the first commercial exploitation in the world.

A Member may provide that the term will lapse 15 years after the creation of the layout-design.

UNDISCLOSED INFORMATION

The protection of undisclosed information relates to secret information with a person or an enterprise, e.g., trade secrets, or to information lodged with the government in the case of pharmaceutical or agricultural products.

A Member must provide to persons or enterprises the possibility of preventing the disclosure, acquisition or use of information within their control without their consent in a manner contrary to honest commercial practices. These practices include: breach of contract, breach of confidence, inducement of such breach, and acquisition of information by a person who knew that such practices were involved in the acquisition or who was grossly negligent in failing to know about it.

There are, however, some conditions for such information to be protected, viz.:

(i) the information is secret;

(ii) it has a commercial value; and

(iii) the person with control of the information has taken reasonable steps to keep it secret.

In respect of such secret information, i.e., trade secret, the independent development of the information or the obtaining of the information from other sources in a lawful manner, will not be considered an infringement. An important feature of a trade secret is that the protection relating to it does not have a limited term; the protection will continue till the conditions mentioned above cease to be fulfilled.

In the case of the data provided to governments in the course of approving the marketing of pharmaceutical or agricultural chemical products utilising new chemical entities, the governments must protect the data against unfair commercial use. Such data must also be protected against disclosure except if: (i) it is necessary to protect the public, or (ii) steps have not been taken to ensure that the data are protected against unfair commercial use.

ANTI-COMPETITIVE PRACTICES

There is a recognition in the Agreement that certain licensing practices or conditions restraining competition may have adverse effects on trade and may impede the transfer and dissemination of technology. Keeping it in view, Members have the discretion to take corrective measures.

Members may specify in their legislation:

(i) which licensing practices or conditions would constitute an abuse of IPRs having an adverse effect on competition;

(ii) appropriate measures, consistent with the Agreement, to prevent or control such practices.

Members have the discretion to make provisions in their legislation on this subject in fulfilment of the basic objectives and principles as contained in Articles 7 and 8, explained earlier.

A Member having reason to believe that a holder of an IPR (of another country) is undertaking anti-competitive practices against the law, may request the other Member, in whose territory the IPR-holder is a citizen or a domicile, to consult on this issue. The other Member must enter into such consultation and provide cooperation in the collecting of information on this matter.

A Member whose nationals or domiciliaries are the subject of such proceedings in another country, may also request consultation with the other Member, and opportunity must be provided for such consultation.

ENFORCEMENT OF IPRs

A good deal of emphasis has been given in the Agreement to the enforcement of IPR legislation. The concern probably flows from the perception of some major technology-leader Members that IPR legislation and procedures are not being effectively implemented in some countries. Elaborate procedures have been included in the Agreement for the enforcement of IPRs. Both civil and criminal judicial procedures have been prescribed. In certain matters, it has been made obligatory on Members to provide authority to the courts. For example, the courts must have the powers to:

(i) in certain circumstances, require a party to produce particular evidence;

(ii) issue an injunction ordering a party to desist from an infringement of an IPR;

(iii) order the infringer of an IPR to pay damages to the IPR-holder;

(iv) destroy or otherwise dispose of goods which have been the subject of infringement, without any compensation;

(v) indemnify the defendant by payment of compensation for wrongful proceedings;

(vi) take interim or provisional measures to prevent an infringement or to preserve relevant evidence with regard to the alleged infringement;

(vii) conduct criminal proceedings and award penalties in cases of wilful trademark counterfeiting or copyright piracy on a commercial scale.

Customs authorities must also be given the authority to suspend the release of goods at the border if they receive an order from a competent authority, administrative or judicial, indicating that the authority has been satisfied that there are *prima facie* grounds to suspect that these are counterfeit trademark goods or pirated copyright goods.

DISPUTE SETTLEMENT PROCESS

The provisions of Articles XXII and XXIII of GATT 1994, as elaborated and applied by the Dispute Settlement Understanding, apply to this Agreement with some modifications, as explained below.

A Member can initiate an action in the Dispute Settlement Body if:

(i) a benefit under the Agreement is being nullified or impaired, or

(ii) the attainment of any objective of the Agreement is being impeded,

as a result of the failure of any Member to carry out its obligations.

There are two other alternative conditions in Article XXIII of GATT 1994 which may be causes for action in the DSB in the case of other agreements, but which have been excluded from this Agreement. These relate to the nullification or impairment of a benefit or the impediment to the attainment of any objective of the Agreement, as a result of:

(i) the application of another Member of any measure, whether or not it conflicts with the provisions of the Agreement [Article XXIII.1(b) of GATT 1994]; or

(ii) the existence of any other situation [Article XXIII.1(c) of GATT 1994].

These two provisions will not be applicable in disputes relating to TRIPS for five years from 1 January 1995. During this period, the Council for TRIPS will examine the scope and modalities for complaints of these types and submit its recommendations to the Ministerial Conference, which may either accept the recommendations or extend the period further.

APPLICATION OF THE AGREEMENT, INTERIM MEASURES

A developed country Member may delay the application of the provisions of the Agreement for one year from the coming into force of the Agreement, i.e., 1 January 1995.

A least developed country Member may delay the application of the Agreement for 10 years from the date of application for developed country Members, i.e., 1 January 1996. Thus, it has to apply it, at the latest, by 1 January 2006. In respect of the MFN treatment and national treatment obligations, it has to apply the provisions of Articles 3, 4 and 5 with effect from 1 January 1996. Further extension may be allowed by the Council for TRIPS for the application of the Agreement to individual least developed country Members on request.

Other developing country Members may delay the application for four years beyond the date of application for the developed country Members, i.e., four years after 1 January 1996. This would mean that the latest date of application for them will be 1 January 2000. The obligations relating to MFN treatment and national treatment will be applicable from 1 January 1996.

If a developing country Member does not have provisions for the patenting of products (as distinct from the patenting of processes) in some areas of technology on 1 January 1995, the application of the provisions of the Agreement relating to the patenting of products in those areas may be further delayed by five years. These provisions should thus be applicable from 1 January 2005.

A Member that is in the process of transformation from a centrally planned economy to a market economy and which faces special problems in the implementation of the IPR laws, may delay the application of the Agreement until 1 January 2000, but the obligations of MFN treatment and national treatment will be applicable from 1 January 1996.

The Agreement creates obligations in respect of all subject matter which exists at the date of application of the Agreement for a Member, and which is protected by the Member on that date or which meets the criteria for protection. However, there are some specific provisions relating to the transition period till the application of the provisions of the Agreement by a Member. Some of these are as follows:

(i) there is no obligation to restore protection to subject matter which has fallen into the public domain by the date of application of the Agreement for the Member;

(ii) if some action had been taken before the acceptance of the WTO Agreement, or if a significant investment had been made before that date, in respect of objects which get covered by IPRs after the application of the Agreement for the Member, provision should be made for the limitation of remedies to the right-holder, and provision must be made for equitable remuneration.

There are also special provisions regarding the acceptance of applications and marketing rights in the transition period for pharmaceutical and agricultural chemical products in the territories of those Members that do not already grant product patent protection in these areas. These are:

(i) arrangements must be made for applications for patents in cases filed after 1 January 1995, even though the applications will naturally not be considered till the Member applies the relevant provisions of the Agreement;

(ii) the criteria of patentability will be applied on the date when these provisions are applied by the Member, but on that date, the criteria will be applied as if on the date of the filing of the application;

(iii) if a patent is then granted, the term will not be the full term from that date, but only the remainder of the term counted from the date the application was filed;

(iv) if a person: (a) files an application for a patent as mentioned above, (b) has obtained a patent and marketing approval for the product in another Member country, and (c) gets marketing approval in the country where the application is filed, he/she must be given exclusive marketing rights for up to five years after the granting of the marketing approval. This provision has been made to tide over the gap until a decision is taken on the patent application in this country. If the application for the patent is granted or rejected during the five-year period, the exclusive marketing rights will end with that decision, and the consequences of the granting or rejection of the application will follow thereafter.

This provision for exclusive marketing rights is important as it gives some right to the innovator even before the application for the patent is considered. The Agreement does not specify the scope or the content of this right. However, it is reasonable to presume that it cannot confer rights equivalent to that of patents during this period. Innovations can be used by other persons. Compulsory licensing provisions can be made. Other public-interest and abuse-of-IPR provisions can also apply.[93]

INSTITUTIONAL ARRANGEMENT, REVIEW, SECURITY EXCEPTIONS

The Council for TRIPS has been formed to monitor the implementation of the Agreement. It will review the implementation of the Agreement after five years of implementation, i.e., after 1 January 2000. Thereafter, there will be reviews at intervals of two years.

A Member may take any action it considers necessary for the protection of its essential security interests relating to fissionable materials, traffic in arms and similar materials. A similar exception exists for actions taken in times of war or other emergencies in international relations, or in pursuance of the obligations under the UN Charter for peace and security.

PART VIII

DISPUTE SETTLEMENT AND INSTITUTIONAL MATTERS

Dispute settlement is an important part of the WTO system, as it provides the mechanism for the enforcement of rights and the observance of obligations prescribed in the WTO agreements. This Part will cover this subject. Besides, it will also cover some important institutional matters, like the Membership of the WTO, the decision-making process and the various subsidiary bodies in the WTO.

Chapter VIII.1

DISPUTE SETTLEMENT PROCESS

INTRODUCTION

THE rights and obligations in the WTO agreements are enforced through the dispute settlement process. A Member may take recourse to this process when it is dissatisfied with another Member for some action it has taken or for its failure to take some action.

There is, however, a serious limitation. The ultimate relief which this process provides is authorisation to the affected Member to take retaliatory measures against the offending Member. It may not be an effective and useful tool in the hands of a Member which is economically weak, because the Member may not find it convenient and practical to resort to retaliation against economically strong Members. Aftcr all, rctaliatory tradc mcasurcs havc thcir costs and other consequences, which may be irksome to a weak trading economy.

Even with this limitation, the dispute settlement process has a discouraging effect on Members in encroaching on the rights of others and ignoring their own obligations. Its effectiveness, however, depends a good deal on the will of the Members to abide by it.

The dispute settlement process has been strengthened significantly in the Uruguay Round. Time limits have been fixed for various stages of the process and firm provisions have been made against obstructing the decisions reached. Now, its effectiveness will very much depend on how these provisions are implemented in actual practice.

There is, however, a significant limitation on the application of general Dispute Settlement Understanding (DSU) provisions to anti-dumping. The role of the dispute settlement panels has been severely curtailed in this area, as will be explained later.

The dispute settlement process is meant to provide security and predictability to the multilateral trading system. Its purposes are to preserve the rights and obligations of Members in the WTO agreements and to clarify the provisions of these agreements, without adding to or diminishing the rights and obligations provided therein.

The original provisions for the dispute settlement process are contained in Articles XXII and XXIII of GATT 1994. These have been clarified and amplified further in the Uruguay Round of MTNs and have also been made more effective. The relevant agreement is the Understanding on Rules and Procedures Governing the Settlement of Disputes (Dispute Settlement Understanding, DSU), which forms Annex 2 to the WTO Agreement.

COVERAGE

The dispute settlement process covers the WTO Agreement (i.e., the Agreement Establishing the World Trade Organisation), GATT 1994, other agreements on goods, services, the DSU itself and the plurilateral agreements. Some of these agreements have some special provisions, either modifying some elements of the DSU or making some additional provisions. These modifications and additions have been discussed in the relevant chapters. These will also be mentioned in brief at the end of this chapter.

In respect of the plurilateral agreements, the applicability of the dispute settlement process will be in accordance with the decisions which may be taken by the parties to these agreements.

To fully understand the dispute settlement process, one must consult three elements, as given below.

(i) Articles XXII and XXIII of GATT 1994, which contain some procedural matters and important substantive provisions laying down the preconditions for starting the dispute settlement process;

(ii) the DSU; and

(iii) the provisions on consultation and dispute settlement in the relevant agreement which is the subject matter of the particular dispute.

The last element has been discussed in the respective chapters. This chapter discusses the first two.

ARTICLES XXII AND XXIII OF GATT 1994

Main Elements

Article XXII of GATT 1994 provides for consultation between Members with respect to any matter affecting the operation of an agreement. The procedural details will be given later.

If no satisfactory solution is reached, a Member may request that a consultation should be held jointly by the Members with any other Member. In actual practice, a Member would generally resort to the process of dispute settlement if consultations do not succeed.

Article XXIII of GATT 1994 lays down conditions which must be satisfied before a Member resorts to the dispute settlement process. These are:

(i) any benefit accruing to the Member under a particular agreement is being nullified or impaired, or

(ii) the attainment of any objective of the agreement is being impeded,

as a result of:

(i) the failure of another Member to carry out its obligations under the agreement [Article XXIII.1(a) of GATT 1994]; or

(ii) the application by another Member of any measure,

- which conflicts with the provisions of the agreement [Article XXIII.1(b) of GATT 1994], or

– which does not conflict with the provisions of the agreement [Article XXIII.1(b) of GATT 1994]; or

(iii) the existence of any other situation [Article XXIII.1(c) of GATT 1994].

Thus, primarily what is essential is that either some benefit accruing to a Member is nullified or impaired, or the attainment of some objective of the particular agreement is impeded. These situations could occur by some action of a Member, by the failure of a Member to take some action, or in any other way.

Violation Cases

If the nullification or impairment of a benefit is caused by a Member failing to carry out its obligations under the agreement [1(a)], or applying a measure which conflicts with some provision of the agreement [1(b), first part], the situation occurs because of the violation of some provision of the agreement. Such situations are commonly called "violation cases".

For example, if a Member impairs the benefit flowing out of its tariff binding by imposing an internal charge on an imported product which it does not apply to the like domestic product, it is violating the provisions of Article III of GATT 1994. This is a violation case of impairment. It will be elaborated later.

Non-Violation Cases

When, on the other hand, a Member applies a measure which does not conflict with the agreement [1(b), second part] and yet causes the nullification or impairment of benefits, it is doing so without violating the provisions of the agreement. Such situations are commonly called "non-violation cases". For example, a Member may grant a subsidy to an industry within permissible limits, and may thereby affect adversely the prospects of the export of another Member. This may, under certain circumstances, be held to impair the benefit accruing to this Member, though it does not violate the disciplines on subsidies. This is a non-violation case of impairment. It will be further explained in detail later.

Clarification of Some Terms

Some of the terms used here need elaboration. In fact, these have been the subject of detailed consideration in several panels in the past during the operation of GATT 1947.

Nullification or Impairment

Article 3.8 of the DSU provides that in cases where there is an infringement of the obligations assumed under a covered agreement, the action is considered *prima facie* to constitute a case of nullification or impairment. There is thus a presumption of nullification and impairment in such cases. It will then be up to the Member against whom the complaint has been made to rebut the charge. However, the experience in the past has been that this presumption is extremely difficult to rebut.

The Panel on US – Taxes on Petroleum and Certain Imported Substances (June 1987) noted that in several cases, such a rebuttal had been tried, but had not succeeded. The Panel concluded that, in actual practice, the presumption had operated as an unrebuttable presumption.[94]

In other cases, the Member bringing the complaint will have to adduce evidence to prove that any benefit which it enjoyed under the agreement has been nullified or impaired. The subject of consideration could be a trade benefit or a systemic benefit, but it must have resulted from the agreement. Some relevant points related to what would constitute nullification or impairment in non-violation cases will be discussed later.

Failure to Carry Out an Obligation Under the Agreement, Application of a Measure Conflicting With the Agreement

In these violation cases, it is necessary to demonstrate that there is some provision in the agreement that creates the obligation which a Member has failed to carry out or which conflicts with a measure taken by a Member. In this process, the establishment of the following elements is necessary:

(i) existence of an obligation in the relevant agreement; and

(ii) failure of a Member to carry it out;
or

(iii) a Member has taken a measure; and

(iv) there is a provision in the relevant agreement which conflicts with the measure.

In this connection, it is relevant to mention that a number of panels in the past have considered the possible occurrence of a "violation" merely by the existence of a legislation, even when no measure might have been taken in pursuance of the legislation. This has been discussed in detail in the chapter on the status of legislation in Part II. These panels held the view that the mere existence of a "violating" provision in the legislation would constitute a "violation" only if the relevant "violating" measure was mandatory in the legislation. If there was a provision of discretion on the part of the implementing authorities, the mere existence of such a provision would not have been considered a "violation".

As mentioned in the chapter referred to above, the situation has changed since the coming into force of the WTO Agreement. Now, Members are required to bring their laws and procedures into conformity with the provisions of the WTO agreements. Hence, if there is a provision in the legislation which conflicts with any provision of these agreements, this obligation would be considered to have been violated. As a result, the mere existence of a "violating" provision in the legislation would amount to a "violation", irrespective of the fact whether it is a mandatory or a discretionary provision.

Non-Violation Nullification or Impairment

The non-violation cases of nullification or impairment can best be explained by some specific examples. Let us consider the case of a Member which has negotiated tariff concessions with another Member, resulting in the binding of the tariff on a product. The Member, after having bound the tariff, grants a subsidy to the domestic industry producing a like product. The subsidy which has been granted is not prohibited by the disciplines governing subsidies. The domestic industry, helped by the subsidy, raises its production substantially, with the result that the export prospect of the Member which had negotiated the tariff concession has dwindled significantly. At the time the negotiation for the tariff concession took place, there was no anticipation that such a subsidy would be granted. In this situation, the exporting Member can validly claim that the benefit which was given to it by the tariff binding on this product has been nullified or impaired by the granting of the subsidy by the other Member.

In this process, three facts are relevant, viz.:

(i) there was a concession of the binding of a tariff which provided benefit to a Member;

(ii) subsequently, the Member binding the tariff granted a subsidy to its domestic industry, which constrained the export prospect of the exporting Member;

(iii) the exporting Member had a reasonable expectation, at the time of the negotiation for the tariff concession, that the competitive conditions for the product in question would not be disturbed.

Thus, the main elements to be determined in non-violation cases are: the existence of a benefit, subsequent action by a Member by which the benefit is curtailed, and the existence of a reasonable expectation that the competitive conditions would not be upset.

It is not necessary, in such cases, that the concession in question should have been negotiated by the complaining Member; what is relevant is that the Member has the benefit of the concession, irrespective of the manner in which the concession came about.

Some specific cases where this subject has been considered will clarify it further.

The Working Party on the Australian Subsidy on Ammonium Sulphate (April 1950) examined the complaint of Chile that the differential treatment accorded to two fertilisers, viz., sodium nitrate and ammonium sulphate, in respect of the subsidy had caused nullification or impairment, even though the measure was not inconsistent with the obligations of Australia. The Working Party found that the competitive relationship had been upset, and also that the action of Australia could not reasonably have been anticipated by Chile at the time it negotiated for the duty-free binding on sodium nitrate. The Working Party concluded that nullification or impairment had been caused.[95]

The Panel on Treatment by Germany of Imports of Sardines (October 1952) considered whether a new tariff schedule of Germany which treated imports of sprats and herrings differently from imports of sardines, though not violating any obligation, would still cause the nullification or impairment of benefits to Norway. The Panel held the view that impairment would exist if the action of Germany resulted in upsetting the competitive relationship between the two types of products, and also that it could not reasonably have been anticipated by Norway at the time it negotiated for the tariff reduction. The Panel found that these two situations did really exist and thus concluded that nullification or impairment was caused.[96]

The Review Working Party on Other Barriers to Trade (March 1955) concluded that a contracting party which had negotiated a tariff concession may be assumed to have a reasonable expectation that the concession will not be nullified or impaired by the other contracting party giving the concession by the subsequent introduction or increase of a domestic subsidy on the product. Thus, the subsequent introduction of a domestic subsidy was found to cause nullification or impairment.[97]

Certain other important principles which have evolved in the course of the consideration of non-violation nullification or impairment cases by some panels are given below.

- Complaints regarding nullification or impairment should be admissible even if there is no statistical evidence of trade damage. These are to be determined based on future trade opportunities also. It has been noted that the market access commitments in the GATT are generally on the conditions of competition for trade and not on the volumes of trade.
  The Panel on EEC – Payment and Subsidies Paid to Processors and Producers of Oilseeds etc. (adopted on 25 January 1990) is relevant in this connection.[98]

- There is no restriction that complaints about non-violation nullification or impairment can be made only by those Members which have the initial negotiating rights. (The term "initial negotiating right" was explained in the chapter on tariffs.)

Generally, the non-violation cases considered have been those relating to the nullification or impairment of benefits accruing through tariff concessions. There has been only one case in which the nullification or impairment of another benefit was considered, but the matter was not conclusively resolved. It came up in the US – EEC dispute on the tariff treatment on imports of citrus products from certain countries in the Mediterranean region. The US had complained that the special tariff treatment accorded by the EEC had nullified or impaired the benefits accruing to it under Article I of the GATT. This matter could not be resolved as an objection was raised that so far, this provision had been applied only in cases in which a tariff binding was at stake and that it would not be proper to extend its application to other situations.

However, it appears reasonable to extend this provision beyond tariff concessions so as to cover benefits under other provisions of GATT 1994.

Any Other Situation: 1(c)

This provision in Article XXIII of GATT 1994 has come up for consideration on some occasions but was not pursued. Hence, specific criteria or guidelines have not been developed.

Attainment of Objectives Being Impeded

Complaints pertaining to this provision have come up on some occasions. The matter has, however, not been pursued. This provision has, therefore, not come up for serious consideration, and criteria and guidelines have not been developed. Some of the important cases in this regard are the following:

- In the Panel on EEC – Refunds on Exports of Sugar (November 1979), Australia had raised the issue that the EEC system of sugar export subsidies had impeded the attainment of the objectives of the GATT. But this question was not examined as no detailed submission had been made as to exactly which objective of the GATT had been impeded.[99]

- In 1983, the EEC brought a complaint against Japan invoking this provision and requested the establishment of a working party. The complaint was not pursued.

- In 1984, Australia complained that the EEC regime of beef and veal had impeded the attainment of the objectives of the GATT, but did not pursue the matter.

The cases relating to the attainment of objectives being impeded either by "violation" or by "non-violation", or by "the existence of any other situation", have not been seriously discussed and, as such, specific principles have not crystallised.

PROCEDURE FOR DISPUTE SETTLEMENT PROCESS

Consultation

The process of dispute settlement starts with a consultation between the Members involved in the issue. If a Member considers that the preconditions for resorting to the dispute settlement process, as mentioned above, have been fulfilled, it has to start the process of consultation.

Notice for Consultation

The request for consultation has to be made to the Member against whom the Member initiating the process has a grievance. The request must be made in writing and must contain the reasons for the request, clearly identifying the measures which are the cause for grievance. An indication of the legal basis for the complaint also has to be given.

Simultaneously, this request has to be notified to the Dispute Settlement Body (DSB), the relevant Committee and the relevant Council by the Member that is making the request for consultation. The relevant Committee is the Committee which monitors the agreement the provision of which is the subject matter of the dispute. The relevant Council for subject matters related to goods is the Council for Trade in Goods, for those related to trade in services, the Council for Trade in Services, and for those related to trade-related aspects of intellectual property rights (TRIPS), the Council for TRIPS.

Response and Time Limits

The Member to whom the request is addressed must accord sympathetic consideration to the request and must afford adequate opportunity with respect to the consultation.

The responding Member must reply to the request within 10 days of receiving the request, except if the requesting Member and the responding Member mutually agree on a longer period.

The responding Member must enter into consultation within 30 days of receiving the request, except if there is mutual agreement on a longer period.

In cases of urgency, for example, those concerning perishable goods, consultation must be held within 10 days of the receipt of the request.

If these time limits are not adhered to, the Member initiating the process may proceed with a request to the DSB to establish a panel.

Process of Consultation

The consultation should be carried on in good faith. The objective of the consultation is to arrive at a mutually satisfactory solution of the dispute. The Members should attempt to obtain a satisfactory adjustment of the matter.

The consultation is without prejudice to the rights of any Member in any further proceedings. The implication is that if a Member has made an offer during the consultation and the consultation does not ultimately succeed, the Member concerned is free to withdraw the offer. The consultation process is confidential.

Members should give special attention to the particular problems and interests of developing country Members during the consultation.

If the consultation has not succeeded in settling the dispute within 60 days of the receipt of the notice for consultation by the responding Member, the complaining Member may proceed to request the DSB for the formation of a panel. A request for a panel may be made even within the 60-day period, if the consulting parties jointly consider that the consultation has failed to produce a solution. In cases of urgency, for example, cases concerning perishable goods, the time limit is 20 days. In cases where the subject of consultation is a measure taken by a developing country Member, the parties to the dispute may decide to extend these time limits. If the time limit has elapsed in such cases and the consulting parties do not agree among themselves that the consultation has concluded, the chairman of the DSB will consult the parties and decide whether to extend the period of consultation and, if so, the duration of the extended period.

Other Interested Members

If any other Member considers that it has a substantial trade interest in the particular consultation, it should give notice to the consulting Members and also to the DSB within 10 days of the date of circulation of the request for consultation regarding its desire to join the consultation. If the Member to whom the request for consultation was made agrees that this Member has a well-founded claim regarding substantial interest, the Member expressing its desire will be included in the consultation. If the request is not accepted, the Member concerned is free to make a request for a separate consultation in accordance with the procedure for initiating a consultation.

Panel Process

The DSU makes a significant departure from the past process of dispute settlement as specific time schedules have been prescribed for various stages, and the decision-making process has been made efficient at all significant stages ranging from the formation of the panel to the final implementation of the decisions.

However, it is not clear in what manner the deadlines at various stages will be enforced. Ultimately, this depends on the moral responsibility of the members of the panel to adhere to the time schedules; the DSB does not have any specific authority to enforce the deadlines.

Formation of the Panel

Request

The Member requesting the DSB for the formation of a panel must make such a request in writing and must give the following information in the notice:

(i) an indication as to whether or not a consultation was held;

(ii) the specific measures which are at issue;

(iii) a brief summary of the legal basis of the complaint which should present the problem clearly.

Time Limit

When a request for forming a panel is made by a Member, it will be placed on the agenda of the DSB. The DSB must decide to establish a panel, at the latest, at the meeting held immediately following the one in which the request first appeared on the agenda. Thus, the matter cannot continue to be considered beyond two meetings of the DSB. The panel will not be formed only if the DSB, at this second meeting, decides as such by "consensus". The provision for a decision by consensus is prescribed in Article IX of the WTO Agreement which says that the body concerned shall be deemed to have decided by consensus if no Member present at the meeting formally objects to the proposed decision. Thus, a "negative consensus", viz., a consensus not to form a panel, is almost impossible, since the Member interested in the formation of the panel will certainly stop such a consensus. Hence, it is a near certainty that the panel will be formed.

There is an additional provision for speeding up the formation of the panel. If the Member proposing the formation of the panel so requests, a meeting of the DSB has to be convened for this purpose within 15 days of the request, provided that a notice of the meeting is given at least 10 days in advance.

Terms of Reference

Normally, standard terms of reference are used by the DSB while forming a panel. They call for: (i) the examination of the issues raised by the complaining Member, and (ii) giving findings which will assist the DSB in making recommendations or in giving its rulings on the issues in question. But a Member requesting the formation of a panel may suggest different terms of reference. In such a case, the proposed text of the terms of reference has to be included in the written request for the formation of the panel. Normally, the standard terms of reference will not meet with any objection. Even special terms of reference, if agreed to by the parties, will generally not be objected to by other Members. However, there is a provision in Article 7.3 that in the case of special terms of reference, any Member may raise any point relating to them in the DSB.

Members of the Panel

Normally, a panel consists of three members. The parties to the dispute have, however, the option to have a five-member panel, but they must reach an agreement on this issue within 10 days of the establishment of the panel.

Nominations to the panel are proposed initially by the Secretariat of the WTO, and the parties to the dispute accept them except if they have compelling reasons not to. In cases where no agreement is reached on the membership of the panel within 20 days of the date of the establishment of the panel, either party to the dispute may request the Director-General of the WTO to make the nominations. The Director-General will make the nominations in consultation with the Chairmen of the DSB and the relevant Council or Committee, and after consulting the parties to the dispute.

The members of the DSB have to be promptly informed about the composition of the panel. In cases where the Director-General has made the nominations, the Chairman of the DSB has to inform the Members about the composition within 10 days of receiving the information.

When a dispute is between a developing country Member and a developed country Member, the panel must include at least one member from a developing country (which is a Member of the WTO) if the developing country Member which is a party to the dispute so requests.

Panel members are expected to function in their individual capacities and not as representatives of governments or of any organisation.

Functioning of the Panel

Right in the beginning, the panel will formulate a timetable for different stages of the working of the panel.

Participation by Third Parties

Any Member (of course, other than the parties to the dispute) having a substantial interest in the matter being considered by the panel may notify the DSB about its interest. These third parties will have the opportunity to be heard by the panel and to make written submissions to it.

Written and Oral Presentations

The initial written submissions will first be provided by the complaining party and then by the responding party. However, the panel may decide, after consultation with the parties to the dispute, that the initial written submissions will be given simultaneously by the complaining party and the responding party. The subsequent written submissions will be given simultaneously.

In the first substantive meeting with the parties, the case will first be presented by the complaining party and then by the responding party. All third parties which have notified to the DSB their interest in the dispute will also present their views.

Written rebuttals will be submitted by the parties after this first substantive meeting.

In the second substantive meeting with the parties, oral rebuttals will be made. The responding Member has the right to make its rebuttal first, and then, the complaining Member will follow.

All presentations, rebuttals and statements will be made in the presence of the parties. The third parties which have notified their interest may remain present throughout the first substantive meeting of the panel with the parties.

Confidentiality

The deliberations in the panel and the documents submitted to it have to be kept confidential. The parties to the dispute may, however, disclose their own positions to the public, if they so wish. When a party to the dispute submits a confidential version of its submission, it must also provide a non-confidential summary, if so requested by a Member.

Expert Group

With respect to a factual issue concerning a scientific or other technical matter raised by a party to a dispute, the panel may request an advisory report in writing from an expert review group.

Time Limit

Generally, the panel has to issue the final report to the parties to the dispute within six months of the date of the final agreement on the composition of the panel and the terms of reference. In cases of urgency, including those related to perishable goods, the panel must aim to reduce this period to three months. If the panel considers that it cannot issue the report within this prescribed period, it must inform the DSB, giving the reasons and also an estimate of the additional period needed. In no case should the period exceed nine months.

If the complaining party so requests, the panel may suspend its work for a period not exceeding 12 months. The authority of the panel will lapse after this duration of suspension.

Report of the Panel

Descriptive Part

After considering the written submissions, oral arguments and rebuttals, the panel will prepare the descriptive sections of its draft report containing the facts and arguments, and give it to the parties. The parties may give their comments in writing within the time set by the panel.

Interim Report

Thereafter, the panel will issue an interim report containing the descriptive sections and also its findings and conclusions. A party may submit a written request for reviewing some specific aspects of the interim report within the time prescribed by the panel for this purpose. The panel will hold a meeting with the parties on the issues raised in the written comments, if there is a request for such a meeting by a party.

Final Report

After such a meeting, or if no comment is received from any party during the prescribed period, the final report of the panel will be prepared. If there had been comments on the interim report, the discussion of the arguments made at the interim review stage will be included in the final report.

Coverage of the Report

In its report to the DSB, the panel must include the following:

(i) an objective assessment of the facts of the case;

(ii) an examination of the applicability of the relevant provisions of the relevant agreement;

(iii) an evaluation as to whether the measures under consideration are in conformity with the provisions of the agreement; and

(iv) any other findings which may help the DSB in its consideration of the issue and in making recommendations or in giving rulings.

A ruling is called for when there is a point of contention on fact or law. A recommendation relates to suggestions for specific action by a party. This distinction has been elaborated by the Panel on Uruguayan Recourse to Article XXIII (November 1962).[100]

Some Examples of Recommendations

Generally, in "violation cases", i.e., where nullification or impairment of benefits, or impediments to the attainment of any objective of the agreement, have arisen because of the violation of any provision of the agreement, panels have recommended that the measure in question be terminated or brought into conformity with the agreement. There has been only one case in the GATT where a panel found a measure to be inconsistent with the GATT and yet did not recommend its termination; instead, it recommended a waiver. The relevant case is the one covered by the Panel on Jamaica – Margin of Preferences (February 1971).[101] In some "violation cases", the panels have also made specific recommendations for action by the Members concerned. For example, in an anti-dumping case, the Panel on New Zealand – Imports of Electrical Transformers from Finland (July 1985)[102] recommended revoking the determination of anti-dumping and reimbursing the anti-dumping duties paid. In a case of countervailing duties between the US and Canada in respect of fresh, chilled and frozen pork, there was a recommendation for the reimbursement of the countervailing duty.

In "non-violation cases", the panels have recommended the restoration of the competitive relationship as it existed before the measure was taken. The important cases of this type are: the Panel on Treatment by Germany of Imports of Sardines (March 1965)[103] and the Panel on Vitamins (October 1982).[104] If a party is a developing country Member, the report must explicitly indicate the form in which account has been taken of the relevant provisions of differential and more favourable treatment for developing country Members.

The final report has to be circulated to the Members promptly.

Consideration in the DSB

A minimum of 20 days is to pass between the circulation of the panel report to Members and the consideration of the report by the DSB. Members who have objections to the report have to give written reasons for their objection which have to be circulated at least 10 days prior to the meeting of the DSB in which the report is going to be considered.

If a party to the dispute has not notified the DSB about its decision to go for an appeal, the DSB has to adopt the report within 60 days of the date of circulation of the report to Members, except if it decides by consensus not to adopt the report. There is no possibility of such a negative decision by consensus, as it will require the agreement also of the Member that benefits from the report. Hence, in actual practice, the report of the panel will certainly get adopted within the time period mentioned.

There is a further time limit. The time taken from the establishment of the panel to the consideration of the panel report for adoption by the DSB shall not exceed nine months.

Appeal Process

The parties to the dispute have the right to appeal against the panel report. The third parties which have indicated their interest in the dispute do not have such a right. However, after the appeal process has started as a result of the move of any of the parties to the dispute, the third party Members may make a written or oral submission to the Appellate Body.

The appeal must be limited to issues of law covered in the panel report and to legal interpretations developed by the panel.

The appeal is considered by the standing Appellate Body. This standing Body will have seven members, three of whom will consider any particular appeal.

The Appellate Body may uphold, modify or reverse the legal findings and conclusions of the panel.

Generally, the appeal process must not take more than 60 days from the date a party to the dispute notifies its decision to appeal against the panel report. When the Appellate Body considers that it cannot give its report within this prescribed time, it must inform the DSB and give an estimate of the additional time required. In any case, the process must not take more than 90 days.

Unlike the case of the consideration of the report of a panel by the DSB, there is no specific minimum time limit for the report of the Appellate Body to be with the Members before it is taken up for consideration in the DSB. The report of the Appellate Body will have to be adopted by the DSB within 30 days of its circulation to the Members, except if the DSB decides by consensus not to adopt it. As explained earlier, there is hardly any chance of such a negative consensus; hence, the report, in reality, will have to be adopted within the time period specified.

In cases where an appeal has been made, the time taken from the establishment of the panel to the consideration of the report of the Appellate Body for adoption in the DSB shall not exceed 12 months.

Implementation of Recommendation

Where a panel or the Appellate Body has concluded that a measure is inconsistent with an agreement, it has the obligation to recommend that the Member concerned bring the measure into conformity with the agreement. In addition, the panel or the Appellate Body may also suggest ways in which the Member concerned could implement the recommendation.

It is expected that the Member to which the recommendation for action is addressed will implement the recommendation promptly. Some time limits have been prescribed in this regard.

Time Limit for Setting the Time Frame

Within 30 days of the adoption of the panel report or the Appellate Body report, the Member concerned will inform the DSB about its intentions in respect of the implementation of the recommendations and rulings. If it is not practical to comply with the recommendations and rulings immediately, the Member will propose a reasonable period for implementation. If this period is approved by the DSB, the implementation will proceed accordingly.

If the DSB does not approve it, the parties to the dispute may discuss and agree on a revised time period. They have 45 days to come to this mutual agreement.

If no such agreement is reached, there will be an arbitration on the time frame within 90 days of the date of adoption of the recommendations and rulings. The arbitration will be done by an arbitrator mutually agreed upon by the parties to the dispute. If there is no agreement on who should be the arbitrator within 10 days of the matter being referred to arbitration, the Director-General of the WTO has to appoint an arbitrator within another period of 10 days of consulting the parties. The guideline to the arbitrator will be that the reasonable period of time to implement the panel or Appellate Body recommendation should not exceed 15 months from the date of adoption of the panel or Appellate Body report. If the panel or the Appellate Body has taken additional time, such time will be added to the 15-month period. But in any case, the time shall not exceed 18 months except if the parties to the dispute agree on a longer period in exceptional circumstances.

Possibility of Compliance Measures Being Inconsistent With Agreements

There is a provision in the DSU regarding the situation when a measure proposed to be taken in implementation of the recommendation or ruling is considered inconsistent with an agreement covered by the DSU. Disagreements in such matters will be decided through recourse to the dispute settlement process, including resorting to the original panel, wherever possible. In such cases, the panel will circulate its report within 90 days of the date when the matter was referred to it. If it is not practicable, the panel will give its reasons to the DSB along with an estimate of the additional time required.

Surveillance of Implementation

The surveillance of the implementation will be done by the DSB. The subject of the implementation will come into the agenda of the DSB meeting six months after the finalisation of the time frame of implementation. It will remain on the agenda until the issue is resolved. Before each meeting of the DSB during this period, the Member concerned has to provide the DSB with a written status report on the progress of the implementation.

Compensation and Suspension of Concession

If the recommendations or rulings have not been implemented within the approved time frame by the Member to which these were addressed (the offending Member), the complaining Member may ask for a negotiation with the former in order to arrive at an agreement on compensation. The offending Member has to enter into such a negotiation. If no agreement on compensation is reached within 20 days of the expiry of the time frame for implementation of the recommendations or rulings, the complaining Member may request the DSB for authorisation to suspend some concessions or other obligations in respect of the offending Member. (The proposed suspension of concessions or other obligations may extend to areas wider than that covered by the recommendations or rulings. It will be explained in detail later.)

The level of the suspension of concessions or other obligations must be equivalent to the level of the initial nullification or impairment, i.e., it cannot be higher. Suspension of concessions or other obligations will not be allowed if it is prohibited by a covered agreement.

It is relevant to point out here that Article XXIII.2 of GATT 1994 provides for a level of suspension which is determined by the Members to be "appropriate in the circumstances". Often, it has been held that in determining appropriateness, purely statistical tests would not be sufficient; it is necessary to consider broader economic elements. The Working Party on Netherlands Action under Article XXIII.2 (adopted on 8 November 1952) applied these criteria and suggested a level of suspension. Another working party was established to assess the level of suspension, and, finally, the level was slightly modified, but similar general principles were followed.[105]

Now, Article 22.4 of the DSU clearly prescribes that the level of suspension will be "equivalent" to the level of nullification or impairment. Hence, one does not have to consider now what is an "appropriate" level of suspension of concessions or other obligations. Further, Article 22.3(d) of the DSU has given guidance regarding the elements to be considered in arriving at a decision on suspension. They are: trade in the area where violation has been established, the importance of such trade to the party, broader economic elements related to the nullification or impairment, and broader economic consequences of the suspension of concessions or other obligations.

The DSB must grant the authorisation of suspension within 30 days of the expiry of the time frame for implementation of the recommendations or rulings, except in the following circumstances:

(i) The DSB decides by consensus to reject the request. As explained earlier while discussing the decisions for the formation of the panel, such a negative consensus is almost impossible. Hence, this exception may be taken to be almost non-applicable.

(ii) The offending Member objects to the level of the suspension proposed, or, in the case of cross-sectoral or cross-agreement suspension (to be discussed later), claims that the prescribed principles and procedures have not been followed. In this case, the matter will have to be referred to arbitration.

If the members of the original panel are available, the arbitration will be carried out by that panel as the arbitrator. Otherwise, the Director-General of the WTO will appoint an individual or a group of individuals as the arbitrator.

The arbitration must be completed within 60 days of the expiry of the time frame for the implementation of the recommendations or rulings.

The parties have to accept the decision of the arbitrator as final. The DSB, at the request of the complaining party, has to authorise suspension if it is consistent with the decision of the arbitrator, except if the DSB decides by consensus to reject the request. As explained earlier, such a negative consensus is almost impossible; hence, authorisation by the DSB is almost a certainty.

The suspension of concessions or other obligations is a temporary relief. It will continue only till the recommendations and rulings are fully implemented. Surveillance by the DSB will continue till then, even if compensation has been given or suspension has been authorised.

CROSS-SECTOR AND CROSS-AGREEMENT SUSPENSION

The DSU permits cross-sector and cross-agreement retaliation by the suspension of concessions or other obligations under certain conditions. The principles and procedures to be followed for this purpose are given below.

The complaining party should first seek to apply the suspension in the same sector in which the panel or the Appellate Body has found a violation or any other nullification or impairment.

If it considers that it is not practical or effective to apply the suspension in the same sector, it may seek to apply the suspension in other sectors under the same agreement.

If it considers that: (i) even such a suspension is not practical or effective, and (ii) circumstances are serious enough, it may seek to apply the suspension in the areas of another covered agreement.

The term "sector" means with respect to goods, all goods. In respect of services, it means a principal sector as identified in the current Services Sectoral Classification List given in WTO document MTN.GNS/W/120. The principal sectors given in this list are: (i) business, (ii) communication, (iii) construction and related engineering, (iv) distribution, (v) educational, (vi) environmental, (vii) financial, (viii) health-related and social, (ix) tourism and travel-related, (x) recreational, cultural and sporting, (xi) transport, (xii) other.

In respect of intellectual property rights, it means each category of rights, viz., copyright and related rights, trademarks, geographical indications, industrial designs, patents, layout-designs (topographies) of integrated circuits and protection of undisclosed information, or obligations relating to the enforcement of IPRs (Part III), or the acquisition and maintenance of IPRs and related *inter partes* procedures (Part IV).

The term "agreement", for goods, means GATT 1994, other agreements listed in Annex 1A to the WTO Agreement and plurilateral agreements in so far as the relevant parties to the dispute are parties to these agreements. In respect of services, it means the General Agreement on Trade in Services. In respect of IPRs, it means the Agreement on TRIPS.

This provision of cross-agreement retaliation means that action can be taken, for example, on goods for some action or for some omission to take action in the area of services or IPRs.

A practical implication of the cross-linkage is that for a perceived violation of obligations in the areas of services and IPRs, there can be the possibility of retaliation in the goods area against countries which are weak in services and IPRs, e.g., almost all the developing countries, as in their case, it can be argued that retaliation in the areas of services and IPRs will not be effective.

SOME OTHER PROVISIONS

Good Offices, Conciliation and Mediation

There is a provision of the Director-General of the WTO offering good offices, conciliation or mediation in disputes. It may be requested by any party to a dispute, but can be effectively undertaken only if both parties to the dispute agree to use this procedure. It may begin and may be terminated at any time, and it may even be continued while the panel process is on. In this process, the objective is to assist the parties to settle the dispute in a way which is satisfactory to both.

When a least developed country Member is involved in a dispute, there is a special provision for good offices, conciliation or mediation. If a satisfactory solution has not been found during the consultation, the least developed country Member which is a party to the dispute may request the Director-General or the Chairman of the DSB to offer good offices, conciliation and mediation.

If a request is made by a least developed country Member, it is obligatory for the Director-General or the Chairman of the DSB to undertake the process, whereas, in other cases, the Director-General may undertake the process at his discretion when a request is made.

Arbitration

An alternative course in the dispute settlement process is arbitration. It will be entered into if the parties to the dispute agree to adopt it. In such cases, the parties have to notify the Members well ahead of the actual commencement of the arbitration. Any other Member may join the process only if the parties which have initiated it agree.

The parties have to agree to abide by the arbitration award. The award will be notified to the DSB where any Member will have the opportunity to raise any point. If a Member considers that it has been adversely affected by the award, this is the occasion to raise it.

The implementation process of the award will be along the same lines as that for the recommendation and ruling of a panel.

Least Developed Country Member

The special provision relating to good offices, conciliation and mediation in respect of cases where a least developed country Member is involved has already been explained. There is a further special provision in respect of these countries. In the dispute settlement process, particular consideration has to be given to the special situation of these countries at all stages of a dispute involving such a Member. Due restraint must be exercised in raising matters involving such a Member and in asking for compensation or seeking authorisation to suspend concessions or other obligations in respect of such a Member, when it is a party to a dispute.

Non-Violation Cases of the Type Covered by Article XXIII.1(b), Cases of the Type Covered by Article XXIII.1(c)

For "non-violation" and "other situation" cases, there are some special provisions.

In "non-violation" cases, the procedure of the DSU will, of course, apply. But a party which has been applying a "non-violating" measure will not be called upon to withdraw the measure. The panel or the Appellate Body has to make a recommendation that the Member concerned should make a suitable satisfactory adjustment. One solution in these cases may be an agreement on compensation.

In cases where an arbitrator is appointed to determine the time frame for implementation of the recommendation and ruling, the arbitrator may, at the request of either party, also determine the level of benefits which have been nullified or impaired and may also suggest a mutually satisfactory adjustment. Such a suggestion will not be binding on the parties.

In "other situation" cases, the procedure of the DSU applies up to the stage when the panel report is circulated to the Members. The procedure thereafter is different. It follows the process contained in the dispute settlement rules and procedures included in the decision of 12 April 1989 (BISD 36S/61-67).

In such cases, the decision on the panel report in the DSB will be by consensus, i.e., the provision of automatic adoption, except in the case of a negative consensus, is not applicable. The tight process for the fixation of the time frame for implementation of the recommendation and ruling is also absent. Instead, the simple provision is that the Member concerned will have a reasonable time frame. Further, there is no provision relating to compensation or suspension of concessions or other obligations.

MULTILATERAL PROCESS IN DISPUTE SETTLEMENT

The DSU prescribes that the violation of obligations, the nullification or impairment of benefits, or the existence of impediments to the attainment of any objective of the agreements must be determined only through recourse to the DSU. Similarly, the determination of the time frame for implementation of the recommendation and ruling, and of the level of compensation or the suspension of concessions or other obligations must also be done in accordance with the DSU.

Though the DSU does not contain a specific provision prohibiting unilateral trade action, it is clear from these provisions that Members can only take recourse to multilateral action in the course of redressing their grievances.

SPECIAL PROVISIONS RELATING TO DISPUTE SETTLEMENT

As mentioned while discussing the coverage of the DSU, some agreements in the area of goods and the agreements on trade in services and TRIPS contain modifications of some of the provisions in the DSU. These are described below.

The Agreement on Textiles and Clothing enters the process of Article XXIII of GATT 1994 and the DSU at the stage of the request for a panel and follows this process thereafter. Ordinarily, disputes on issues covered by the Agreement are to be settled by the Textiles Monitoring Body (TMB). However, if the dispute remains unresolved after the TMB has given its recommendation and continues to remain unresolved even after the TMB has given a reconsidered recommendation, either party to the dispute may bring the matter to the DSB and request for a settlement of the dispute. Thereafter, the process of the formation of a panel and subsequent procedures will be followed.

The Agreement on Anti-dumping has its own preconditions for starting the dispute settlement process. If a Member considers that any benefit accruing to it under the Agreement is being nullified or impaired by another Member, or that the achievement of any objective of the Agreement is being impeded by another Member, it may seek consultation with the other Member to resolve the issue. If the issue is not resolved in this manner and if a final action has been taken by the other Member to levy definitive anti-dumping duties or to have a price undertaking imposed, the Member against whom the action is taken may refer the matter to the DSB. Also, if a provisional measure is taken which has a significant impact and if the Member against whom the action has been taken considers that it has been taken without the preconditions having been fulfilled, it may refer the matter to the DSB. Thereafter, the process of the formation of a panel and further action in the DSB will follow.

In the case of customs valuation, there is a provision for the Technical Committee to provide advice and assistance to Members engaged in consultation, if so requested. Further, the panel may also request the Technical Committee to carry out an examination of any question requiring technical consideration.

The General Agreement on Trade in Services has also stipulated its own preconditions for resorting to the provisions of the DSU. If a Member considers that any other Member fails to carry out its obligations or specific commitments, it may take recourse to the DSU. A Member may also take recourse to the DSU if it considers that any benefit which it could have reasonably expected to accrue under some specific commitments of another Member is being nullified or impaired as a result of a measure which does not conflict with this Agreement. The process will involve the formation of a panel and further follow-up in the DSB.

The Agreement on TRIPS follows Articles XXII and XXIII of GATT 1994 as elaborated and applied by the DSU. However, an action can be initiated only if a benefit under the Agreement is being nullified or impaired or if the attainment of any objective of the Agreement is being impeded as a result of the failure of any Member to carry out its obligations. The two other alternative conditions contained in Article XXIII of GATT 1994, viz., those related to the provisions whether or not in conflict with the Agreement [1(b)] and the existence of any other situation [1(c)], are excluded for a period of five years from the entry into force of the WTO Agreement.

In some of the covered agreements, there are some additional provisions which have been described in the respective chapters dealing with those agreements.

The special provisions in the Agreement on Anti-dumping which restrict the role of the panels are particularly significant. In disputes relating to this Agreement, the panels have been asked not to give their findings as to whether or not the measures are consistent with the provisions of the Agreement. The panels have been authorised only to determine whether the establishment of the facts by the authorities has been proper and whether the evaluation of the facts has been unbiased and objective. Even if the panels come to a conclusion different from that of the authorities, the evaluation of the authorities will not be overturned. Further, if the relevant provisions of the Agreement allow more than one permissible interpretation, the panels must declare the anti-dumping measure to be in conformity with the Agreement if it rests upon one of these permissible interpretations.

This is a serious curtailment of the role of the panels. It is particularly significant because a very large proportion of disputes in recent years has been about dumping.

Further, a decision of the Ministerial Meeting in Marrakesh says that this provision must be reviewed after a period of three years with a view to considering the question whether it is capable of general application. Thus, the restriction of the role of the panels is not sought to be limited to only anti-dumping cases; there is a possibility of it being extended to other areas as well. If this actually takes place, it will make the whole dispute settlement process almost totally ineffective.

Chapter VIII.2

INSTITUTIONAL MATTERS

MEMBERSHIP

THERE are two types of Members of the WTO, viz.:(i) original Members, and (ii) Members by accession.

Original Members

Original Members are those:

(i) which were contracting parties to GATT 1947 on 1 January 1995;

(ii) which accepted the WTO Agreement and the Multilateral Trade Agreements (the Agreement was open for acceptance for a period of two years from 1 January 1995);

(iii) for which schedules of concessions and commitments were annexed to GATT 1994; and

(iv) for which schedules of specific commitments were annexed to the General Agreement on Trade in Services.

Thus, for a contracting party to GATT 1947 to be a Member of the WTO, it was necessary to conclude its schedules on goods (including tariff concessions, and commitments on domestic support and export subsidies in agriculture) and services. This was a process which was conducted through bilateral and plurilateral negotiations.

These schedules were considered complete when all interested Members (or would-be original Members) had agreed. Simultaneously, the contracting party had to go through its domestic procedure for accepting the Agreements. When all this was done, the contracting party communicated its acceptance.

Members by Accession

A government or a customs territory which has full autonomy in the conduct of matters covered by the agreements may express its desire to accede to the WTO. There will be negotiations between itself and the Members of the WTO; if there is an agreement on the terms of its accession, the decision on the accession will be taken by the Ministerial Conference of the WTO (by a two-thirds majority). Thereafter, this government or customs territory will become a Member of the WTO.

Generally, the process of accession is rather long. When a country applies for accession, a Working Party is usually established in the WTO to determine the terms of accession. The country has to enter into very detailed and often very tough negotiations in the Working Party and also bilaterally with several countries on an informal basis. It has to bring its legislation and procedures into conformity with the WTO agreements and it has to enter into commitments to reduce its tariffs and to eliminate its non-tariff barriers within a given time frame. Sometimes, countries have taken up to four to five years to have their accession finalised.

Date of Application

The WTO Agreement and the Multilateral Trade Agreements entered into force on 1 January 1995.

For an original Member, the application of the Agreements will start on the thirtieth day following the date of acceptance. Even if the acceptance is after 1 January 1995, the Member must discharge its obligations in the prescribed time frames as if it had accepted the Agreements on 1 January 1995.

For a Member joining by accession, the date of application will normally be prescribed in the terms of accession.

Withdrawal

A Member may withdraw from the WTO. For this purpose, it has to send a notice to the Director-General of the WTO. The withdrawal will be effective upon the expiration of six months from the date when the written notice was received by the Director-General.

DECISION-MAKING

General

Decision-making will generally be by consensus. There is a specific meaning of the term "consensus" here. A decision will be deemed to be made by consensus if no Member present at the meeting when the decision is being taken formally objects to the proposed decision. Thus, even one Member may withhold the consensus.

If consensus is not possible, the decision will be arrived at by voting. Each Member will have one vote. Generally, the decision will be adopted by a majority of the votes cast. There are some exceptions, as will be explained later.

The WTO Agreement mentions one-Member-one-vote and decision by majority in the case of the Ministerial Conference and the General Council. Perhaps the implication is that other bodies will be taking decisions only on the basis of consensus. In practice, if these other bodies are unable to decide on a matter, it will come for decision to the General Council or the Ministerial Conference.

Decision on Interpretation

The interpretation of the Agreements can be done only by the Ministerial Conference or the General Council. The decision to adopt an interpretation needs a three-fourths majority of the Members.

Decision on Waiver

A decision on the waiver of an obligation will be taken by a three-fourths majority of the Members. Decisions on such a matter can be taken only in the Ministerial Conference.

Decision on Amendment

Amendment of Provisions Relating to Waiver, MFN, Tariff Binding, Provision of Amendment

Amendments to (i) the provisions on waivers mentioned above; (ii) provisions relating to tariff binding in GATT 1994; and (iii) MFN provisions related to goods, services and intellectual property rights will come into effect only when accepted by all Members. A similar process also applies to amendments to the provision on amendments.

Amendment of Other Agreements in Goods Area and Agreement on TRIPS

There are two types of decision-making for amendments to the other provisions to various agreements in the goods area and of the one in the IPR area, viz.:

(i) Amendments which are of a nature that would not alter the rights and obligations of the Members can be decided by a two-thirds majority of Members.

(ii) Amendments which are of a nature that would alter the rights and obligations of the Members can be decided on acceptance by two-thirds of the Members. These will take effect for only those Members that accepted them at the time of the decision, or those that accept them later within the time specified by the Ministerial Conference.

In fact, all provisions in these agreements contain, in some ways, rights and obligations; hence, it will be extremely difficult to categorise provisions as not altering the rights and obligations, except for totally routine provisions, in which case the amendment may not be necessary or significant.

Amendments in GATS

There are two types of decision-making for amendments to GATS, viz.:

(i) Amendments to Parts IV (progressive liberalisation), V (institutional provisions) and VI (final provisions) of the Agreement and the related annexes will be decided on acceptance by two-thirds of the Members.

(ii) Amendments to Parts I (scope and definition), II (general obligations and disciplines, except the MFN clause) and III (specific commitments) can be decided on acceptance by two-thirds of the Members. The amendments will be applicable only to those that accepted them at the time of the decision, or to those that accept them later within a time frame prescribed by the Ministerial Conference.

Removal or Withdrawal of Members Not Accepting Some Amendments

There is a provision for the withdrawal or removal of a Member from the WTO in case the Member does not accept some important amendments. It applies to amendments in the agreements relating to the goods area and the IPR area, in case the amendments are of a nature that would alter the rights and obligations of the Members, as well as to amendments to Parts I, II and III of GATS.

In these cases, the Ministerial Conference may decide by a three-fourths majority that the amendment is of such a nature that if any Member does not accept it within a specified period (the period to be specified by the Ministerial Conference), the Member is free to withdraw from the WTO. In such a situation, the Member can continue only with the consent of the Ministerial Conference.

This is a very important provision, as it provides for the expulsion of a Member for not accepting an important amendment.

STRUCTURE OF THE WTO, COUNCILS, COMMITTEES

Ministerial Conference

The Ministerial Conference is the highest body in the WTO. It is composed of the representatives of all the Members. This Conference is to meet at least once in two years. It has the authority to carry out the functions of the WTO and to take actions necessary to this effect.

General Council

The General Council is composed of the representatives of all the Members. In the intervals between the meetings of the Ministerial Conference, the Conference's functions are conducted by the General Council.

Dispute Settlement Body

The Dispute Settlement Body (DSB) has been envisaged in the Dispute Settlement Understanding. It is responsible for the settlement of disputes among Members. The General Council has the authority to convene, as appropriate, to discharge the responsibilities of the DSB. In actual practice, the DSB, which is constituted of the representatives of all Members and which has its own Chairman, is operationally a separate body.

Other Councils

There is a Council for Trade in Goods, a Council for Trade in Services and a Council for TRIPS. These Councils operate under the general guidance of the General Council. The membership of these Councils is open to representatives of all Members.

Committees

There is a Committee on Trade and Development (CTD), a Committee on Balance-of-Payments Restrictions (BOP Committee) and a Committee on Budget, Finance and Administration.

Secretariat

There is a Secretariat of the WTO, headed by a Director-General. The Ministerial Conference appoints the Director-General who, in turn, appoints the staff members of the Secretariat.

ENDNOTES

1. For a historical perspective and a preparatory history, see John H. Jackson, *World Trade and The Law of GATT*, Bobbs-Merritt, Indianapolis, 1969, pp. 249-54.
2. BISD II/12.
3. BISD 35S/245,289-290.
4. John H. Jackson, op.cit., pp.263-4.
5. BISD II/188,191.
6. BISD 25S/49,63.
7. BISD 28S/112.
8. BISD 1S/59,60.
9. BISD 1S/94,98.
10. BISD 20S/34,36.
11. BISD 28S/102,111.
12. BISD 28S/92,98.
13. BISD 18S/149,154.
14. This illustration was given in the preparatory work for this provision and has been quoted in John H. Jackson, op.cit., p.282.
15. BISD 7S/60,64.
16. BISD 36S/345,385-386.
17. BISD 34S/83,113-115.
18. BISD 18S/97,102.
19. BISD 34S/136,154-155.
20. BISD 39S/206,276-277.
21. BISD 7S/60,63-64.
22. BISD 39S/206,277.
23. BISD 30S/140,159-161.
24. BISD 25S/49,65.
25. BISD 28S/90.
26. BISD 39S/206,279-280.
27. BISD 39S/27,84-85.
28. BISD 37S/345,385-387.
29. BISD 39S/206, 276-277.
30. BISD II/181,182.
31. BISD 37S/132,191-192.
32. BISD 36S/387.
33. BISD 39S/206,274.
34. BISD 34S/136,158.
35. BISD II/181,185.
36. BISD 39S/206,270-271.
37. BISD 37S/86,124-125.
38. BISD 39S/206,271-273.
39. BISD 34S/136,163-164.
40. BISD 37S/132,198-199.
41. BISD 37S/200,227.

42. BISD 34S/136,160.
43. BISD 36S/167,197-198.
44. BISD 28S/102,111.
45. BISD 31S/114, 131-133.
46. John H. Jackson, op.cit., p.558, makes the following observation regarding relative increase: "This concept of 'relative increase' seems inappropriate in an escape clause that is based on a policy of allocating the burdens of market readjustment...Here no actual increase in imports has occurred, so it seems very difficult to justify placing this burden on the foreign products. It appears that the 'relative' increase concept is a protective device. It is a device that may have little relevance in a general period of increasing economic wealth, but it is a potentially dangerous device if general world economic conditions tend to decline."
47. BISD 35S/336.
48. BISD 27S/98,113,116.
49. BISD 36S/93,130-131.
50. BISD 1S/28-30.
51. BISD 3S/170,182.
52. BISD 26S/205.
53. BISD 26S/209.
54. BISD 6S/112,113.
55. BISD 36S/202,234,268.
56. BISD 20S/47-49.
57. BISD 18S/48-53.
58. BISD 18S/49, paragraph 3; 26S/205, paragraph 12.
59. For a comprehensive analysis of this issue and other issues relating to technical barriers to trade, see Edmond L.M. Völker, "The Agreement on Technical Barriers to Trade", and Reinhard Quick, "The Agreement on the Technical Barriers to Trade in the Context of the Trade and Environment Discussion", in Jacques H.J.Bourgeois, Frédérique Berrod and Eric Gippini Fournier (editors), *The Uruguay Round Results – A European Lawyer's Perspective*, College of Europe, Bruges, 1995.
60. BISD 36S/345, 392-393.
61. BISD 37S/200, 222-226.
62. BISD 39S/155, 198-200.
63. The developing countries (other than LDCs) included originally in this list are: Bolivia, Ghana, Guatemala, Guyana, India, Indonesia, Kenya, Morocco, Nicaragua, Nigeria, Pakistan, Philippines, Senegal, Sri Lanka and Zimbabwe.
64. BISD 27S/69,97.
65. BISD 26S/290,319.
66. BISD 32S/55,67-68.
67. BISD 39S/411,435-436.
68. BISD 32S/55,68.
69. BISD 39S/436,446-447.
70. For a comprehensive history of negotiations on this subject and analysis of conflicting interests, see Mark Koulen, "The New Anti-Dumping

Code through its Negotiating History", in Jacques H.J.Bourgeois, Frédérique Berrod and Eric Gippini Fournier (editors), op.cit.

71. Various governments have enacted their legislation to prescribe how the determination of dumping, injury and causation is to be done. For a concise review of the relevant implementing legislation of some major trading countries, see UNCTAD, TD/B/WG.8/6, 15 November 1995.
72. For an analysis of the effects of actual commitments of major importing developed countries, see Stefan Tangermann, *Implementation of the Uruguay Round Agreement on Agriculture by Major Developed Countries*, UNCTAD, Geneva, 1995.
73. UNCTAD, TD/B/WG.8/2/Add.1, 26 July 1995, Table I.1.
74. See Sanjoy Bagchi, "The Integration of the Textile Trade into GATT", *Journal of World Trade*, Vol. 28, No. 6, December 1994, p.36. See also UNCTAD, TD/B/WG.8/2, pp.10-1.
75. See UNCTAD, UNCTAD/ITD/17, 6 October 1995, table 9, col. 4, p.50.
76. This explanation has been communicated by the Chairman of the Trade Negotiating Committee to the Chairman of the Textiles Monitoring Body formally in a letter which is a part of the decision of the Trade Negotiating Committee.
77. Para 4 of the Final Act Embodying the Results of the Uruguay Round of Multilateral Trade Negotiations, in GATT Secretariat, *The Results of the Uruguay Round of Multilateral Trade Negotiations: The Legal Texts*, Geneva, 1994, p.4.
78. BISD 36S/268, 301-302.
79. BISD 30S/140, 163.
80. BISD 9S/28, 170-172.
81. For a detailed analysis of the Agreement on TRIPS, see J.H. Reichman, *Implications of the Draft TRIPS Agreement for Developing Countries as Competitors in an Integrated World Market*, UNCTAD Discussion Paper No. 73, Geneva, November 1993, and South Centre, *The Uruguay Round Intellectual Property Rights Regime – Implications for Developing Countries*, Geneva, 1995. See also Arvind Subramanian, "Trade-Related Intellectual Property Rights and Asian Developing Countries: An Analytical View", in a forthcoming publication of the Asian Development Bank.
82. For a detailed discussion, see Abdulqawi A.Yusuf and Andrés Moncayo von Hase, "Intellectual Property Protection and International Trade – Exhaustion of Rights Revisited", *World Competition,* Vol. 16, No. 1, September 1992.
83. See South Centre, op.cit.
84. The relevant provisions have been reproduced in WIPO, *WIPO Publication No. 223(E)*, WIPO, Geneva, 1996.
85. UPOV, *Publications Nos 221(E), 293 (E)*, WIPO, Geneva (available in WIPO Secretariat).
86. South Centre, op.cit.
87. See WIPO, op.cit.
88. See South Centre, op.cit.

89. See J.H.Reichman, op.cit.
90. See WIPO, op.cit.
91. See South Centre, op.cit.
92. See WIPO, op.cit. This treaty was concluded in Washington in 1989, but it has not entered into force (till the time of writing, May 1998) as there have not been adequate ratifications.
93. See South Centre, op.cit.
94. BISD 34S/157,158.
95. BISD II/188, 193-194.
96. BISD 1S/53,58.
97. BISD 3S/222,224.
98. BISD 37S/86,130.
99. BISD 26S/290,291.
100. BISD 11S/95,99.
101. BISD 18S/183,187.
102. BISD 32S/55,70.
103. BISD 13S/45,48.
104. BISD 29S/110,117.
105. BISD 1S/62,63-64.

Bibliography

Abbot, Fredrick M. *Law and Policy of Regional Integration: The NAFTA and Western Hemispheric Integration in the World Trade Organisation System*. Dordretch, London: Martinus Mishoff, 1995.

Agra Europe, London. *Agricultural Trading – Post GATT: A Guide to the Implementation of the GATT Uruguay Round Agreement*. London, 1995.

Colins, S. *The New GATT*. Washington, D.C.: Brookings Institution, 1994.

Croome, Hohn. *Reshaping the World Trading System: A History of the Uruguay Round*. Geneva: World Trade Organisation, 1995.

Dearforff, Alan V. *Analytical and Negotiating Issues in the Global Trading System*. Ann Arbor: University of Michigan Press, 1994.

European Communities. *GATS: The General Agreement on Trade in Services: A Guide for Business*. Brussels: EC, 1995.

European Communities. *Report on United States Trade Barriers to Trade and Investment*. Brussels: EC, 1995.

Evans, Philip. *Unpacking the GATT: A Step by Step Guide to the Uruguay Round*. London: International Organisation of Consumers Unions, 1994.

Hallastorm, Par. *The GATT Panels and the Formation of International Trade Law*. Stockholm: Jurisforlaget, 1994.

Hoekman, B. *Trade Law and Institutions: Good Practices and the World Trade Organisation*. Washington, D.C.: World Bank, 1995.

Jackson, John Howard. *Legal Problems of International Economic Regulations: Cases, Materials and Text on the National and International Regulation of Transnational Economic Relations*. St. Paul, Minn.: West Publishing, 1995.

Martin, Will. *The Uruguay Round: Widening and Deepening the World Trading System*. Washington, D.C.: World Bank, 1995.

Organisation for Economic Cooperation and Development. *The New World Trading System: Readings*. Paris: OECD, 1994.

Petersmann, E.-U. "The dispute settlement system of the World Trade Organisation and the evolution of the GATT dispute settlement system since 1948" in *Common Market Law Review*, 31, 1994.

Qureshi, Asif Hasan. *The World Trade Organisation: Implementing International Trade Norms*. Manchester: Manchester University Press, 1996.

United Nations Conference on Trade and Development. *The Outcome of the Uruguay Round: An Initial Assessment: Supporting Papers to the Trade and Development Report, 1994*. New York: United Nations, 1994.

World Trade Organisation. *Analytical Index*. Geneva: WTO, 1995.

World Trade Organisation. *Regionalism and the World Trading System*. Geneva: WTO, 1995.

World Trade Organisation. *The Results of the Uruguay Round: Market Access for Goods and Services*. Geneva: WTO, 1995.
World Trade Organisation. *The Results of the Uruguay Round of Multilateral Trade Negotiations: The Legal Texts*. Geneva: WTO, 1995.
World Trade Organisation. *The WTO Dispute Settlement Procedures: A Collection of Legal Texts*. Geneva: WTO, 1995.

Index

A

actionable 202
actionable subsidy 157, 170-3, 200
ad valorem 56-7, 61, 200, 279, 300-2, 305
adjustments to transaction value 284
advantage 4, 16, 21, 26, 42, 140, 151, 163, 340, 358, 368
Aggregate Measurement of Support (AMS) 241-4, 247-9
agricultural machinery 33, 37
agricultural products 6, 227-9, 231-2, 234-5, 253, 387
agriculture 6, 7, 9, 10, 12, 96, 155, 171, 174, 182, 225, 227-9, 231, 235-6, 239, 241, 244, 249, 252, 255, 427
alcoholic and malt beverages 36-8, 40-1, 43-4
amendment 9, 10, 145, 430-1
animal feed proteins 19, 38
Annecy 5
Annual Bound Commitment Level 242-3, 248
anti-competitive practices 373, 388
anti-dumping 10, 26, 49, 75, 205-6, 216-7, 219-21, 223-4, 306, 397, 414, 424-5, 436
anti-dumping duty 216-22, 299
appeal 172, 291, 295, 312, 415-6
arbitration 161, 173, 338-9, 416-7, 419, 421
Arrangement Regarding International Trade in Textiles – see *Multi-Fibre Arrangement*
Article I of GATT 1994 15, 18, 22
Article III of GATT 1994 29, 30-1, 37, 39, 42, 44, 49, 315, 400
Article XX of GATT 1994 26, 40, 120, 131, 147, 231
Article XXI of GATT 1994 26
Article XXIV of GATT 1994 24, 347
authorisation for supply of service 343
automatic licensing 294

B

balance of payments (BOP) 10-1, 27, 45, 99, 100-13, 142-3, 231, 336, 344-5, 348, 350, 432
balancing 22, 41, 141-2, 279, 362
Base Total AMS 242-3, 249
beef 23, 102, 232, 314, 406
Belgian family allowances 20
benefit 4, 6, 15-7, 19, 20-2, 27, 42, 45, 72, 90, 102, 144, 153-6, 165-6, 170-1, 173, 175, 180, 199, 200, 205, 212, 221, 246-7, 253-4, 317, 330, 338-9, 353, 356-7, 359, 360, 390, 399, 400-1, 403-5, 414-5, 422-4

best endeavour 318
binding 20-1, 59, 60-1, 63, 67-8, 72, 103, 232, 253, 402-3, 430
bound 16, 21-2, 25, 41, 60-3, 65-6, 72, 79, 103, 227, 229-32, 240, 242-3, 248-9, 291, 327, 329, 345-6, 402
bovine meat 5, 10, 27, 321
broadcasting 374, 377-8
bullion 149
burden of proof 166, 200, 214, 248, 374

C

carry forward 259, 263, 270, 369
carry over 259, 263, 270
causal linkage 78, 174, 180, 183, 189-90, 193-4, 202
change in classification 301, 305
charge 10, 12, 17-8, 23, 30-1, 36, 65-6, 93, 153, 163, 240-1, 246, 274, 284, 289, 377, 400-1
circumvention 19, 22, 272-4
civil aircraft 5, 10, 27, 321
classification of products 22, 57, 301
clothing 10, 257-9, 261-2, 264-6, 272, 275-6, 299, 423
Code of Good Practice 123-5
combined tariff 57
commercial level 287
commercial presence 326-8, 330-3, 350
Committee on Trade and Development 319, 432
Common Declaration 306
compensation 48, 78, 87-8, 91, 95, 173, 240, 247, 353, 389, 417-9, 422-3
compensatory concession 63, 101
competent authority 76-8, 84, 389
competition-restrictive practices 349
competitive condition 29, 34, 42-3, 403
competitive opportunities 11-2
compilation of data 376
compulsory 30, 32-3, 149, 370, 373, 386, 393
compulsory licensing 361, 370-2, 380, 386, 393
computed value 285, 290-2
computer programs 376-7
conciliation 421-2
conditions 11, 20, 24, 29, 30, 33-4, 39, 42-3, 61, 71, 73, 83, 89, 93, 96, 100-2, 105, 132-4, 139, 141-3, 155-61, 166-7, 180, 187, 190-1, 193-4, 201-2, 209, 211, 214, 218, 233-5, 237, 240, 245-6, 248, 253-4, 266-7, 269, 280-2, 284-6, 288-9, 294-6, 311, 318, 327, 329, 335-7, 340-2, 348, 350, 352, 357, 359, 361, 366-8, 370-3, 375-9, 381, 383-4, 387-8, 390, 399, 403-4, 406, 419, 424
conformity assessment procedure 117, 126-7
constructed export price 208

consultation 64, 78-9, 80-2, 84, 87-8, 91, 95, 100, 106-10, 112, 125, 136, 144-5, 160-1, 171, 177, 198, 217-8, 221-2, 240, 252, 255, 268-71, 273-4, 276, 291, 297, 307, 312, 340, 349, 352-3, 388, 399, 406-11, 421, 424
consumers 35, 115, 117, 154, 179, 189, 205-6, 246, 268, 334, 360, 362
consumption abroad 330-3
CONTRACTING PARTIES 9, 23-4, 90, 349
contracting parties 5, 9, 25-6, 42-3, 110, 317-9, 427
conversion of currencies 215
copyright 105, 112, 148, 357, 374-7, 389, 420
cost of production 210, 212-4, 284-5, 290-1, 311
Council for Trade in Goods 63-4, 90, 95, 143-5, 275, 316, 407, 432
Council for Trade in Services 338, 340, 343-4, 353, 407, 432
Council for TRIPS 367, 390-1, 393, 407
countermeasures 157, 160-1, 173, 200, 202, 265, 338
countervailing duty 155-6, 170, 173-5, 180-1, 188-94, 198-9, 202, 206, 216, 219, 253-4, 414
countries in transition 202
coverage of unbound duty 21
cross-agreement 419-20
cross-border supply 330-4
cross-sector 419
current access opportunity 233
Current Total AMS 242-4, 248
Customs Co-operation Council (CCC) 57, 291, 304
customs duty 4, 16, 18, 21, 55, 61, 238, 279, 281
customs fee 17
customs union 10, 24-5, 28, 187, 300
customs valuation 5, 10, 279, 291-2, 424

D

dairy 5, 10, 27, 233, 321
decision-making 395, 408, 429-31
decoupled income support 247
deduced value 285, 288
dependent patent 373
determination of equivalents 369
developing countries 5-8, 23-4, 27, 44, 55, 68-9, 91, 95-6, 99, 100-1, 113, 127, 143, 149, 154, 164, 176-7, 196-9, 201-2, 223-4, 228, 232-3, 241, 243-5, 247, 250-1, 255, 257-8, 269, 272, 275, 292, 296, 317-9, 336-7, 347, 352, 357, 375, 420
differential and more favourable treatment 5, 8, 23-4, 414
Dillon 5
directly competitive product 73, 75, 267-8
disadvantaged region 157, 159, 248
discrimination 15, 19, 22, 33, 36-7, 39, 43, 67, 93, 119, 124, 133, 143, 275, 294-5, 348, 362-3, 370

dispute settlement 42, 96, 128-9, 136, 145, 170-1, 196, 199, 221, 223, 254-5, 275-6, 291, 297, 307, 312, 317, 352-3, 390, 395, 397, 399, 406, 408, 422-3, 432
dispute settlement process 7-8, 12, 26, 42, 47, 128, 136, 155, 161, 170-2, 196, 199, 200, 202-3, 221, 223, 253-4, 260, 325, 353, 359, 389, 397-9, 406, 417, 421-2, 424-5
Dispute Settlement Understanding (DSU) 96, 128, 136, 145, 165, 171, 173, 196, 221, 223, 255, 276, 291, 297, 307, 312, 353, 389, 397-8, 401, 408, 417-9, 422-4, 432
dissemination of technology 358, 388
distribution 17, 30, 36, 39, 140, 163, 296, 367, 420
domestic food aid 247
domestic industry 34, 71-2, 74-5, 78-9, 83-4, 95, 160-1, 174-5, 179, 181-2, 184-9, 191-2, 201, 205-6, 217, 224, 253, 257, 259, 267-9, 402-3
domestic product 29, 30-9, 40-5, 55, 73-6, 105, 111, 124, 126, 136, 139-40, 143, 148, 153, 159, 175, 184, 186-7, 199, 235, 253, 400
domestic support 228-9, 230, 241-5, 249, 252-3, 255, 427
due restraint 254, 422
dumping 5, 11, 151, 205-7, 210-1, 214, 216-21, 224, 275, 425
duration 83-6, 95-6, 111, 190-1, 271, 297

E

economic integration 347
Enabling Clause 23-4
enquiry point 128, 134-6, 346
environment 45, 110, 115, 119, 122, 126, 129, 147, 149, 363
equal opportunities 29
equivalent measurement of support 243
exception 5, 8, 15, 18, 23-4, 26, 43-4, 68, 71, 92, 96, 117-8, 120, 122, 127, 131, 147, 149, 156, 163, 168, 172, 216, 231, 281, 327, 336, 345-6, 348, 350, 352, 359, 363, 366-8, 375-6, 378, 380, 382-5, 393, 419, 429
excise duty 17, 43
excise tax exemption 36-7
exhaustion 272, 359-60, 367, 386
expert group 129, 412
export competitiveness 164, 197-8
export price 207-8, 214-7, 219
export subsidy 154, 164, 197-9, 249, 252
export tax 17

F

false origin 274
favour 15-6, 24, 64, 158, 211, 329, 366
Final Bound Commitment Level 242-3
financial facilities 37

fixed external reference price 243-4
food security 246, 252
Foreign Investment Review Act 38, 314
formula approach 60, 63
free-trade area 10, 24-5, 28, 68, 300
full consultation 107-10, 112

G

GATT 1947 9, 10, 27, 227, 401, 427
GATT 1994 9, 10-2, 17, 19, 20, 23-6, 28, 32, 40, 43-4, 47, 50, 53, 56, 63-4, 66-8, 71, 73-4, 80-1, 88, 90-1, 93, 96, 99, 100, 102, 112, 120, 133, 136, 139, 140-3, 145, 147-8, 155, 165, 196, 200, 206, 223, 229, 231, 234-5, 253-5, 257, 260-6, 271, 275-6, 279, 290, 299, 306-7, 312-4, 316, 319, 325, 348-9, 352, 389-90, 398-9, 400, 405, 418, 420, 423-4, 427, 430
General Agreement on Tariffs and Trade (GATT) 3-9, 10, 21, 24-5, 50, 90, 105, 267-8, 329, 331-3, 335-6, 360, 365-7, 415-6, 423
General Agreement on Trade in Services (GATS) 325, 335, 350-1, 431
General Council 106, 112, 345, 429, 432
general exceptions 26, 40, 120, 147, 149, 231, 336, 345, 348
general obligations 94, 325, 330, 339, 347, 358, 431
general rules of origin 299, 300, 307
Generalised System of Preferences (GSP) 24, 68, 300
Geneva 4-5
geographical indications 357, 381-2, 420
gold coins 35
good offices 421-2
government procurement 5, 10, 26-7, 44, 117, 321, 346, 351-2
grey-area measures 90-1, 93-4
gross national product (GNP) 102, 164, 197
growth rates 258-9, 262-3, 272, 275

H

Harmonised System (HS) 57-8, 66, 165, 198, 252, 260, 301, 304-5

I

identical goods 285-8
immunity 16, 157
implementation period 230, 232, 236, 240-3, 250-1, 253, 255
import licensing 5, 10, 68, 104, 293-7
import surcharge 17, 103
import-substitution subsidy 165, 199
income insurance 247
income safety-net 247
incorporated products 254
industrial designs 357, 361, 382-3, 420

initial negotiating rights (INR) 63-6, 240, 405
injury 75, 78, 84, 95, 97, 165, 170-1, 174-9, 180-9, 190-4, 199, 200, 201-2, 206-7, 216-7, 220, 224, 235, 253-4
input subsidies 245
inspection entities 311
intellectual property rights (IPRs) 3, 6, 8, 12-3, 275, 323, 355-60, 370, 388, 392, 420-1, 430
interested Members 135, 178-9, 181, 188, 193, 234, 240, 296, 315, 340, 344, 408, 428
internal taxes 17, 30-2, 35-6, 41-2, 49, 120
international standards 115, 118, 121, 124-5, 127, 130, 133, 135, 310
interpretation 19, 29, 33-5, 47, 64, 66, 80, 121, 168, 185-6, 188, 222, 313, 415, 425, 429
investigation 50, 76, 78-9, 80, 84, 89, 94, 173-4, 176-9, 180, 189, 192-6, 212-3, 215-9, 221, 224, 254, 267, 273
investment 6, 35, 44, 139, 140-2, 144-5, 166, 182, 213, 244, 247-8, 267, 392
investment aid 247
isolated markets 186-7

K

Kennedy 5

L

labelling practices 35
layout-design 357, 383-6, 420
least developed countries (LDCs) 8, 24, 44, 164-5, 197-9, 255, 347
least developed country Members 45, 108-9, 231, 249, 255, 271, 337, 391
like product 15-6, 18-9, 20, 23, 31, 33-6, 39, 40, 45, 75, 119, 124, 126, 144, 167, 174, 181, 185-8, 201-2, 205, 207-8, 210, 213, 219, 310, 402
limitation 9, 44, 83-5, 100, 104, 121, 132, 158-9, 170, 180, 189, 229, 253, 265, 281, 327-9, 330-1, 334-7, 342, 350, 356-7, 359, 360, 365, 367, 370-3, 376, 378, 392, 397
liqueurs and sparkling wines 35
local content requirement 44
local government 13, 47-8, 118, 123, 125-6, 128-9, 144
Long-Term Agreement 258

M

manufacturing or processing criterion 300
market access 53, 69, 130, 147, 229-31, 233-5, 240-1, 318, 327-32, 335-7, 346, 350, 352, 404
market price support 243
mediation 421-2

Members by accession 427-8
minimal operations 305
minimum access opportunity 231, 233
minimum-price requirement 39
Ministerial Conference 304, 306, 340, 345, 390, 428-33
Ministerial Decision 223, 255, 280, 292
modes of supply 326-7, 334-5
modification of schedules 337
monopoly 169, 313-5, 349
monopoly supplier 348
moratorium 89
most favoured nation (MFN) 8, 13, 15, 21-2, 24, 26-7, 59, 62, 64, 68, 119, 133, 314, 325, 341-2, 430-1
most-favoured-nation (MFN) treatment 8, 15-6, 18-9, 20-3, 27-9, 32, 34, 68, 72, 75, 124, 126, 187, 306, 325, 338-40, 342, 345-8, 350-1, 359, 391
Multi-Fibre Arrangement (MFA) 91, 258-64, 266, 269
Multilateral Trade Agreements 10, 427-8
Multilateral Trade Negotiations (MTNs) 4-6, 9, 60-1, 66, 131, 227, 275, 357

N

narcotic crops 245
national treatment 8, 13, 29, 34, 40-5, 75, 119, 124, 126, 139, 143-4, 268, 306, 310, 314, 327-32, 336, 345-6, 352, 359, 361, 375, 391
natural persons 326, 328, 330-2, 334, 353-4
negligible effect on trade 41
newcomers 221, 296
1979 Declaration 99, 107-8, 110, 112
non-actionable 161
non-actionable subsidies 157, 162
non-automatic licensing 295
non-discrimination 15, 27, 29, 92, 310, 325, 339, 352
non-tariff measures (NTMs) 4-5, 11, 24, 79, 230-2, 235
non-violation cases 253, 400-3, 405, 414, 422
normal value 207-8, 210-1, 214-7, 219
nullification and impairment 42, 401

O

ordinary course of trade 207-11, 213
original Members 427-8
other duties and charges 10, 66, 241

P

panel 18-20, 22-3, 33, 35-44, 49, 59, 67, 81-2, 102, 120, 129, 149, 169-73, 184-5, 188, 222-3, 234-5, 291, 311, 314-5, 397, 401-2, 404-5, 407-17, 419-25

parallel import 360, 367
Paris Convention 360-1, 370, 379, 381
Part IV of GATT 1994 317
patent 40, 105, 112, 148, 323, 357, 360-4, 367-74, 377, 386, 392-3, 420
payments and transfers 350-1
performers 377-8
phonograms 374, 377-8
plurilateral agreements 10, 27-8, 225, 233-4, 321, 398, 420
preferential rules of origin 306
preferential tariff 67-8
preshipment inspection 10, 309, 311-2
presumption 27, 48, 118, 156, 162, 166, 200, 281, 374, 401
previous representative period 81
price 4, 11, 31, 37, 39, 93, 103, 153-5, 167-70, 180-3, 185, 190, 194, 205, 207-12, 214-7, 219, 222, 228, 235-6, 238-9, 243-9, 251, 267-9, 279-85, 288-90, 301, 309, 311, 314-5, 356, 360, 371, 424
price gap 244
price trigger 236, 238-9
price verification 311
price-based measures 103-4
principal supplying interest 63-4, 66, 80
privilege 16, 313-4, 365-6
process patent 374
processes and production methods (PPMs) 116-7, 129, 132, 134
producer retirement 247-8
product patent 362, 392
progressive liberalisation 86, 95, 110, 260, 431
prohibited subsidies 155, 162, 202
protection 3, 4, 6, 11-2, 26, 29, 31-2, 34, 36-7, 40, 43, 55, 70, 72-3, 112, 119, 124, 126, 129, 131, 133-4, 148-9, 160, 227, 254, 345, 355-7, 359, 361-2, 364-6, 375-9, 381-7, 391-3, 420
provisional duty 180
provisional measure 79, 80, 84, 134, 192-4, 217, 219-20, 222, 389, 424
purchase 17, 26, 30, 33, 36-8, 43, 140-1, 156, 216, 246-7, 284, 310, 314-5, 331

Q

qualifications 329, 336, 342-3, 347, 352
quantitative regulation 30-3, 44
quantitative restriction 11, 72, 80-1, 87, 93, 95-6, 103-4, 140, 237, 265, 295, 306
quantity trigger 236-7, 239

R

recognition process 344
regional government 47
regional trading blocs 28

related 15, 43-4, 90, 100, 108, 116-7, 120, 129, 132, 139, 141-2, 149, 159, 163, 175, 180-1, 186, 209, 221, 231, 247-8, 269, 282-5, 290, 306-7, 311, 326, 329, 344, 350, 354-5, 370, 383, 401, 407, 412, 418, 420, 424, 430-1
related buyer and seller 282
related process and production method 129
related rights. 374, 420
relative increase 74, 77
removal 190-1, 219, 431
rental right 376-7
repeated application 85
request-offer approach 61, 63
resource retirement 247-8
retaliation 8, 70, 87-9, 91, 397, 419-21
retroactive application 192
reverse notification 94, 106, 195, 316, 346
risk of discrimination 43
Round of MTNs 4, 7, 66, 131, 357, 398
rules of origin 10, 22, 187, 299, 300, 302-4, 306-7

S

safeguard 10-1, 71-4, 76, 78-80, 82, 84, 86-9, 92-6, 100, 231, 235-6, 240, 257, 260, 262, 264-6, 306, 351, 361, 375
safeguard measure 71-4, 76-9, 80-1, 83-9, 90, 92-6, 231, 265-7, 269-71, 351-2
sales below cost 210-1
sanitary and phytosanitary (SPS) measures 10, 118, 131-5, 137
schedule 9, 10, 19, 39, 56, 60, 62-3, 65-8, 103, 106-9, 143-4, 229-30, 232, 234-5, 238, 240-2, 249-52, 304, 325-31, 335-8, 340-2, 350, 352, 404, 408, 427-8
schedule of market access 330
Secretariat 105, 108, 110, 122-3, 135, 144, 307, 312, 315-6, 335, 410, 433
sectoral balance 275
security exception 26, 345, 348, 393
selectivity 92-3
semi-conductor 374
serious adverse effects 157, 160-1
serious damage 259, 267-9
serious injury 73-6, 78-9, 80-1, 83-4, 94-5, 97, 235
serious prejudice 156, 165-7,169-71, 199, 200-1, 253, 363
service operations 328
service supplier 326-9, 333-4, 337, 342-5, 347-9
services 3, 6, 8, 9, 13, 156, 158, 163, 246, 323, 325-9, 331-5, 337, 339, 342-3, 345-7, 349, 352-4, 356, 379-80, 398, 420-1, 427, 430
Short-Term Agreement 258
similar goods 283-5, 287-8, 311, 379-80
simplified consultations 107

site of inspection 310
social and cultural matters 148
special credit facilities 37
special factors 81-2, 111
special minimum access opportunity 231, 233
special safeguard provisions (SSP) 96-7, 235-40
specific 7, 11-2, 15, 17-8, 26, 32, 35, 42, 57, 73-4, 83-4, 90, 93-4, 96, 99, 100, 102, 106, 110, 112, 118-20, 134, 153, 157-60, 168, 171, 174-5, 180, 187-8, 195-6, 201, 206, 209, 225, 234, 244, 248, 253-4, 257-9, 271, 275-6, 282, 294, 296, 302, 305, 319, 326-7, 335-6, 342, 344, 346, 350-1, 353, 359, 363, 371, 374-5, 391, 402-3, 405-6, 408-9, 413-5, 423, 429
specific commitments 230, 325-7, 329-30, 335-7, 342-4, 347-8, 350-4, 424, 427, 431
specific operation 302
specificity 157
SSG 235, 240
standards 12, 35, 101, 115-8, 123-8, 130, 133, 169, 303, 310, 329, 336, 342-4, 355, 357
state trading enterprises 10, 313, 315, 348
stockholding 246
structural adjustment assistance 247
subsidies and countervailing measures 43-4, 153-4, 196, 217
subsidy 5, 9, 10-1, 43-4, 75, 151, 153-74, 176, 178-80, 182-3, 185, 188-90, 193-9, 200-3, 205, 216-7, 219-20, 227-30, 241, 244-9, 250-5, 275, 306, 331, 351-2, 400, 402-5, 427
substantial interest 64, 66, 80-2, 84, 87, 265, 408, 411
substantial transformation 304-5
substitutable product 31
Superfund Act 49
suspension of concession 48, 90, 95, 353, 417-9, 423
swing 258, 263, 270

T

tariff 4, 5, 7, 9, 10-1, 16-7, 19, 20-2, 24-5, 27, 29, 33, 36, 40-1, 53, 55-7, 59, 60-9, 70, 72-3, 79, 80, 87-8, 93, 95, 103, 106, 165, 206, 223, 227, 229-35, 240-1, 252-5, 260, 275, 279, 301, 305, 318-9, 400, 402-5, 427-8, 430
tariff escalation 68-9, 319
tariff measure 79
tariff nomenclature 57, 301
tariff quota 23, 67, 79, 233-4, 241
tariffication 231, 233, 235, 240
tax refund 37
tax remission 37
technical barriers to trade (TBT) 5, 10, 115, 117-9, 121, 124, 127-9
technical regulations 115-9, 123-7, 129-30
technological innovation 356, 358, 360

terms of reference 171-2, 410, 412
textiles 10, 12, 91, 96, 225, 257-62, 264-5, 272, 275-6, 383, 423
Textiles Surveillance Body (TSB) 259, 264
third country action 224
threat of injury 182, 192
Tokyo Round 5-8, 24, 27, 115, 279, 292, 295
Tokyo Round Codes 5, 8
Torquay 5
trade in services 10, 12, 28, 325-6, 329, 338, 340, 343-4, 346-7, 349, 353, 407, 420, 423-4, 427, 432
trade-related aspects of intellectual property rights (TRIPS) 10, 325, 355-6, 361, 370, 390, 393, 407, 420, 423-4, 430, 432
trade-related investment measures (TRIMs) 10, 43, 45, 139-41, 143-5
trademark 105, 112, 148, 287, 357, 361, 379-82, 389, 420
transaction value 280-7
transition period 300, 302, 306-7, 391-2
transitional safeguard 96, 262, 266-7, 269-71
transparency 13, 50, 66, 134, 144, 231, 346
transportation 17, 30, 36, 126, 140, 289, 314
triggers for SSP 236

U

unbound 21-2, 330-2, 335-6
unbound duty 21, 40
undertakings 38, 180, 190, 194-5, 217, 222, 315, 379
undisclosed information 357, 387, 420
unfair practice 151, 153, 205
unfair trade 4, 5, 11, 151
unroasted coffee 20, 22, 59
UPOV 365-6
Uruguay Round 4, 6-9, 10, 24, 28, 44, 73, 77, 105, 140, 177, 238, 254, 265, 397, 419, 438
use 6, 17-8, 26, 30, 32-4, 36, 39, 44-5, 70, 93, 100, 104, 111, 113, 118, 127, 140-3, 149, 154, 162, 199, 216, 236, 240, 258-9, 262-3, 270, 281, 285, 306, 316, 341, 346, 360, 362, 365, 367-70, 372-4, 378-82, 385-7, 421
use without authorisation 370-1, 374, 386

V

variable levy 17
violation cases 400-1, 414

W

waiver 10, 340, 414, 429-30
wholly obtained 304-5
withdrawal 64, 66, 68, 72, 100, 161, 173, 337, 339, 351, 353, 429, 431

World Trade Organisation (WTO) 3-4, 7-9, 11, 16, 24, 28, 50-1, 56, 62, 105-8, 110, 113, 122, 135, 144, 149, 249, 259, 260, 275, 304, 307, 312, 315, 321, 335, 354, 357, 361, 395, 398, 410-1, 417, 419, 421, 427-9, 431-3
WTO Agreement 44-5, 50, 74, 96, 99,144, 258, 275, 325, 336, 340, 346, 392, 398, 402, 409, 420, 425, 427-9
WTO agreements 3, 9, 10-2, 15, 26-9, 42, 47, 50, 71-2, 99, 115, 139, 151, 223, 229, 231, 234, 254, 259, 276, 279-80, 299, 323, 325, 355-6, 395, 397-8, 402, 428